# BACKROADS
# INDIANA

## By WENDELL TROGDON
### Cover by Gary Varvel

THE HIGHLANDER PRESS

Distributed by Wendell Trogdon, P.O. Box 651,
Mooresville, IN 46158, and by
The Highlander Press, Evanston, Illinois

ISBN 0-913617-17-2

Art by Gary Varvel
Book design by Martin Northway

This book is based on conditions and situations
in late 1992 and early 1993. It is possible lives
of some persons mentioned may have changed and
that some places may be slightly different
now than when they were visited.

# ACKNOWLEDGMENTS

Chambers of Commerce, county tourism officials and town officials contributed to this book. *Indiana: A New Historical Guide* and a dozen or so local histories provided invaluable background information, as did brochures and newspaper features. It was, however, the residents, proud of their towns and happy with their lives, who shared their time and their thoughts and allowed us to write about people as well as places.

# DEDICATION

To my wife, Fabian, who was on the backroads of Indiana with me on many trips and shared in the experiences recorded in this book.

# INTRODUCTION

It is a land of contrast, this area called southern Indiana where the terrain changes as suddenly, as dramatically, as the weather in a summer storm.

One mile is unlike the last, different from the one ahead. Changes come, one after another, as inevitable as the roll of the odometer.

No two towns are the same. Each, like individuals, has its own appearance, its own past, its own personality.

This is not a book for the pessimistic, for those who seek the dregs of life, or who expect the negative. It is, instead, an unabashed tribute to rural Indiana, a sometimes unappreciated area some would call rustic, sylvan, bucolic or provincial.

We traveled the backroads, seeking out towns just tiny dots on maps, far from the interstates, bypassing tourist attractions in search of an Indiana little-known except by the people who live there.

We took roads that turn back on themselves, forming zigzags, series of S curves on alpine-like hills that stretch jaggedly upward over gorges far below, then bottom out like roller coasters . . .

Roads that meander through wooded hills, maples stretching their limbs on one side to greet oaks on the other. . .

Roads that stretch straight as arrows through lush grassland, between almost endless rows of crops, past farms with silos, granaries and manicured lawns. . .

Still other roads that snake through brush and wasteland, scarred hillsides, plots scraped level for mobile homes, cars on concrete blocks . . . and roads with illegal dump sites and junk yards—unsightly sores and pimples on otherwise scenic terrain. . .

This is southern Indiana, "Backroads Indiana," we have chosen to call the land where we were born, the land we have grown to love, and the land we traveled for four seasons, visiting three hundred or so towns, talking with scores of residents, observing the land's people and places.

Call "Backroads Indiana" a journal, a diary, a romantic affair, an adoration for and about a special place and the ordinary people who call it home. It is a place of beauty unlimited only by the seasons for which it was intended.

Join with us as we set out on our adventure . . . as Fall, 1992, arrives, days on end of golden sun on a golden harvest. No one remembers a better yield. Giant harvesters rumble through fields, shelling 200-plus bushels of corn an acre, reaping bumper crops of soybeans. The high yield is good news; the low price for the abundance bad news.

Trucks creak out of giant fields, line up at grain elevators and at shipping locations, waiting to unload grain at sites like the new Maritime Center outside Mount Vernon.

Leaves turned the dense woods of the Hoosier National Forest from Nashville to Tell City into a marvel of color, free for the viewing. The backroads offer sights without sounds of traffic, isolation where time knows no clock, appointment or deadline.

Then Winter, the senior citizen of the seasons, strips itself of cover, exposing the craggy awesomeness of hills, the bareness of fields, giving those who make their living from the land a chance to rest before a new start.

Trees become bare and wait for their new spring outfits. Cattle gnaw at hay, the grass gone with the first deep freeze.

Snow, glistening in the sun, brings a new landscape, marred only by the footprints of wildlife and livestock. The chill leaves icicles dangling from waterfalls, clinging to cliffs, thawing in the warmth of the afternoon sun.

Spring comes slowly, reluctantly, for it has too much to offer to unload it more quickly than it can be appreciated. Redbud paint the hills red against the multi-colored wildflowers. Then come the dogwood, overshadowing the red with white, turning stretches like those on Ind. 58 and Ind. 45 in Greene County into pictures to be recorded by the video of the mind and stored in the recesses of memory.

Finally, Summer comes. The corn grows, first dark green, then fades to light brown; wheat heads, ripens to amber, except for fields reddened by the dreaded rust that has sapped the yield. Giant rolls of clover and alfalfa, each packaging 1,500 pounds of hay, dot the landscape.

Other changes have been as inevitable as the seasons. Towns, especially those in "Backroads Indiana," have their own life cycles, birth, growth, decline, a few born again on the lessons of the past.

Flatboats came, then came no more. Railroads chugged into town, stopped, and, after a time, ran no longer.

Cars came, roads were improved, and the itch to go to the "city," be it a county seat or just a bigger town, became irresistible. Some towns thrived, waned and died. Others withered, yet survived, "downsized" in the lexicon of the '90s. A few prosper.

Many have retained the charm and influences of the Old World from which their settlers came. Such communities still embrace the virtues brought by the Germans, the Swiss, the English; the traits acquired by pioneers as they moved from the Carolinas, up through Kentucky, or east through Pennsylvania and Ohio.

We looked for towns off the interstates, off main highways, off the beaten paths, as we listened to FM stations with country music and sell-and-swap shop radio programs.

We traveled roads with little traffic, roads filled with pot holes, twisting roads that seemed engineered by a snake and paved with stone from a bucket of gravel.

We found towns so quiet, so barren of traffic, that dogs slept in the streets. We traveled country roads where buzzards, unafraid of cars, finished dining on road kill before soaring away. We saw bantam roosters strutting bravely in front of houses with no fear of approaching cars.

We saw churches on lonely roads, coming alive on Sundays to give congregations a sense of life's purpose; cemeteries with history etched on tombstones, classrooms for descendants in search of genealogy.

We saw farmsteads abandoned, their owners surrendering to the inevitable surge of bigness, selling their land to more prosperous operators down the road where silos stood tall, surrounded by six, eight, maybe 12 granaries.

We recorded what we saw, places that linger now in our minds, pictures that flash from the recesses of the mind like movies on a screen. Pictures like:

The sun on the bend of the Ohio at Buzzard's Roost, the remote village of Alton upstream, the rays of the sun filtering onto gravel roads roofed with limbs, the vastness of fields in the delta where the Wabash meets the Ohio . . .

Farms with names like DeLovely, Clear Spring, Frost Hill, Cedar and Hedgerow . . .

Stores closed, rusting gasoline pumps out front . . .

Well-kept parks, even in small towns, gymnasiums, the schools closed for consolidation, still open to residents. And gyms now used for farm storage...

Sprawling consolidated high schools, grounds neatly landscaped around playgrounds, football and baseball diamonds . . .

Kudzu-like vegetation on dense trees in swampy areas . . .

Drag lines, huge machines, bringing coal to the surface at strip mines. Gaping holes in the landscape, the coal already removed, and mine land reclaimed and its the unsightliness gone . . .

Working oil wells, the pumps nodding up and down, slowly, endlessly...

Signs like "Beware of Dog" . . . "No Trespassing" . . . "School Bus Stop Ahead" . . .

American flags, I.U. flags, Purdue flags, high school athletic booster signs at farm homes . . .

Barns, seemingly becoming things of the past as farmers specialize, yet also barns that remain with hip roofs, rounded roofs, sloped roofs; round barns, pole barns, collapsed barns . . .

Fire towers, satellite dishes, rusted farm machinery on hillsides, farm lakes created by dams in ravines between hills, giving farmers fishing and recreation sites . . .

The cleanliness of Dubois County, the beauty of Franklin, Crawford, Jefferson counties; the diversity of Daviess County with its fertile farms, coal mines and oil wells . . .

Historic towns almost as old as the nation; river towns, farm towns, church towns; suburban subdivisions as new as tomorrow . . .

Towns that have become favorites, towns frozen in time, like Laurel, Millhousen, Magnet, Bridgeton, Cannelton and Bethlehem . . .

The remote communities of New Amsterdam, Calvertville, Newark . . .

Towns, or unplatted communities, with names like Sassafras, Solitude, Surprise, Eureka, Lena, Letts, Dogwood, Cuba, Carp, Siberia, Azalea, Cumback, Tulip . . .

Favorite views, like the Ohio, at almost any spot—but especially at Alton, Magnet and Aurora; the Merom Overlook above the Wabash; the ridges of Dearborn County; the isolation of northeast Jefferson and northwest Switzerland Counties; the remoteness of the Hoosier National Forest . . .

But it was the residents who impressed us most, individualistic yet concerned about the places where they live: common, ordinary men and women, candid, easy to talk with, helpful, seemingly free of any distrust of strangers . . .

We found the residents in restaurants, barber shops, post offices, general stores, antique shops, taverns and town parks.

No one failed to stop when we flagged them down on desolate roads to ask for directions or information.

We talked with men who wore matted hair under seed-corn caps, men in tailored suits with styled hair; women in pickup trucks, women in BMWs; the young and the wealthy, the poor and the old caught in the crevices of life.

We met folks with time on their hands and stories in their minds, ready to tell them to the first person who will listen.

None were empty people filled with themselves. All were too busy with life to have become neurotic.

Join with us, now, in our journey of rich discoveries, as fresh as today in our memories. Discover with us Backroads Indiana . . .

# BACKROADS INDIANA

## Contents

*The Trips*

*Trip 1*
# THE BEGINNING

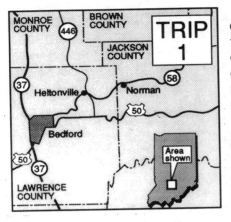

Our first journeys were over gravel roads, dusty when dry, squishy when wet. They led to a country church, to a school at Heltonville, down the road to the highway that stretched from the country to the county seat at Bedford.

It is these backroads that lead from the innocent isolation of the farm, from the remoteness of the country, to the world beyond. They have become roads drawn on the maps of the mind as clearly as if in ink on an atlas.

They are roads, some now paved, some still not, that are again worth retracing as we begin this trek across the changing terrain of southern Indiana.

## Hickory Grove
### CHURCH IN THE WILDWOOD

The road out of Norman to Hickory Grove begins with pavement—tarvy, some folks still call it—and continues with crushed stone. It is a route where the present is much like the past, little changed for a half-century, maybe longer.

Hickory Grove is four minutes from Norman, 12 minutes from Heltonville, 35 minutes from Bedford and light years from Indianapolis.

It is a place where, in the 1990s, time stands still, measured not by clocks, but by seasons and calendars. It is a place of serenity, not turmoil, a place where pretense and formality are alien, a place where the lowly and the mighty are made equal in the vastness of the wooded hills and hollows.

It is a place which, in one of the U.S. government's rare acts of foresight, was preserved by being purchased at $7 to $10 an acre in the 1940s and 1950s, creating the Hoosier National Forest.

It is here the late Dee Terrell, a retired Norman merchant and 83 at the time, stood eyeball-to eyeball with government agents more than 25 years ago and forced them to forget plans to remove the log Hickory Grove church.

The people who occupied the land are gone, but the trees have prospered. Their branches now meet over the narrow one-lane, crushed-stone roads, forming arches, leaving tunnels for motorists who want to drive backward in time.

Foliage is so thick in places, the Rev. L. D. "Sam" Axsom jokes, "sunshine has to be piped in." It is here to this little church in the wildwood that "Brother" Axsom, "a Pentecostal by handle," has come home in an attempt to brighten the darkness with "The Light."

Axsom, seventy-plus, grew up as a child of the Great Depression a hill or two over, in Lincolnback Holler, attended the one-room Hickory Grove school and listened to other revivalists preach.

Now he is back on this October weekend for four nights of old-time religion, preaching "The Word" much as it has been ever since the logs were shaped and the church built in 1881.

Not much has changed in the church. The pews, seven on each side, room for six in each, were built by men who cared, not in a factory by faceless people. A linoleum carpet, covered by a rug runner between the aisle, stretches wall to wall.

Overhead, three bare bulbs attract heat-seeking wasps. There are no other lights. No electric lines reach out here into the forest. A generator on a pickup truck powers the lights and the electric musical instruments.

Cloth curtains cover the four small windows. A chimney remains unused as it has for years.

An oil heater sits in the aisle, glowing red. It will not be needed long on this Friday evening. The fire of "Brother" Axsom's preaching will heat up the night.

A banner at the front of the church proclaims: "You must be born again. John 3:7." It will be the theme of the sermon and the preacher will let no one forget it.

Brother Axsom calls on "Sister Sharon" to lead the singing. She does so, as most of the sixty people who have come for the service join in the words to "Beulah Land" and clap to the music of "An Old Account Settled."

Sister Sharon is Sharon Lee, a member of Pastor Axsom's Ellettsville Pentecostal Church.

The preacher explains he is here "to see God's will accomplished." He asks for testimonials. A woman asks for prayers for her husband who is unsaved. A man requests prayers for his wife who has "an awful cold and couldn't be here tonight."

Others will testify later about the power of God in their lives.

It is time for the free-will offering. There are no collection plates in the church. Someone offers a felt hat. Paul Axsom, the preacher's brother, passes it down the pews.

But not before he jokes, "I do better working for money."

That doesn't stop the men and women from placing folded $1s, $5s, $10s into the hat. The money will help the musicians who will perform later.

Brother Axsom talks about the Sears Roebuck catalog. "I once took a catalog to a service and explained to the congregation, 'You have more confidence in Sears Roebuck than in God. If you order something from Sears Roebuck you are sure what you are getting. It will send you what you want. When we ask the Lord for something, we ought to believe we will get what we ordered.'"

"Amen," a voice in the congregation says.

The preacher continues. "We don't even have to tell Him the right color. He knows our needs even before we ask."

"Right," adds a woman.

The preacher picks up a newspaper. "The news of the day is so tremendously prophetic," he says. "More people read the newspaper than the Bible. When you pick up a newspaper it is almost like reading the Bible.

"More people read the headlines in a newspaper than read the Bible. The signs of the coming of the Lord are all around us. That has been the expectation of the church since Jesus went away.

"And, friends, if you don't go in the Rapture, you've had it. Time is running out. . . . All you can do is to get ready. That's why we are here tonight."

It is time for music. Ron Hawkins is on the keyboard, Troy Jacobs on the bass, Nicholas Jones on the drums for Keith Hunt, who sounds like Johnny Cash in voice and delivery. They have come from Bloomington for the service.

There are more testimonials. From "Sister Dixie," the preacher's wife of 49 years; from "Sister" Sylvia, his mother-in-law; from "Sister" Epsie Louise, his sister.

Lloyd White, a preacher from Heltonville who has come to hear his long-time friend preach, turns down the heater.

Brother Axsom is back at the pulpit. "Yes, the Lord is here . . . even way out here." Out here, which Dixie thinks is a foreign country.

He starts his sermon. "We have big problems. But we have a big Lord."

The people in the pews, many of them descendants of the men and women who pioneered the area, agree. "That's for sure," "Amen," "Thank God," "Yes sir!", "Beautiful," they say.

Brother Axsom talks about procrastination, using the eighth chapter of Exodus for his sermon.

"The devil is after you every day," he insists. "He wants to destroy you. He knows where he is going and he wants you to go with him.

"He will do everything he can to keep you from being saved. Even in this revival, if you please.

"The devil doesn't care what you do for God as long as you wait until tomorrow. The Bible says today, not tomorrow, is the day of salvation."

The sermon continues. The preacher welcomes anyone who wants to be saved to come to the tiny altar. (He hopes to have an outdoor baptismal later in the water at the humpback bridge over Henderson Creek.)

No one steps forward into salvation. Those who have not been saved procrastinate. Brother Axsom is not deterred. There is still Saturday night. But there will be no one saved then, either. The baptismal will have to be canceled.

Pastor Axsom is disappointed but not discouraged. He has returned "home" for a few days to the church he knew as a boy.

Once again the church grows dark. It will remain unlocked, as it has been for 109 years.

Outside, the air is crisp and silent. In a few days, the leaves on the hickories, maples, oak, gums and ashes out on the ridges and down in Lincolnback Holler will be brilliant in color.    To the procrastinators, the leaves and the beauty of nature may be silent testimonials to the power of "The Word" the preacher has spoken.

# Hoosier National Forest
### AN IDEA THAT WORKED

It was an idea that came out of Washington, an act of Congress, a gem among a passel of legislative junk.

It has become a living monument to wisdom, a vision realized, a seed that grew into a vast woodland.

It is the Hoosier National Forest, chunks of Indiana where hardwood, pine and cedar stand tall on rugged hills overlooking valleys of almost-hidden meandering creeks.

It is a timeless treasure, where animals, mosses, shrubs and fungi can flourish next to springs, caves and sinkholes.

It is a place free from commercialization, where silence is broken only by the sound of crows overhead, a snake slithering underfoot, the fluttering of grouse.

It was a simple mission, compared to most government legislation: A large area of southern Indiana would be bought for reforestation, the work done by the Civilian Conservation Corps.

Back in the late 1930s, landowners debated the merits of creating the forest. Some called it "government intervention," "make-work"; others argued that over-farming had gullied the hills, that over-cutting had destroyed the woods.

Objectors calmed down when they learned that the Forest Service would neither force landowners to sell their property nor encourage them to do so. And eventually, they decided, it wasn't a bad idea to plant trees, prevent erosion, help stop creeks from flooding and set aside some scenic areas away from people and pollution.

They saw the fast-growing pines and cedars planted on "government land by the CCC boys" were beginning to cover red clay hills left barren by poor farming practices.

The government had bought almost 7,000 acres in Lawrence, Monroe and Jackson Counties by 1941, when World War II delayed further acquisitions. Once the war ended, the Hoosier National Forest grew again, its outer boundaries finally stretching from the Ohio River north into Brown and Monroe counties.

Inside those boundaries there now are 187,812 acres, with areas set aside for primitive camping, hiking, hunting and fishing.

It is enough to restore faith in government.

# Norman
## CHANGE FOR A $10

Horace George is alone in his store on this Saturday morning in September when a friend from another time walks in.

Horace hasn't changed much. He is still friendly, sharp-witted. It's the town that is different.

His place has been the only store in town for the last 15, maybe 20 years. There is nowhere else to shop in a five-mile circle, but he says he doesn't have much business.

It doesn't bother him. "I'm not looking for much," he admits.

Horace is 83, old enough to have seen the town change from a bustling rural community to a quiet wayside on Ind. 58 near the Jackson-Lawrence county line.

He remembers the day he bought the store, which was then closed, and reopened its doors. "It was 48 years ago, 17th of April, 1944."

It was the third store in Norman and business was good. Gasoline was rationed and no one traveled far from home, except to go to war. People were close, neighborly.

C.E. Cummings, who owned a store a block or so to the east, showed free movies on Saturday nights, bringing in enough customers to crowd all three stores.

Things changed gradually, almost unnoticed for a time. World War II ended, young men and women who had grown up around town moved to cities, families drifted apart. Movies could be seen on television; groceries bought in supermarkets in places like Bedford and Seymour.

Norman was no longer a hub around which a community revolved.

\* \* \*

A youngster of about 10 walks into the store, opens a display case and removes a treat. He drops coins into Horace's hand. Horace nods thanks. There are no longer many children in town.

\* \* \*

Horace shows off a wood stove he built himself to heat the store. He still cuts his own wood.

"I used to open at 6:30 and have the place heated so about twenty school kids would have a place to keep warm while they waited for the school bus," he recalls. He would remain open until 10 p.m. back then.

Now he's available for customers whenever they arrive. If he's not in the store he can see them arrive as he tends his garden or cuts wood.

\* \* \*

A man walks in and asks Horace to break a $10 bill. Horace does. The man leaves without a purchase.

\* \* \*

Chances are Horace could have gained some business if he had chosen to accept food stamps. He refused, though. He remembered his own hard times, the Great Depression, of the struggles then to make do with what he had.

"I read the food stamp regulations two or three times and got so aggravated (with the red tape) I never bothered."

Someone once suggested he "jack up the prices" and accept food stamps. Horace recalls his response: "If I have to do that I'll just get a gun and get it all at one time."

He doesn't want to jack up the price of his store now. He just wants to find someone to keep it open, maybe rebuild business, fire up the wood stove so school kids and farmers can stay warm on cold winter days, break a $10 bill now and then, or just talk to a motorist passing through town.

Every town needs at least one place like that.

# A Country Place
## BLUEGRASS AND BIB OVERALLS

Welcome to Larry's Country Roadhouse where, briefly, time will stand still, locked between the past and present.

Larry's, mid-way between Bedford and Brownstown on U.S. 50, is not a roadhouse of the Depression years where couples danced and drank cocktails made from the bottles they carried.

There is no dancing here, no drinking, no liquor licenses, no carry-ins, no set-ups, just food and music, country-Western, bluegrass and, on this night in 1992, some gospel songs.

About forty people are here, fewer than on a normal Saturday night. There are annual events at nearby towns that have reduced the crowd.

No one is well-dressed. One man is in bib overalls, one or two wear caps, for this is down-home country.

Larry Rollins owns the place, opened it a few months ago. He once performed at the Little Nashville (Indiana) Opry house, cut some records and sang the title song in John Mellencamp's movie, "Falling From Grace."

Rollins is busy in the kitchen on this night, fixing T-bones, country-fried steaks and chicken while waiting for a phone call announcing the birth of a grandchild.

Brian Tolbert of Williams starts the entertainment. Country-Western, Not bad.

Pat and Jack Hamilton are up next with the religious music, previewing some of the songs they'll perform at the Heltonville United Methodist Church's all-day homecoming tomorrow.

The tempo picks up. The Back Creek Tomato Pickers are on. There is Greg Norman, Heltonville, on the guitar; Danny Young, Heltonville, on base; Dean Fisher, Norman, on mandolin; his son, Frank Fisher, Clearspring, on banjo; Roy Branaman, Seymour, on the violin, and Ron Jarvis, Bedford, on the steel guitar.

All pick and play. Norman and Young sign. There are songs like "Faded Love," "Thirty Acres of Bottom Land," "Long Black Veil" and "You Are My Flower." A black hat stays firmly on Jarvis' head, his expression unchanging despite what looks like a wade of "chawin' tabaccer" planted firmly in his right jaw.

The music is older than the musicians, songs as dated as the mountains from which they came.

Rollins is finished in the kitchen. He's ready to sing, right after a news flash. "The grandchild has been born. It's a girl. All is well."

He begins his music with "Pretty Fraulein," follows with four or five more songs.

He is the star in his own establishment, as big here as Loretta Lynn and others he has preceded are in shows at Nashville.

He is eager to leave to see that granddaughter, but he agrees to let Johnny Horton, who lives on a nearby farm, join him in singing "The Old Country Church."

It still is not 10 p.m.

"See you all next week," Rollins says as the customers wait at the cash register to pay their bills.

It has been two nonstop hours of music. Hardly anyone pays more than $10 for his or her meal. The music has come free with the food.

The entertainers have performed without pay. Their own enjoyment and the applause has been their reward.

Some guests book reservations for the next Saturday when the past again merges with the present, blending as smoothly as summer into fall.

# Zelma
## AN ENDLESS FOUNTAIN

Some people came to Zelma on this day to bid on the antiques and blacksmith tools. Others came to remember Sherm Umphress and his wife and the era in which they lived.

Sherm had been the blacksmith. His wife had collected the household items that with time became antiques.

The antiques sold for a pretty penny. The memories went at no cost.

Sherm had been dead 30 years or so. He would have been proud to know the crowd came out as much in tribute to him as they did for the auction.

Sherm and his wife raised seven boys in Zelma from the earnings Sherm made at his blacksmith shop. The sons grew to manhood in the first third of the century, when Zelma was a bustling stop on the Chicago, Milwaukee and St. Paul Railroad between Heltonville and Norman Station on Ind. 58.

It was a time when farmers drove horses instead of tractors and depended on the village blacksmith to keep plow points sharpened, harness mended and tools repaired.

It was a time Elmer Harrell, who attended the one-room school in Zelma from 1925 to 1931, recalled away from the chant of the auctioneer.

"The school sat down there," he said, pointing north from Sherm's now abandoned house. "Sherm's blacksmith shop was just beyond the school. The depot was over there," he continued, turning to point toward where Fred Evans lived. Fred is dead now, too, but his house is still there, abandoned, growing old, alone, without attention.

Passenger trains took riders east to Seymour, west to Bedford. Freight trains took farm produce to market and limestone to Washington for use in government buildings.

Elmer talked about the canning factory Jimmy Cummings once operated across Ind. 58, and about the two stores that were in business when he was in school.

But it was the school that he talked about most. Elmer, Waneta and Thelma had entered the first grade together. They learned from Evie Henderson, the teacher, and the students in the other five grades.

Elmer remembered strange noises from out of the clouds when planes began to soar across the sky. "It was automatic recess when a plane went over. We all went outside to watch as long as we could see it."

And he remembered the time a blimp went over. "That turned out to be an hour recess. It floated slowly from the north to south and we watched until it drifted out of sight."

Elmer recalled when the first diesel-powered engine came through Zelma. "I remember an old milk cow Sherm had. The diesel made such a loud and unfamiliar sound, that old milker's legs shook so much she just dropped to her knees trembling."

He wiped the sweat from his brow and talked some more as he looked around at the town as it is today—just three or four homes.

It was time for Elmer to get back to the sale.

* * *

Zelma was founded along the railroad, platted by Stephen Fountain in 1889, named after one of his daughters. Eight years earlier, he had built a two-story Gothic-Revival style house and moved in his family. It's still there up a lane a quarter-mile or more from Ind. 58, just north of the railroad. It is now occupied by the fourth generation of Fountains.

Stephen's great-grandson, George, lives there now with his wife, Laverne, keeping a part of Zelma's history alive as a memorial to its founder.

Their son, Mike, and their daughter, Paula Brooking, both live between the Zelma town-limit signs. And there are five grandsons, sixth-generation descendants, to continue the tradition.

Zelma has again become a family town. Stephen Fountain would be proud his town is still there, even if his ancestors are about the only residents who remain.

# Heltonville
## EVERY TOWN NEEDS ONE

Ind. 58 still twists and turns as it winds through Heltonville, but the railroad warning signs are gone, the tracks motorists crossed three times in less than a mile removed.

Gone, too, are the feed mill Jerry Jones operated, Ray Roberts' General Store, Jim East's blacksmith shop, Doc Cain's office, Lute Thompson's restaurant, Stan Hanner's barbershop, the Oddfellows Hall, the Milwaukee depot where "Pop" Ammerman was the agent.

The school is still on the hill, but it's for grades K-6, not 1-12 as it once was.

The Jones Funeral Home still conducts services for the deceased; residents still comfort the survivors of the departed.

Residents now pick up their mail in a new location. The post office is now in a brick building across from the school.

New generations of Todds, Baileys, Normans and Bartletts live in or around town. No Heltons remain to brag that Andrew Helton founded the town in 1845. The march of time is eternal.

Old houses have been torn down, others improved, new ones built on the fringes now that rural water is available. The population is somewhere between three hundred and five hundred, depending on how far out a person wants to count.

Ind. 446 now cuts north and south east of town, crossing Ind. 58, taking boaters to Lake Monroe or motorists to Bloomington. A caution light slows traffic at the Ind. 58 crossing, giving passing motorists a chance to read the signs that point into Heltonville.

One of the signs proclaims "Heltonville—Home of Damon Bailey." Bailey became a legend as a teen-ager, setting new standards for high school basketball scorers at Bedford North Lawrence before going on to Indiana University.

Limestone again is being cut at the Heltonville mill, which was closed for years until it was reopened in the early 1990s. Most people, though, work in Bedford, a 15-minute drive, and come home each night to the serenity of the small town.

Men no longer gather at the feed mill or the barber shop. If there is a gathering stop, it's at Larry "Bonehead" Faubion's Heltonville Store, where the coffee is hot and the pop cool.

It is there—at the only store in town—where residents can buy groceries, supplies, gasoline, and lottery tickets, rent movies, check the bulletin board for sales or community events, trade news.

If a town is people, "Bonehead" is Heltonville's heart. He grew up in town, took over the only store, made it the community's center when school isn't in session.

He has coached the grade school basketball team, supported bowling and softball teams, given his time to boost the town and the people in it.

In a small town, one person can make a difference.

# Bartlettsville
## APPLE PIE AND AMERICANA

A grave is opened at the Bartlettsville Christian Cemetery, awaiting the funeral procession led out of Heltonville by the Jones Funeral Home ambulance.

Virgil Mikels, 83, a retired carpenter and a Navy veteran of World War II, will be buried in the area where he grew up, spent most of his life and once owned the town's store.

Graves are decorated in observance of Memorial Day the following weekend.

It is the church and the cemetery that have for decades been the anchor of the Lawrence County community.

The community was founded in 1860 by Samuel J. Bartlett, a century before the sprawling Monroe Reservoir was built just a couple of hills and hollows over, on Salt Creek.

Bartlett still is a prominent name here, 130 years later. For example, enter Maxine's Restaurant and Store in Bartlettsville and meet Maxine Smith. Before she married Herman Smith, she was a Bartlett, one of "Doc's" children. "Doc" was a farmer and the Pleasant Run Township trustee back in the 1950s when it was the trustees who ran the school systems in Indiana's townships.

Most of Maxine's brothers and sisters, "eight of us," she says, still live within a few miles of the area. Joe is one of them. He played on the 1954 Heltonville basketball team that won the county championship and reached the finals of the Bedford sectional. A cousin, Fred, now owns "Doc's" old home place.

Maxine's is the only business in town, a place to buy gasoline, a few groceries or comforts, have a cup of coffee, order a complete meal or a single piece of the homemade pie any day of the week except Sunday.

Scott Callahan, the Lawrence County prosecutor, is just leaving. An office holder needs to get out among the people from time to time.

"We opened the restaurant when the lake went in," Maxine explains. Business varies. "It goes in spurts, sometimes it's good, sometimes not."

A customer comes in to make reservations for rib dinners the following Monday at lunch. "There will be between seven and eleven of us," she says. Maxine says she'll be ready for the guests, be they seven or eleven.

A visitor eyes the apple and peach pies. They look good and it takes courage to refuse a piece of either . . . or both.

"It is quiet around Bartlettsville now. We don't have much crime. It's not like it used to be out here," Maxine explains.

"Back when drugs first came around, no one would believe me. They didn't believe it when I told them how much drugs were being used."

She recites a quote from a sheriff who once told the *Bedford Times-Mail,* "We don't have a drug problem in Lawrence County."

"He didn't know. We had big problems," she adds.

"They [police agencies] are picking up the little guys, but when they get to the big dealers, it seems to me they back away. That's disgusting to people.

"I try to convince kids who come in here not to get mixed up in drugs—don't haul it for them, don't do this, don't do that."

But she also is a realist. "You know if you were 15-16 years old and someone offered you $100 to go to Bedford or go to Mitchell, you know truthfully, you would have gone. You wouldn't have known the difference."

She tells a story to illustrate her point. "A boy was in here the other day, who said he had made himself a fast $100. An older youth in Bloomington claimed his car was torn up and that he'd pay that much for someone to drive down to this area and pick up a package. The boy came down, picked up a plastic sack of 'weed,' marijuana, and returned it to Bloomington.

"He told me later that when he got back to Bloomington he was given $100. He took the money, but told the dealer, 'That's it! Don't ever ask me to take you down there again.'

"I didn't find out where he picked up the marijuana, but somebody down in this area is growing the weed."

That bothers Maxine Smith. Small towns need more adults like her to care for their young people, set them straight, give them ears to listen.

## Chapel Hill
### TOWN WITHOUT LIMITS

Chapel Hill is just up the hill on the ridge—across Knob Creek, across the county line in Monroe County, up on Ground Hog Ridge—above Bartlettsville.

There are no road markers, no town-limit signs, for Chapel Hill is more of a community than a town with defined limits. Houses line the road that leads to Monroe Reservoir and it is difficult to tell where Chapel Hill begins and ends.

A big sawmill is in operation here in the heart of the hardwood area. Some visitors, perhaps genealogy tracers, check the tombstones in Pentecostal Cemetery. An old store is barely visible through vegetation that has grown up around it, almost hiding the rusting Phillips 66 sign. An old log house nearby is still in use with an addition of modern construction.

A sign at Chapel Hill Church invites young people to Vacation Bible School.

\* \* \*

Beware of the aromas of the country on rural roads. We decide to go cross-country from the Bartlettsville-Chapel Hill area to Ind. 37. A pickup loaded with mulch leaves a trail of aromatic scent for us to follow. The road twists and turns above deep ravines and we slow to enjoy the view and drop far behind the mulch. Suddenly the timber-lined road opens into level farm land. It is another example of Indiana's changing terrain.

A mile or so later, the road drops down a steep hill. We are again behind the truck and its mulch as we creep through the Salt Creek bottoms below the Lake Monroe dam. Up on a sharp turn is Valley Mission, a big rural church here in the valley. The road continues up hills, along gorges, passing among trees, northwest, past the Monroe dam, before reaching Ind. 37.

We leave the backroads for another day.

*Trip 2*

# *Trip 2*
# BACKROADS ARE FREE

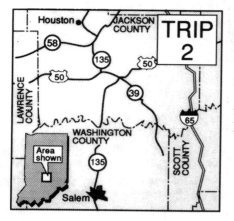

It could have started anywhere, this odyssey through "Backroads Indiana."

"Begin at Salem," a friend suggests. "At the Backroads restaurant."

We compromise. We head south toward Salem, stopping at towns off Ind. 135 along the way.

## Houston
### A DIFFERENT HOUSTON

Houston (pronounced House-ton) is a Jackson County town accessible only on county roads, almost surrounded by the Hoosier National Forest.

Its school is gone, its grocery abandoned, its 15 residences eight miles or so from the nearest food store. It's a town insulated from the noise of the city, the pollution of the highways, the concrete pavement of shopping centers.

Chances are its demise started fifty years ago or so, back when its high school closed, when the Pirates basketball team ended play, when student were transferred to Clearspring, later to Brownstown.

No matter! It's a place that exists, and will continue to exist, as long as there are Hoosiers who prefer life off the beaten path.

We leave Houston, exchanging waves with a farmer in a pickup truck, and return to Ind. 135. There are no strangers on the backroads of Indiana.

## Freetown
### FREE AND INDEPENDENT

Unlike Houston, Freetown is on two state roads, Ind. 135 and Ind. 58.

Students are in recess at the grade school, but there is little activity on the streets of the Jackson County town at mid-morning. Freetown is like this on most days. It is different though, each summer when the park up on the northside is filled with visitors who come to town for the annual July 4 celebration.

This is, after all, *Free*-town, a place that's free and proud to be.

On this day, a lone customer is at Mowery's Freetown Grocery and she is more interested in conversation than in shopping.

Up the street sits the old high school gym, little changed since the days almost a half century ago when Dean Zike, Bill Brown and Chuck Scott played for the Spartans.

It now is a community building, a monument to the foresight of townspeople who didn't let it fall into ruins like gyms in dozens of other town.

We enter the gym and listen closely. Ghosts of the past flash across the mind; names like Fields and Forgey emerge from mental scorebooks. The swish of nets, the carom of basketballs on hardwood can be heard on most weekends and on some nights, for the love of the game is alive in generations that now call Brownstown Central their high school.

# Vallonia
## BLUEBIRD OF PARADISE

Doris Wheeler cups her ear and leans over the bar in the Bluebird Tavern in order to carry on a conversation. Forty-eight years of juke box country music has dulled her hearing, caused her to ask customers to repeat their order, to talk a bit louder.

Doris and her late husband, Dan, bought the Bluebird back in 1944 when a beer sold for 15 cents and men too old to fight talked about the war that raged in Europe and the South Pacific.

The tavern became her second home and she kept it when Dan died, serving the same type clientele. "Lots of farmers. And business is still good," she says, before asking the three men at the bar if they need another round.

It is 11:30 a.m., a bit to early for the lunch customers. Before the day is over, the tavern will see the kind of crowd that led the *Louisville Courier-Journal* in 1980 to name the Bluebird the best neighborhood bar in Indiana.

The pool table will be in use, the stools filled, maybe a few customers standing, holding beers that now go for $1.05 each.

Fort Vallonia Days (the third weekend in October) are coming in a few weeks, an event that likely will see the place wall-to-wall with customers more interested in suds than in crafts, flea markets and parades.

It was a quarter-century ago that Vallonia decided to share its heritage with visitors, noting that it was the site of a stockade built in 1812 on an old Indian trail; that a year later Maj. John Tipton led his garrison of militia rangers into that stockade.

It has been Fort Vallonia Days which have provided the revenue for the town to rebuild the stockade and to restore old Fort Vallonia.

And it is that event that has allowed new generations to watch apple butter being made, rugs being braided, chairs being caned, wool being spun, apples being turned to cider.

Old ways, old virtues. But not all is perfect, not even in this town that has kept its past its present. A sign, handwritten, is taped to a soft-drink machine on the main street: "$50 reward for return of camera. No cops will be called." Folks in small towns have a way of taking care of their own problems.

We return to Ind. 135, driving past roadside stands with elbow squash, watermelons and pumpkins. A round barn is surrounded by sheep. Holsteins graze on the still green meadow of the Indiana autumn, across the fence from round hay bales that will be their feed when the freeze comes and the grass dies. Cox Comb flowers surround a rural church on the road.

We remember a section of old Ind. 135 near the Jackson-Washington County line, leave the new road that goes almost straight over the hill, and drive again into the past. The old route is now a county road, but it still has the 35 sharp turns we recall from a drive decades earlier.

Signs on Ind. 135 toward Salem point to Milport, Plattsburg, Kossuth, wide spots in the backroads of northern Washington County.

# Salem
## BEER AND BACKROADS

Salem, county seat of Washington County, isn't on the backroads, not with four highways, Ind. 135, Ind. 56, Ind. 60 and Ind. 160, joining there. It is those highways, though, that lead into the small towns we have chosen to visit on this particular trek into the bucolic beauty of rural Indiana.

Owner Jack Schlichtenmyer isn't sure how the Backroads Restaurant got its name. He bought the place in January, 1992, and renamed it Jack's Backroads Restaurant & Lounge.

George Bowers, a former owner who still tends bar at times, might know, Schlichtenmyer says. Sure enough, George knows: "Back when I was younger, I'd get a friend, drive out into the country on a back road, sit under a tree and write songs while sipping beer.

"I called one of the songs I wrote 'Backroads.' I said then that if I ever had a lounge, I'd call it 'Backroads.'"

He bought the restaurant in 1984, and called it "Backroads," sometimes included the song, which was recorded, when he entertained guests.

"Great fish, steaks and ribs," the Backroads menu promises. It offers a Friday night special: Jack's Backroads famous seasoned and breaded fish, all you can eat for $6.95. On Saturday night the specials are prime rib for $12.95, shrimp and crab legs for $16.95.

Schlichtenmyer wasn't like the General Morgan's raiders, the Confederate soldiers who rode into Salem back in 1863, took what they could and left. He was transferred to Salem 15 years ago by the G.C. Murphy Co., grew to like the town and chose to stay. When the Murphy Co. closed its stores in Indiana, he declined a transfer to Boston.

He liked Salem. It was more like his hometown of Kendallville than were Fort Wayne or Chicago, where he had also worked, certainly different than Boston would be.

Schlichtenmyer has kept the $1 bill tradition Bowers started. Hundreds of $1 bills, each autographed, are posted around the bar section. Thus, a person who signs his name on a dollar and leaves it at the Backroads will never be broke.

We dine at the Backroads and continue our adventure.

# Harristown

## B.S.—Before Smog

Cattle graze on the grassy hills along undulating Ind. 160 southeast of Salem in Washington County. "Harristown," promises a sign pointing to the north. The county road crosses a railroad a mile to the north, near a half dozen or so houses. But there are no signs to mark the town.

"This Harristown?" we ask a man at a small engine repair shop.

"You found it," we are told. "Don Motsinger," the man says, introducing himself. He owns the shop, which is in a grocery that closed three years earlier.

Gone is the Monon Railroad depot. Trains don't even slow down now, let alone stop. Few motorists, except those who live along the route, travel the road.

Motsinger gave up his job in Salem when he opened the shop to enjoy the peace and quiet of Harristown.

He points to a ridge off to the south, calls it the highest point of elevation in Washington County. "My dad told me that years ago boys would sit atop the hill and watch for the lights on steamboats on the Ohio. That's a distance of thirty miles or so," he explains, then adds:

"That, of course, was before smog and pollution."

Harristown is no longer on many road maps, but geologists know about the community. College professors and students from universities as far away as Colorado have come to dig among the glacier deposits. "Two or three car loads at a time," says John Dawalt, 83.

Dawalt recalls when there were children around. Now the birth of a baby is big news to those who still call Harristown home.

He talks about the town as it once was but will never be again. Like a hundred other hamlets, it grew up with the railroad, withered when its importance declined.

Dawalt tells us about a place called Canton "on up the road." It's a town that still has a store, a place people in Harristown sometimes go to shop.

# Canton
## THE LIARS' BENCH

Canton, too, is on a county road, not far off Ind. 56.

It's Traci Purlee's shift at the store her parents, Odetta and Orval Purlee, have owned for the last five years.

Take a seat on the liars' bench in Fox's Country Corner Store at Canton and you'll be sitting on a piece of history. "My brother, Rick, made that from lumber cut from a log that was used to build Ind. 135," explains Traci.

That would have been decades ago, back when logs were used to build corduroy roads, long before Ind. 135 became a paved north-south state highway through the county.

The liar's bench gets lots of use. "Certain people come in every day, sometimes more than once a day," Traci adds, for the store is the community center. It's a spot for the neighborhood kids to gather when they return home each day from school five miles away in Salem.

A coffee pot is on for visitors who stop in from 6 a.m. to 9 p.m. It's a convenience store in a rural setting, a place where customers can find items like video rentals that will save them a trip to a bigger town.

If some residents want to drive miles to shop for some of their groceries, that's okay. The coffee at Fox's Country Corner will be fresh and warm when they return.

And there may be a spot on the liar's bench for a discussion of the economy . . . or to weave tall stories.

Every community needs a place like the Country Corner.

# South Boston
## IT RAN IN THE FAMILY

South Boston is in southeastern Washington County, on Ind. 160, a route marked by 90-degree turns and a constantly changing roadside.

Marjorie Mull is picking up cigarette butts and paper from the asphalt in front of Mull's Store in South Boston on this Friday afternoon.

"Field stripping, that's what my husband said they called it in the service," she explains.

Her husband is Elgin, the fourth generation of Mulls to run the general store, a holdover from an earlier time, a place where shoppers can find almost anything they need for any purpose.

Look around. There are shoes, clothes, plumbing supplies, nuts and bolts, coal buckets, groceries. Seed, fertilizer, salt blocks, cattle feed, supplements, fencing, fence posts, shovels are in an attached building.

A stop at Mull's may save a farmer or homeowner a long trip into a bigger town.

A loafer's bench is near the pot-bellied stove, still heated by coal. If the coal doesn't heat the place, the conversations may. A gas heater is turned on when the store is closed. Back when nails came in kegs, boards were stretched across the barrels, providing additional seats for the daily conversations men carried on around the warmth of the stove.

Elgin returned to South Boston after World War II, joined his father, Roscoe, in the business and married Marjorie, who lived nearby.

They've operated the business ever since. Elgin, 71, isn't interested in retiring. He tells Marjorie, 71, that "people go crazy when they retire."

Besides, there likely will be no fifth generation to operate the store, not like when Willis took over from his father, Roscoe for Willis, and Elgin for Roscoe. None of Elgin and Marjorie's three children are interested in taking over the business.

Royce Smith, 73, crosses Ind. 160 from the store to the garage Willis Mull built years ago. He had one of the first cars around and thought the town ought to have a garage.

Smith still works in the garage, but it's for sale now. Change is inevitable in South Boston, just as it is everywhere.

# Little York
## KEEPING POSTED

A jar sits in Colwell's Grocery at Little York. It is a depository for cash for funeral flowers or for contributions in case of need.

Little York, on Ind. 39 in northeastern Washington County, is a town where residents care about each other, where they see each other almost every day. Most of them meet at Colwell's Grocery and the adjoining post office, which can be entered from the store.

It is at the store where residents like George Trueblood, pastor of the Christian church, come each morning to sip coffee and share a copy of the *Louisville Courier-Journal*—and whatever is new in town.

Once in a while they may talk about the three-member council that runs the incorporated town, or recall the days when Little York had a high school and some good basketball teams called the Wildcats.

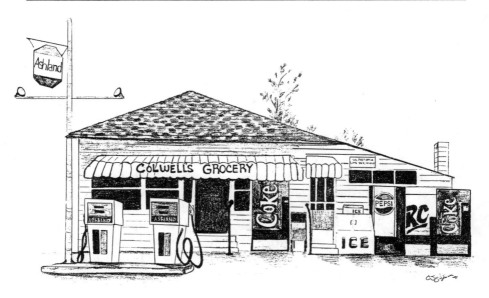

"We usually have about three crews that come in each morning. When one crew leaves, another drifts in," Mrs. Colwell says, pointing to a rocking chair: "A man who had a $600 bill offered me the chair as part payment. That's all I got back from the $600 before he skipped town."

Mrs. Colwell grew up in a family grocery in Austin and bought the Little York grocery from her brother, Doug Campbell, when he went into politics, becoming the Washington County auditor.

Marcia Bush runs the post office, Zip Code 47139, open from 9 a.m. to 1 p.m. Monday through Saturday. It is where about fifty residents pick up their mail, buy stamps, have letters stamped with the "Little York" postmark. "We can provide almost any postal service except overnight express," the postmaster explains.

Little York, she adds, is "a quiet, peaceful town. Everybody looks after each other, cares about each other. If anyone is sick, we all know about it.

"This is sort of the information center. If we learn something new, we wonder why we didn't know about it first."

That's how small towns are.

It is quiet here, the seats in the store are comfortable. It would be easy to sit longer, ignore the clock, continue the conversation.

* * *

Ind. 39 beckons. It stretches through the Muscatatuck River bottom, into Jackson County through a place called Tampico. It is quiet on this Saturday morning. Traffic is light enough for a young man on a skate board to roll through at near the speed limit.

It's a town that's seldom in the news since the school closed and the Tampico Bobcats became part of the Brownstown Central Braves.

# Skyline Drive
## HILLS OVER BROWNSTOWN

One of Indiana's most scenic drives is hidden in the hills of the Jackson-Washington State Forest south of Brownstown off Ind. 135.

Ask residents who've lived in the area and some may not know about Skyline Drive, a narrow three-mile paved roadway that traverses the ridge line of the Brownstown hills.

It's a series of turns, some sharp, through the hardwood forest that peaks high above the valleys, each turn a prelude to spectacular beauty. Off to the north is a picture view of Brownstown, to the southwest a panorama of the Starved Hollow Lake area.

Traffic is light, except in October when the hills become nature's palette, a canvas of changing colors attracting those fortunate enough to know about Skyline Drive.

It is a jewel that brings mixed emotions—a creation of nature too good to share, yet too good to keep from others.

# Clearspring
## A QUIET SATURDAY

Indiana's official highway map doesn't show a road off U.S. 50 to Clearspring. We know it from earlier visits, take it north past Wrays Church, where our parents once took us to revivals on hot summer nights.

Only county roads lead to Clearspring and the town, which has no post office and gets its mail from a Norman rural route, is free of traffic on this morning.

Dogs, appearing somewhat bored, amble down the streets, for there are no cars to chase. What vehicles that have come into town are parked across the way at a garage sale.

The school that housed all 12 grades is now used for farm storage, the gymnasium no longer in use. From out of the memory bank comes a mental movie of Dan Bowman, scoring baskets on long arching shots through the rafters, of the Cummings boys in action, of the nights back in the 1940s when Crispus Attucks brought its all-black team from Indianapolis to meet the Warriors.

Any athletes from the area now perform for Brownstown Central.

There are no stores, no businesses now. Like a lot of other such places, Clearspring lost its heart when it lost its school.

Sometimes traveling the backroads is bittersweet. We return home, to travel another day.

## Trip 3
# DOWN BY THE RIVER

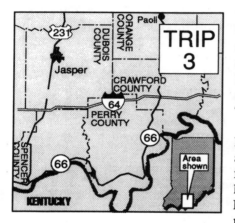

Paoli is the Orange County seat. On two major highways, it is too big to be called "backroads Indiana." It's a town that greets visitors with signs like "Heart of Hoosier Hospitality" and "Home of Paoli Marching Band." The band is one of Indiana's best.

We drive south through Paoli on Ind. 37, stopping a mile or so south to appreciate the view to the north. Seen from this vista, Paoli could be a village in New England, or southern Europe. It's an image that will be recorded and stored in the memory bank of the mind.

The Pioneer Mother's Memorial Forest is in the area. It's an 88-acre National Natural Landmark, an original and undisturbed presettlement forest. There are oak, hickories, sugar maples, American beech and black walnuts reaching skyward, a view of Indiana two centuries ago.

Ind. 37 is rolling, winding and rustic. A mailbox is attached to an old plow, a reminder of when a moldboard plow turned over soil behind real horse power.

\* \* \*

We drive past a sign pointing southeast to Valeene, a Orange County town. We have been there on earlier trips, have read about the days when it was a commercial and social center where residents from miles around came on Saturday nights.

Those days are gone. The old grocery which was occupied for most of its 130 years is now "Grammy and Grampy's," a restaurant run by Mary and Andrew Smith.

# Youngs Creek

## DOWN IN THE VALLEY

A sign about six miles south of Paoli points west off Ind. 37 to "Youngs Creek."

It is three miles over a paved county road to the Orange County community. Along the way a bantam rooster struts across the road, king of his own domain. A vulture, less brave than the rooster, soars from a road kill as a car approaches.

A floral tribute hangs from a bridge railing, a memorial to the victim of a traffic accident. A turtle plods across the road, oblivious to time or to distance.

At Youngs Creek a calico kitten runs across the road. A tree house is at the edge of town, but it is too early for youngsters to begin their escape from watching TV. A rubber tire swing hangs on a rope from a tree, the grass gone from the area below it, rubbed bare by tiny feet.

The town is in a small valley, elevation 591 feet, far below the 912-foot peak a half-mile or so to the northeast.

What had been a store is abandoned, an old "Pepsi" sign still on one outside wall, "Gilliatt's Fabric Center" written on the other. It has been years since the building was a fabric center, longer since it was a neighborhood store.

Three men work on the roof of the Youngs Creek Church of Christ on this Friday morning. It's near the center of town, which has six or eight houses, some manufactured homes. Each residence appears to have a boat on the lawn, for Youngs Creek, the town, is on Youngs Creek, the stream, which runs into Patoka Lake, two miles downstream.

Youngs Creek is far from any major city, but close to nature. Chances are the few people who live here prefer it that way.

*  *  *

Back on Ind. 37, Orange County becomes Crawford County, an area more blessed with scenic beauty than with resources. There is little industry in the county and many workers have to travel to Jasper, Louisville or other places for employment. There are no stop-and-go lights in Crawford County but, it is reported, one may be erected at Marengo to replace a caution light.

All high school students attend Crawford County High south of Marengo. It's a consolidation, the English Red Raiders, the Leavenworth Rivermen (also called Wyandottes), the Marengo Cavemen and the Milltown Millers now members of the Wolfpack.

# English

## TOWN ON THE MOVE

English, the Crawford County seat of government, is a town in transition. It's tired of being flooded out and it's moving to higher ground.

Two creeks meet, one from the north, one from the east, and sometimes inundate what was once the heart of the town. It happened in 1979, bringing water seven feet deep in the town library. That was, experts said, a "once-in-a-100-year flood." They were wrong. Eleven years later, a second deluge engulfed English, leaving the business district and houses in the valleys flooded. Damage was extensive, but no lives were lost.

If it could happen twice, it could occur three times. Most of the buildings were old, their foundations in bad shape. The town had pushed its luck far enough. It was time to take action. The three-member Town Council, supported by petitions, had made the final decision to move the town to a ridge out on Ind. 64, even before the 1990 flood.

But with government there is red tape. Grants and government assistance take time. The move has been slow, but steady.

Janice Holzbog, Crawford County librarian, says some older residents are biding their time. If the relocation takes long enough . . . well, they won't need to worry about making a move.

Out on Ind. 64, new stores are open for business. Soon the library, which serves the county's 9,914 residents, will be relocated there.

Down in the valley, storefronts are empty, the shoppers gone. The Crawford County jail and courthouse are now atop a hill overlooking what is becoming a ghost town.

It is a far different place than it was 35 years ago. Lucille Stroud, a retired teacher, has lived around English for seventy years. She recalls "when it was a big thing to come into town on a Saturday night. We just went into the stores, walked around, didn't do anything big, but it was important for those of us living out in the country."

Businesses may be duplicated, but it's doubtful the charm of the past can be recaptured.

\* \* \*

Ind. 37 continues to wind its way through Crawford County south of English. A campaign poster urges voters to elect "Mutt" as a county commissioner. It is good to know that men with names like "Mutt" and "Bull" can seek offices, just like men with more sophisticated names.

The road passes through Grantsburg, a hamlet of ten houses and a closed "cash and carry" store.

A sign on Ind. 37 near Grantsburg points west to Hemlock Cliffs. The road is narrow, unimproved at times, not much more than a farm lane.

It is early morning, an ideal time to make the trip. The only sounds belong to nature. The air is pure, clear, only a contrail marring the blue skies. There are no cars to be heard, no man-made noise, only stillness and the beauty of the hemlocks, wildflowers and wildlife.

A trail leads into a captivating wilderness of sandstone cliffs and deep canyons, along a clear rushing stream, to the giant waterfall that cascades down the bluff.

Civilization seems miles away. The venture back to reality is made with reluctance.

# Sulphur
## A STOPPING POINT

Ind. 37 runs into Ind. 66 at the I-64 interchange just north of Sulphur. It is a hamlet that seems to have prospered from traffic off the interstate.

Lutz's Grill and Arcade at Sulphur sells hunting and fishing licenses. It also is a place to check in deer killed during the hunting season.

Edward and Treva Tucker own the Ole Country Store at Sulphur, which is almost surrounded by the Hoosier National Forest. Hunting and fishing licenses are for sale in the store, forest fires can be reported there, and almost anything a person needs to hunt or survive seems to be available. Shirts and caps that carry the name "Ole Country Store" are for sale.

The Tuckers also have a deer processing plant about two miles south of town near Sulphur Springs. Sulphur Springs was the site of a spa around 1900, when visitors claimed they were soothed by the water from the artesian wells.

Here in the present, a woman who needs her nerves soothed enters the store with with two small children. She has locked her keys in the car and needs help. A customer offers to take her home, until it is learned she lives in Louisville.

Instead, he tells her about a wrecker service that will send someone to open the car door. The woman, now wiser about the hazards of cross-country travel, agrees and her crisis is solved.

# Alton
## "BEAUTIFUL COUNTRY"

The librarian back at English has told us Alton is a must on any visit to Crawford County. We enter Perry County, drive to a community called Oriole on Ind 66, turn east onto a county road and re-enter Crawford County.

There is no traffic, no people, only an occasional house on the road to Alton. Trees extend their branches from each side of the road, form a roof above the crushed stone, shutting off light except for slithers of sunshine.

A hill drops from the west into the Ohio River bottom, and there on a pocket against the Ohio River, is Alton. It is a stunning sight, the sun glistening against the smooth water, disturbed only by a single speed boat.

If there is a "Backroads Indiana" this is it.

Alton may be remote, but it is not isolated. It has an Indian museum, the center of the town's annual Festival of Fallen Leaves on the second weekend of October.

The only store has been abandoned for some time, and Glenn DeLong wants to change that. DeLong is at work, turning a building on the main route through town into a store.

"Going to give it a try. Want to sell general merchandise. And my wife wants to sell new and used clothing." Nothing fancy, mind you. Items like children's clothing and jeans.

DeLong moved here from Vincennes, but grew up in Ohio. "I guess you could say I'm a Buckeye, but I call myself an adopted Hoosier."

"I'm having a little yard sale to get rid of some of this stuff," he says as he continues to remove items from the building that was a store years ago.

"Have to move in some showcases and furniture, but we're pretty well on our way," he says.

"I love it down here. If the good Lord is willing, I'll be here the rest of my life. It is quiet, the river is nice, it is beautiful country."

And it is different than places like Vincennes and other towns he has lived.

"We saw five wild turkeys just outside of town the other day," he says to prove the point.

"The only thing bad right now is that we don't have a general store or anything like that, but we're trying to work on that," he says in case anyone doubts he is serious.

He expects the store to become a gathering spot. "We'll probably put a liar's bench out front," he adds. My grandfather had a general store in Ashland, Kentucky. When I was a kid, that was my life."

The serenity DeLong has grown to appreciate may change, eventually. Alton could be a busier place if a proposed development is successful.

A 500-acre tract is being developed on the east side of Alton on the bow in the river called Bull's Point. It is a scenic site, and there are reports the development could combine housing with a golf course and possibly a marina.

A drive to its peak offers a panorama of the river both upstream and downstream, and of Alton down at river's edge. The development could change Alton, bringing improvements, but also altering its rustic setting.

A steel one-lane bridge with wooden planks for a floor crosses the now-placid Blue River that empties into the Ohio. It was not built for tourism, for heavy traffic. It is almost 100 years old, having been built in 1897. "Twelve Ton Weight Limit," a sign says.

The road east out of Alton is unpaved. A hand lettered sign pleads: "We need a road. It's been too long. Vote for Tucker." (A week after the sign was seen, Curtis Tucker won election as a Crawford County commissioner, one of only two Republicans in the county to win in the 1992 general election.)

* * *

We return to Ind. 66, called the George Rogers Clark Trail through the scenic Lincoln Hills area of southern Indiana. A sign warns "Hill, 15 mph," and it means it. South of Mt. Pleasant, the road makes a 110-degree turn to the right. This is not a road for those who prefer interstate driving.

Further south in Perry County the road continues its curves and twists, making at least three 90-degree turns before easing along the Ohio to Derby.

## Derby and Rome
### LORE OF THE RIVER

Derby has a boat dock and ramp, but the town is quiet on this Friday morning.

A few customers are parked at the store in town, which, fittingly, has a brown derby painted on its concrete side. There are few houses, no more than ten, and a post office.

High school students, once Derby Warriors, are now Commodores up at Perry Central High School near Leopold.

* * *

Ind. 66 straightens to follow the river south from Derby. A historical marker near the river notes an incursion on June 17, 1862, by Capt. Thomas H. Hines and 62 Confederate soldiers. Their mission, to pose as Union troops looking for deserters, failed. Most of the invaders were ambushed on an island near Leavenworth and killed. Hines escaped to return a year later with John Hunt Morgan and his raiding Confederate cavalrymen.

* * *

Nestled in a curve on the Ohio off Ind. 66, Rome was the Perry County seat from 1818 to 1859. The old handmade brick courthouse built about 1820 still stands. Two story, square with an octagonal cupola, the courthouse was

designed to resemble the state capital in Corydon.

Rome gave up the seat of government to Cannelton, but it retained the Courthouse, using it as the Rome Academy, then as a public school until 1966.

There are no judges around, no lawyers, no elected officials, no real estate agents transferring deeds, no sheriff's cars around the old courthouse—only ghosts of the past.

The building is now a town hall and a community center with a playground on the grounds. There are a dozen or so houses, but no businesses, except for the post office.

Rome's significance is in the past . . . and in the people who call it home and appreciate its serenity.

\* \* \*

Back on Ind. 66, goldenrod is in bloom as the road leaves the river and cuts cross country past neat farms on graceful rolling hills, then turns south to a place called Rocky Point. Ind. 66 and Ind. 160 meet here and a marker indicates it is six miles south to Tobinsport, one of the southernmost towns in Indiana. Ind. 160 is as rough as a washboard even at 15 mph, but the pavement finally grows smoother and teeth stop chattering.

# Tobinsport
### A PLACE TO RELAX

A man is target-practicing with a pellet gun down at the Tobinsport boat ramp. It is a pleasant Indiana autumn afternoon and he is relaxing at the river's edge, sipping on a beer now and then.

He extends his hand, says he is "Jim Morris from Tell City." He knows Tobinsport well, though, recalls when the town had a store and high school. The store is closed, the high school merged with Perry Central, "Pirates" becoming "Commodores."

Morris recalls that a ferry once plied the river, connecting Tobinsport and Cloverport, Ky. It is gone, the nearest connection now the bridge downstream at Cannelton.

"The state took over the dock one time, but couldn't get enough money appropriated and had to let it go back to the owner," Morris says. When a community is this far from the state capital in Indianapolis it is not easy to get anyone to listen.

It is obvious Morris appreciates the river. He talks about other towns on the Ohio, recalls when railroads carried more traffic and there were few barges.

"When a barge went by, people used to go down by the river and watch. Now there is so much traffic no one pays much attention."

No one except men and women who appreciate the river as much as Jim Morris does.

* * *

The drive back to Ind. 66 is no smoother. It is past time for lunch and we take Jim Morris' advice about where to dine in Cannelton.

# Cannelton
## A TOWN TO COTTON TO

It is early afternoon at Yaggi's Bar and Restaurant. The men are solving the world's problems, talking about baseball, medical costs, health insurance and whatever else comes to mind. One says a new doctor in town doesn't like golf. "But he did say he'd join us at the 19th green for drinks afterwards," one of them says, breaking into laughter.

A sign at the bar says, "My bank and I have a deal. If I don't lend money, it won't sell beer.

There are no strangers at Yaggi's. Emory Yaggi, the owner, sees to that. If a visitor acts interested, Emory will want to know his name, make him feel at home.

In a few weeks, the college basketball season will be under way and three TV sets will be on, especially when I.U. plays.

Down at the courthouse, a custodian who won't reveal his name doesn't mind talking about Cannelton, Perry County or its sandstone courthouse. He takes visitors through the courthouse, now outgrown, offices spilled over into a brick annex which seems out of place among its surroundings.

The custodian talks about crime, which is no stranger to these seemingly serene surroundings. "We've had 43 people in jail at one time. Lot of drunks on weekends, usual kinds of crimes."

There has been talk, and likely there will be more, about moving the county seat from Cannelton to Tell City. Tell City has more voters, more employees who work for the county. But Cannelton won't give up without a fight, because the loss of the courthouse would be a difficult blow to the

town, as it was to Rome back in 1859.

The custodian takes his guests to historical markers, tells them the present courthouse was built in 1896 on land donated by the American Cannel Coal Company.

There is history here in Cannelton, a river town founded in 1837. Another marker calls attention to Gilbert du Marquis de Lafayette, "who spent a night and day at Rock Island four miles from here May 9, 1825. His steamboat was wrecked. Pioneers for miles around came to see him. The spot is now called Lafayette Springs."

A block or so from the Courthouse, Mike Tierney is at work at Sweetbrier & Company, a flower shop and antique store. Mike takes time out to talk about a sandstone house he and his wife, Tara, are restoring across the street. It just isn't any house. It's one that is filled with reminders of the past. Built about 1850, it once was a tavern and bakery. It is just 20 feet wide as it faces the street, but it has three stores above-ground, a basement and a subbasement with a tunnel.

There is good reason to believe the tunnel led from the river and the house and was used as part of the underground railroad that helped slaves escape in the days before the Civil War. Workmen on scaffolds are restoring the south outer wall to its original look, preserving a bit of history that might otherwise be lost for future generations.

Nearby, the sounds of music drift over town from Cannelton High School, with 110 students one of the smallest high schools in the state. The school is 70 years old, "1922" etched on the front. The gymnasium is old and small, but a sign proudly proclaims, "Home of the Bulldogs, Cannelton Gymnasium."

Not small is the old Indiana Cotton Mill, a decaying landmark in town. Weeds grow in cracks in the sandstone walls of this monument to King Cotton.

Started in 1847, the mill is almost a block long, three stories high, an achievement of American ingenuity at the mid-point of the 19th Century. It began operating in 1850 and employed 400 people on 372 looms and, for a time, was Indiana's largest industry. It remained in continuous operation until 1954, making uniforms for the Civil War and materials for both World Wars.

Towns like Cannelton shouldn't be forgotten.

# Troy

## No Fulton's Folly

We bypass Tell City, with 8,800 residents Perry County's largest town. It is another river city worth visiting, and we make a note to spend more time there later.

Troy, just a few miles away on Ind. 66, is the focus of our attention.

The 18-foot "Christ of the Ohio" monument is on a hill above Troy, standing watch, extending a silent message of peace and a guide to pilots and rivermen on the Ohio. It was sculpted by Herbert Jogerst, a German who was an American prisoner in World War II. He came to America after the war, worked at the St. Meinrad seminary and was commissioned to design the statue.

Enter Troy from the west and even more visible is the 142-foot-high steeple of St. Pius V Roman Catholic Church, now more than 100 years old.

Troy, like most river towns, has a long history. It was platted in 1815 on a site where the Anderson River empties into the Ohio.

Abraham Fulton, brother of Robert Fulton, inventor of the steamboat, is buried at the Troy cemetery, having been killed cutting trees to build a family home. The Fultons had bought land from Nicholas A. Roosevelt, great-uncle of Theodore and Franklin D. Roosevelt, about 1811.

It is said Nicholas Roosevelt commanded a steamboat modeled after the one Robert Fulton invented. The boat, the New Orleans, stopped at Troy, one of the few fueling sites on the Ohio at the time.

The sandstone Nester House, down near the Ohio, was built in 1863 and was a hotel from the late 1860s until the 1950s. It is now privately owned and known as Riverplace.

Its high school is gone, the Troy Trojans have become Tell City Marksmen and Troy's boom days as a river town have past, but more than 500 residents still call Troy home. It is a scenic stop, a quiet place to pause and listen . . . and perhaps visualize a time faded in history.

*　*　*

It is time to head north. We cross the Anderson River into Spencer County and take Ind. 545 north.

Up ahead is New Boston, a community platted in 1870 with 44 lots. It still is a small town with two churches, a tavern and a gas station.

We ask about Evanston, a community southeast of New Boston, and learn it was founded in 1888 when a railroad built a line through the scenic area.

The big thing in Evanston, we are told, is the annual hog roast (the third Saturday in September) that raises money to improve the community park built by the Evanston Civic Association.

The community of Lamar, over on Ind. 245, also grew up with the Huntingburg, Tell City and Cannelton Railroad (later the Southern Railway). Lamar, surrounded by farms and strip mines, has a service station, a bar and restaurant, post office and a construction company.

# Fulda
### A STOPPING PLACE

Fulda, further north on Ind. 545, is another southern Indiana town that grew up around a Catholic church. The Rev. Joseph Kundek, the priest in charge of Catholics from Troy to Jasper, aware of the slow travel of the times, established parish communities at Fulda and Ferdinand, spacing them a day's ride apart.

St. Boniface parish, begun in a log church, has been the core around which the community revolves since 1847. Its building is accentuated with a 150-foot tall steeple, that was dedicated in 1866.

At one time Fulda thrived as a stopover for travelers between Troy on the Ohio River and Jasper. It now has five hundred residents, two bars, two garages and a convenience store. When basketball isn't being discussed, chances are you may find customers at Louie & Mary's Cafe playing euchre, Indiana's second most favorite game.

Drive around Fulda and notice a community building, tennis courts, picnic area and playground equipment, evidence that the people here care about their quality of life.

\* \* \*

Ind. 545 turns and twists as it continues north, past farms and strip mines, toward St. Meinrad. St. Meinrad is home to St. Meinrad monastery and seminary, which surround a prosperous town that's a living postcard, a community that appears to belong to another place and time. We will return on another day, include it in another chapter.

It is time to drive west on Ind. 62 from St. Meinrad, turn north on Ind. 162 to Ferdinand.

# Ferdinand
## NEAT AND ORDERLY

Like St. Meinrad, Ferdinand (accent on Ferd) is another town for artists and photographers in search of charm. It is a busy community, with stores, businesses, a commercial center for its 2,300 residents.

And like Fulda, it owes much of its past to Father Kundek, who laid out the town in 1840 as a stop on the pioneer Troy-to-Jasper trail. With the church came settlers, Germans and Austrians who built Ferdinand into one of Dubois County's more important towns.

The Convent of the Immaculate Conception, home of the Benedictine Sisters, and St. Ferdinand's Church, rise above the town from the east side of Ind. 162. Nothing is in disarray. Everything is neat, orderly, in place.

The church, now almost 150 years old, is believed to be the oldest building in Ferdinand, evidence of the care and dedication it has received.

Not far away is Forest Park High School, a consolidation of Ferdinand and Birdseye, its athletes, appropriately, called the Forest Park Rangers.

* * *

Ind. 161 slices gently through central Dubois County, past Bretzville, allowing a review of images snapped into memory during the day.

It has been a day when the surroundings, it seems, have changed with each mile. There has been no time, and no reason, for boredom while traveling miles over crazily twisting roads, straight stretches, hills, valleys and rolling landscapes.

There are mental pictures of "Visit Meramec Caverns" on barn roofs. Signs for Red Man tobacco slowing fading on side of barns filled with harvested tobacco. Barns falling into disrepair as farming becomes more specialized. Hogs, the least pretentious of all animals, wallowing in pools, content with their surroundings.

Up ahead is Jasper, a good place to spend the night.

## Trip 4
# ORANGE & LAWRENCE COUNTIES

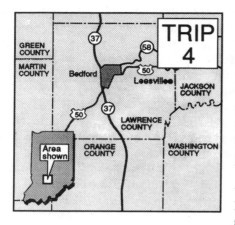

It is Columbus Day, exactly 500 years after the discovery of America, and it is a day to enjoy a part of this land the Italian aboard the Santa Maria encountered.

Landscapes change daily in October on this route through southern Indiana. Leaves, red, yellow, sienna and an assortment of other colors, paint a masterpiece no artist can copy.

It is cool enough for heat and wood smoke, scented oak, rises slowly from chimneys along Ind. 446 as it snakes across Monroe Reservoir, on its southward path toward U.S. 50.

A caution light slows traffic on Ind. 58 east of Heltonville.

Off to the west, a couple of miles south is the neat, orderly Hunter place, a farm that has been in the same family as long as Indiana has been a state. Hereford cattle graze on the still green meadow.

Off to the east, a sawmill is in operation, a reminder that timber still is a big product of these southern Indiana hills.

Ind. 446 ends at U.S. 50. A few miles east, a county road leads south to Leesville, the oldest community in Lawrence County.

# Leesville
### 40TH AND PLUM

Leesville was settled in 1810, platted in January 1818, named for Lee County, Virginia. It was the site of a Potawatomi Indian massacre on March 10, 1813.

Lawrence County's first school was opened in Leesville in 1813; the first high school in 1858.

Students now are bused elsewhere, but a school remains, well maintained as a community center by the civic minded. It has been money from Thursday and Saturday night bingo games that has allowed the center to remain open, for equipment to be placed on the surrounding playground.

It is Rhea Canfield's day to mind the Leesville Village Store. She and her sister, Louanna Robbins, operate the store for their parents. "One of us works three straight days, 11 hours a day, the other the next three days," Rhea explains. "The hours are long, but the work isn't hard."

It is 9 a.m. and there are no customers.

The store, like the old school, is a community center, a place to share information. The portable sign out front proclaims "Happy 17th Birthday Tabatha Bair."

This is a town where people know each other, care about each other, their town and their country. The American flag flies from a number of homes.

Leesville is not incorporated, the streets are not named, but a residence boasts a sign, "40th and Plum," from a street elsewhere.

* * *

A county road leads from Leesville east out of Lawrence County into Jackson County. A fat ground hog waddles across the pavement.

Off to the north is the Hemlock Bluffs nature preserve. Visitors are warned: "Everything is protected. Do not disturb or remove anything from the area. Hike on marked trails only. Hunting and trapping prohibited. No fires, camping, picnicking. Your cooperation will protect and preserve the unique natural area."

Despite that plea, Styrofoam cups, paper sacks, soft drink and beer cans, plastic bottles and debris litter the grounds. It is obvious some people have come to enjoy the outdoors, but not to preserve it.

The road drops sharply, winding down from the ridge into the valley, past wooded hillsides and house trailers before entering Medora.

# Medora
### HITTING THE RIGHT NOTES

Founder West Lee Wright, must have been a musician. He chose three notes from the scale, me-do-re, and called the town Medora. Medora grew up on the Ohio and Mississippi Railroad (later the Baltimore & Ohio, now CSX) and continued to prosper when U.S. 50 passed through town. The east-west road, however, was relocated in the 1930s, taking much of the traffic from town. Ind. 235 now connects Medora with U.S. 50 to the north, Ind. 135 to the east.

Medora may have lost its U.S. highway, train traffic may have declined, but it is a small town that has kept its schools and much of its business area.

Doomsayers insisted the community was too small to maintain a high school, that with an enrollment ranging from 100 to 110, the Medora school would be unable to resist consolidation. They were wrong, the school is still here, a mom-and-pop operation in an era of Wal-Marts.

A new school and a gymnasium for its "Hornets" basketball team are monuments to the independence, the pride of the people of this community.

Medora's eight hundred residents do not need to leave town to bank, buy groceries, dine out or participate in the annual Christmas parade.

It may be Columbus Day, but an employee in the post office puts the mail in the boxes, holiday or not.

Bundy Brothers grain elevator, the old mill where farmers brought wheat from the threshing rigs fifty years ago, is still here but has changed with the times.

At Betty's Rainbow Grill, three men argue whether marijuana should be legalized, recall the rambunctious days of their youth and, now that they are older, discuss retirement at 62 vs. 65. They agree the Indiana Lotto and Powerball games could save them from financial worries in their golden years.

Next door, the Plastic Company, Inc. plant is closed, its workers now employed elsewhere or not at all.

On the opposite corner of town, the old brick yard is no longer in operation, even though its kilns are in place.

Times change, factories close. Towns with community spirit continue to survive.

*  *  *

A Jackson County road follows the railroad southwest toward Sparksville. Trash in plastic bags outside rural homes awaits the scavenger truck. Hoosiers are becoming more environmentally conscious, although there still are roads cluttered with debris.

An old steel bridge is off to the left, crossing the East Fork of White River into Washington County. We resist the temptation to take the road into an unfamiliar area.

Not much remains in Sparksville except a church. The only business is a house that advertises "Brown eggs for sale."

We remember a farmer named "Squirrely Birge" who once farmed the White River bottoms fifty years ago. A person doesn't forget a good man named "Squirrely."

# Fort Ritner
## HOMETOWN HERITAGE

A viaduct covered with graffiti and initials spray-painted in hearts that may outlast the romances leads into Fort Ritner at the southeast edge of Lawrence County.

A "Fort Ritner" sign puts the town population at 70. This town may be small but it is a community that is preserving its past. The Fort Ritner Heritage Museum opened in September, 1992, in a concrete block building in Heritage Park.

The dedication came during Fort Ritner Heritage Days, an event when former residents returned to join those who remain for the fifth annual town reunion. It is now a month later and folks here are still talking about a crowd of four hundred that showed up on that Saturday for a big pitch-in dinner.

The Museum has a collection of old pictures, railroad memorabilia, reminders of the Fort Ritner of an earlier time.

The Fort Ritner Heritage Corporation operates the park and the museum, keeps it going through donations.

Liberty C. Root, corporation secretary and museum curator, said in a report on the Heritage Days that the museum's creation has been "a labor of love": "It is the wish of all involved that the park will serve as a memorial to those who withstood the hardships of depressions, wars, floods and epidemics . . . and be an incentive to future generations."

Across the street, pictures of the Fort Ritner of old hang on the wall at the Hudson Store, where the post office occupies one corner. There are pictures of the 1913 flooding of the White River, a 1919 picture of the depot where trains stopped in the days when Fort Ritner had a hotel. A plaque recalls October 6, 1856, the day the "Big Tunnel" between Fort Ritner and Tunnelton opened: "The train stalls midway. Smoke and soot ruin passengers' clothing and everyone has to walk out."

This is heartland America, and the Bill of Rights hangs on the wall, as does a roster of all postmasters from "M. Ritner," appointed September 4, 1856, to Sheila Hudson, who got the job September 22, 1979.

Mrs. Hudson is still postmaster, serving thirty families. She still owns the store, which handles groceries and, just like the supermarkets, tabloids like *The Star* and *Weekly World.*

A woman enters the store with two young men and a boy. She asks for two dozen eggs, picks up a few other items. "Fixing breakfast for the entire family," she says.

Linda Brewer, who grew up in the area, is assistant postmaster. She likes the area, explaining, "A small town is a better place to raise kids. People are friendly, but nosy." Just like in any small town, she might have added.

Sheila Hudson interjects, "And we have more excitement around here than what people think."

A woman walks in as she talks. She wants to tell Hudson and Brewer about the arrest of a man they all know. "Washington County's got him now, but there is a warrant out from the [Lawrence County] sheriff's office in Bedford."

Not every one is perfect, not even in a small town.

* * *

A road to the west out of Fort Ritner leads up on Devil's Backbone, a scenic overlook north to the Guthrie Creek bottoms, south across White River. Old mattresses and kitchen appliances, dumped over the edges of the bluffs, mar the beauty nature created.

We decide to take the paved county road to Buddha, a community to the northwest, toward Bedford. The isolation of the hill country changes, houses begin to line the road outside Buddha, a crossroads that has grown to an unincorporated, undefined area of three hundred residents.

Buddha (called Boo-dee around these parts) may have been named for a tramp who drifted in and out of town, or it may have come from Buda, as in Budapest, Hungary. John Beasley, who named the town when a post office opened in his store a hundred or so years ago, is no longer around to say for sure.

The post office is gone, the community has a Bedford zip code, but the Sallee Grocery keeps folks from driving into town to buy something they'd forgotten on an earlier trip.

# Tunnelton
## "PEACE OF MIND"

From Buddha we backtrack, then go south into Tunnelton, a town down on the river named after the two tunnels near town. It is a place far older than the railroad, though, for a church was built here in 1816.

Off to the left is the Guthrie Mansion, a huge Italianate brick structure accentuated with limestone blocks, surrounded by a wrought-iron fence. It is named for Alfred Guthrie, who built a general store in Tunnelton, acquired more than 3,000 acres, and served in the General Assembly before becoming president of the Stone City Bank in Bedford.

The post office Guthrie established is still here, open (the sign says) from 9:30 a.m. to 1:30 p.m.; the general store is not.

We arrive too late to join the "Older Americans," a group of senior citizens who gather each weekday morning for coffee, pastries and conversation at the United Methodist Church.

Tunnelton is quiet on this holiday morning. Larry McCart, director of the Lawrence County Family and Children's Service in Bedford, is using his day off to work at home. He moved from Bedford to Tunnelton, the place where his mother was born, 15 years ago.

"We like it out here. It's a whole different kind of life. There are no stoplights, no sirens, no traffic tie-ups," he says.

"It's a good place to raise children. [He has four.] You can turn kids loose and not worry a lot about them. Everyone knows who they are, and if anyone gets out of line their parents will hear about it.

"People take care of each other. They care about one another. No one is a stranger for long.

"You can leave your property unattended. There is peace of mind. There aren't many places left where—day in and day out—you don't have to lock your house or worry about your car."

No town is free of crime and Tunnelton is no exception. "Sheriff's deputies made a marijuana bust the other night," McCart says.

Now that the store is closed, the nearest places to pick up loaves of bread are at Sallee's Grocery in Buddha or Hudson's Grocery in Fort Ritner.

A visitor looks toward the old high school gym, still standing but surrounded by tall weeds. It now is owned by an antique/collectible dealer.

A civic group bought the gym for $1 when the school closed to become a part of the North Lawrence School Corp. The group opened the gym for basketball, community events and parties, holding fund-raisers to maintain the building.

Interest slowly dwindled, fewer and fewer people were left to do the work that needed to be done, and it was decided, reluctantly, to sell the school.

Like other small towns, there is too much to do, too few to do it.

# Bono, Saltillo, Leipsic
## How Now, Brown Cow?

We drive south out of Tunnelton through the one-lane viaduct under the railroad, headed south toward a place on our map called Bono, an early settlement dating back to 1816.

A half-dozen vultures dining on road kill do not fly off until a car is within fifty feet of them.

A man and woman who appear to be past retirement age stop their pickup under a tree to gather black walnuts.

It is a splendid day, one in which the mind can become lost in the appreciation of the surroundings.

Up ahead, a farmer is herding 75 Guernsey dairy cows across the road from barn to pasture. We stop a few feet away and study the map.

Another man, older than the herdsman, walks by.

"Whatcha looking for?" he asks.

"Bono," we say.

"You missed it. It's back the way you came. It was back there at the turn in the road where there were four or five houses."

There obviously isn't much to see in Bono. We have driven through it without realizing we were there and have crossed from Lawrence into Washington County.

We decide to look elsewhere. "Where does this road go?" we ask.

"To Campbellsburg," he says.

"How do I get to 'Saltillo'?"

The man is patient. "Go back to the crossroads there," he says, pointing to a stop a few hundred yards behind us. "Just go south 'til you get there."

We find the community of Saltillo a few miles down the road. What had been a grocery is closed. There are no businesses open and the town has no post office. The ruins of a Massey-Ferguson dealership remain after a fire. A farm center once operated by the Farm Bureau Co-op is abandoned.

It is three weeks until Halloween and an artist in straw sculpture has created a straw horse, a straw man on a manure spreader, a straw woman holding a basket. It is an elaborate Halloween exhibit that will not be seen by a great number of people. Excellence has been its own reward for the person who fashioned the exhibit.

We drive west from Saltillo, cross from Washington into Orange County, and take a county road off Ind. 60 to Leipsic.

Formed in 1861, the town was known as Lancaster, then Lancaster Station, then Leipsic after the post office came.

A few people remain who remember when Leipsic had two stores that operated huckster trucks selling household and farm goods over much of southern Indiana, or when patients from miles around came to town to get eye examinations and glasses from "Doc" Colglazier.

The Leipsic United Methodist Church congregation is about all that's left of the community that grew up along the old Monon Railroad.

We take county roads west of Leipsic toward Orleans. The roads seem to be atop the world, and a 360-degree panorama opens across level fields to the vastness of the horizon beyond.

The Orleans water tank is in the distance. We are not lost, but it would be a beacon if we were.

Grain bins with giant elevators dot the landscape. It is another bountiful Indiana grain harvest. Outside Orleans a rural home offers square-dance clothing for sale.

Orleans, on Ind. 37 and Ind. 337, isn't a backroads town, but it is time for lunch. Herle's restaurant in the center of Orleans proves to be a good choice. No one enters without offering a greeting. It is a friendly place and no one is a stranger for long.

It is Herle's second anniversary. The occasion is observed with coffee for 10 cents.

# Orangeville
## ITS RISE AND FALL

We can't leave Orange County without driving south, then west to Orangeville for a look at one of nature's mysteries. It is at Orangeville where Lost River, one of Indiana's wonders, rises from its subterranean course. At the Orangeville Rise Nature Preserve, a national landmark, a sign calls the site one that possesses "exceptional value as an illustration of American heritage."

Greenish-blue water rises in a pool, edged by a semi-circle of stone shaded by trees growing on the ledges.

Lost River sinks underground southeast of Orleans, travels about eight miles through waterways and caverns before rising at Orangeville and staying above ground until it empties into White River.

From Orangeville, roads wind from Orange into Lawrence County and onto U.S. 50.

# Huron
## GETTING A HEAD START

Ralph Riggle is back home in Huron, a Lawrence County town across the old B & O tracks from U.S. 50, this time to operate Riggle's Grocery & Deli.

Riggle was born here, moved across the county to Fayetteville when he was in the sixth grade, then stayed in Fayetteville, where he operated a service center ("a garage, wrecker service and car crusher") for 20 years.

He and Ada, his wife for 36 years, read a "for sale" ad, knew that the store was the only one between Mitchell on the east and Shoals on the west, and bought it in March, 1992. So far, Riggle says, the store has done "pretty well" even though it is not the best of times, economically: "We get a lot of food stamps. There is just no work available around the area."

There is deer hunting, though, and six or seven hunters have checked in deer killed with bow and arrow even though the season is just getting started.

Hunters have to eat. "Our restaurant business is picking up. We're selling a lot of sandwiches," Riggle explains. It is a full-time business, operating a general store that is open from 8 a.m. to 8 p.m. Mondays through Saturdays, 11:30 a.m. until 6 on Sundays.

The old Huron school, where the "Beavers" once played basketball before high school students were sent to Mitchell, is now used by the Hoosier Uplands Head Start Program. The school is in good condition, the playground equipment well-maintained.

A block away, a tractor tire dangles on a rope from a tree limb. A parent need not be rich to fashion a delight for his children.

* * *

We cross U.S. 50 and take a Lawrence County Road north toward Williams. There is no traffic, except for a slow-moving car with two retired couples enjoying the scenery off busy highways.

The trees are taking on their fall colors and there is no need to rush. The road meanders into a covered bridge over the East Fork of White River. It is 368 feet long, said to be the longest covered bridge still in use in Indiana.

Its floor is wooden and the planks clatter beneath cars. The pavement drops off at the north edge and, unfortunately, there is no good place to pull off for a closer look.

The memory unwinds back to the 1940s when Williams High School burned and its students bused across the bridge to school at Huron, the basketball players from two rival Spice Valley Township teams joined together as teammates for two years.

The county road leads onto Ind. 450 southwest of Williams and we drive into town, notice that the Williams Milling Company is closed, and decide to return later to talk to the owner, Leland Williams.

*- Claude Parsons*

West of Williams, we turn north on a county road across the western edge of Lawrence County, the road dropping down over a hill, across Indian Creek, into Silverville on Ind. 158 which terminates at the Crane Naval Surface Weapons Center.

Silverville has no stores, but houses along Ind. 158 are neat and clean. The Monday wash is on the lines. Wood is stacked neatly, awaiting the winter ahead.

Another adventure in driving awaits us north of Silverville. A county road meanders up the northwest edge of Lawrence County, through Boone Hollow, past the Boone Cemetery, then onto Ind. 58.

# Owensburg

### END OF AN ERA

A sign on a building in Owensburg says "Lehman Store—Since 1867."

Inside, Darlene Lewis is asked about the sign and confirms it is accurate. "This has been a store since 1867. The front part is the original store. The rest was added later. "When we [she and her husband, James], bought the place, we decided to keep the name which is what everyone knows it as."

The wooden floor is original, unchanged in 125 years. "It takes a lot of work to keep it clean," Mrs. Lewis says.

The Lewises are busy. They run the store and farm; Jim raises Hereford cattle, Darlene feeder pigs. The store is open daily except Sunday; livestock need daily attention. "We need Sunday off to go to church," she says. And, chances are, to rest.

"People depend on the store and we try to sell a little of everything . . . groceries, seed, feed, plumbing." It is a convenience store, because Bedford is 30 minutes away, Bloomfield 35 minutes, Bloomington 45 minutes.

Mrs. Lewis talks about the town: "People are friendly and nice. If someone moves in, they are made welcome. If you need help, people will come to help."

POSTSCRIPT: *Not enough people came to Lehman's Store and a lack of business forced Jim and Darlene Lewis to close its doors three months later. The contents were auctioned February 13, 1993, and the Lewises returned to farming full time.*

*"It was kind of sad, a difficult thing, but something we almost had to do," Jim said. He cited a combination of reasons for their decision.*

*Competition from bigger stores in Bedford and Bloomington hurt. Older, faithful, customers died off, and new residents weren't as likely to shop at home. More and more husbands and wives worked in bigger towns where they did their shopping.*

*"We were working 11 hours a day and about all we were getting out of it was what we were eating," Jim Lewis said.*

*It is a decision that likely will be repeated in other towns along the backroads of Indiana.*

## *Trip 5*
# MILLER'S TIMES

New houses built on hills are scattered along Ind. 158 as it winds west toward Fayetteville from Ind. 37 at the west edge of Bedford. Some houses are small, some large, almost mansions, some on wooded lots, others without shade. Trees grow almost against the pavement, leaving drivers only a small margin for error.

And, *Eureka!* We are in Eureka (Lawrence County, not the one in Warrick County). It is a community of several houses built against sharp bends in the road as it continues to run up and down and around, a roller coaster in an amusement park created by nature.

West of Eureka traffic slows behind a scavenger truck making its weekly rounds.

A John Deere tractor is parked under a car port across the highway from the Fayetteville town limits sign, a blend of town and country.

## Fayetteville
### NOMADS IN THE BARBERSHOP

Fayetteville Store, operated like the one in Heltonville by Larry "Bonehead" Faubion, is in a big stone building with an additional shelter for spring flowers.

There is a lot of activity in town. We enter Crane's Barber Shop, where Harold Crane, the barber, is at work. He's just in—on the next-to-last day of classes—from the bus route he drives for the North Lawrence School system. He has finished his first customer, has started on his second.

It is obvious he is an Indiana University basketball fan. A montage of Bob Knight pictures is in a frame with a Knight autograph under a greeting, "Best wishes, to Linda and Harold."

"That's just some of my pictures. I've got a lot of others, too," Crane says.

We mention we're visiting small communities off the main highways. One of the men says, "Down in Greene County, them little backroads communities are like that 'cause the damned roads are so rough nobody can get in."

The man says his name is Leonard Soper, his age 78, that he grew up in Owensboro, Kentucky, and now lives over in nearby Owensburg, Indiana.

We tell him we've been over most of the roads of Greene County. He looks at us and asks, "How the hell did you get over them? You're not riding a donkey." He's outspoken, this Leonard Soper.

"I was raised a Democrat. But we had Republicans in for four years and they did more for the roads than the Democrats have in 26 years," Soper says.

But he isn't optimistic roads will ever get much better. "Hell, if they blacktop the roads, some S.O.B. will get out there with a tractor or something and tear it up."

The customer in the chair agrees. "Or somebody will drive a bulldozer over it," he adds.

That customer is Max Linkenhoker, who describes himself as sort of a nomad in a travel trailer. He, too, spends some time over in Greene County when he's in Indiana. "I spend part of my time in Florida, part of it in Tennessee and part of it in Indiana over on a friend's place.

"Everything I own is on wheels," he says. "I've got a travel trailer here, one in Florida and I got a camper that sits on my truck in case I want to go somewhere I don't have one. I've been doing that for the last five or six years and I enjoy every damned minute of it. I've got no place to go and nothing to do when I get there."

Linkenhoker keeps talking, now that he has taken the conversation from Soper. "I sold all my real estate, except for a farm up in Hamilton County which doesn't have any buildings on it," he continues.

He talks about traveling being more difficult, traffic more crowded, and admits that with age he can see "the handwriting on the wall. But I'm not going to hurry it up."

Soper speaks up. "Every damn thing I own is on wheels, too, except my place, and if I could jack that up, I'd put wheels under it, too. But I've gotten so I don't give a damn whether I go anywhere or not."

Soper is still hot about the roads. "There're holes in the road this big," he says, circling his arms. "They come out and fill them with gravel. That does a hell of a lot of good 'cause the first rain that comes the hole is back again."

Linkenhoker says, "It takes all kinds of people to make a world."

Soper adds, "And, by God, we've got 'em, too."

Crane is too busy, or too smart, to join in the conversation. He concentrates on Linkenhoker's hair.

Linkenhoker pays his bill and leaves. Soper stays to talk a while longer. "I can remember things that happened back when I was a kid, but I can't recall what happened last week. If I get as bad the next ten years as I have the last ten, they'll have me in a hospital somewhere."

It is just a few days after President Bill Clinton had a $200 haircut at Los Angeles International Airport.

Crane has a sign on the wall, "Haircuts $3."

"You need to raise your prices," a visitor says.

Crane replies, "We don't have very many ignorant people in this country. I think we only have one, right now. Anyone who'd pay $200 for a haircut is a little bit ignorant."

Soper says, "He [Clinton] may have paid for it with food stamps. You can't tell. I voted for him, but now I have my doubts. One thing about it, and it's my opinion, he can't be any worse than Bush or Reagan."

Soper pays his $3 and says he'd better be leaving. He's admonished not to let his car drop into any of those Greene County chuckholes.

We ask for directions to Williams. Crane says that's where he went to school, a graduate with the class of 1951.

## Williams
### IT'S THE MILLER'S TIME

Harold Crane gives directions as well as he cuts hair. We reach Ind. 450, turn southwest and find Williams. A banner—"Welcome Home Jason"—hangs from a trestle for motorists to see as they pass under a viaduct. We wonder about Jason. Is he home from the service, back from college for the summer? No matter! Someone is happy to have him back home.

The Spice Valley fishing area, a state facility open to anyone, is just outside Williams. It's above the old dam that has given Williams much of its identity for decades. Two dogs meander along the highway at the entrance to town, unafraid of the traffic.

Leland Williams is at the Williams Milling Company where he has been a fixture for more than four decades. He knows the milling business, the town and its people. It's no wonder. He's a descendant of the founders of Williams. His grandfather, T. H. Williams, was a county commissioner when the covered bridge downstream across White River was built in 1884.

He's 79, but sharp, interesting, as enthusiastic about life as a teen-ager. He's at the mill six days a week, 8 to 5, except on Thursday afternoons. Chances are you'll find him then at the 900-acre farm he sometimes helps son Dave operate.

Williams is wearing Big Mac bib overalls and a red "Beck's Hybrid" cap. He drove a Model-T Ford to Williams High School, graduating in 1931, played for the basketball team, the Bulldogs ("I was just a hamburger specialist"), recalls many of the games, and almost every play in the battles with rival Huron, especially a game in which he was thrown out for roughness by a Huron man who refereed for the home team when an official didn't show up.

"A real homer, huh?" we ask. "He was a piece of art," Williams replies.

"You know how primitive some of us used to be. Well, I was maneuvering around, got some Huron kid off his feet, and he landed on my shoulders. I bent down, stuck his head between the two rows of bleachers, picked up the ball and started dribbling. That's when I got thrown out.

"We won. I don't think we ever had any problems with Huron," he said. Old rivalries never die.

For 15 years, Williams would keep score for the Williams team, recalling names of storekeepers from rival schools. He is loyal to friends, family and school, and has missed but one Williams High School alumni dinner since he was graduated.

He and his wife, Anabel, live in the same house where he was born. He attended Purdue University for two years, still remembers the names of his professors, the grades they gave him, the friends he made there.

The mill sits on White River at the dam site, along the old Southern Indiana Railway (later owned by the Milwaukee). It is a reminder of the days when farms were small, and millers ground wheat into floor, grain into livestock feed for customers.

"We don't grind much grain, except for a few small farmers who don't have facilities on their farms," Williams says.

A woman customer enters the mill, asking for "mouse killer." Williams points to a sack. "Two and a quarter," he tells her.

"It's like a cafeteria here. Somebody will come in an carry out a sack of dog food, or another customer might drop by and leave with a calf starter."

Williams talks about the old electric generating plant that operated at the dam for about fifty years, earlier in the 1900s. He shows pictures taken when the plant was under construction, seems to know its operation as well as its history, is happy a potential buyer may be able to restart the power plant.

It is obvious his interests extend beyond the mill, beyond the farm, beyond the town.

His office is in a corner of the mill. The room is a bit dusty, befitting a feed mill. "Sit down, if you can find a place," he says. The wooden desk is an antique, the kind merchants once used to store 3 by 5 inch credit books. The cash register is old, too. ("It's about a 1905 edition.")

He looks at the old wood stove in the office. "We sit around it in the winter and tell a lot of tales. When I sit back in the chair at my desk, I tell people that's my rush hour."

Williams trusts his customers, citing the honesty of a farmer whose hog business failed back in the mid 1950s.

"I hadn't seen him for 25 years. He came in here two or three years ago [about 1990], handed me $2,000 in cash and said, 'I owed you $1,700, I think. The interest would have been at least $300. It's the first time I've had that much money.'"

The man had sold his farm and was paying off his debts . . . more than thirty years later.

"We don't mail out any statements. We quit that years ago. If I can't get them [customers who owe money] on the telephone to keep them on their toes . . . We don't lose much. And we haven't lost anything the last few years. We just don't let the credit get out that far."

Williams may be as old as yesterday, but he's as new as tomorrow. He talks about the county's high cost of trash disposal, cites the need for recycling, talks about Indiana Department of Environmental Management regulations and says, They are plumb nutty up there [in Indianapolis], as far as I'm concerned."

We leave, wondering if there is some way to make Leland Williams' common sense contagious.

We head out of town, slowing again for the two dogs we saw in the road earlier. There may be no policemen in the unincorporated town . . . but there are dogs to patrol the streets.

*   *   *

Anyone who likes Indiana backroads should plan to travel Ind. 450 from Shoals to Bedford in the fall. It passes through Dover Hill, skirts the site of Trinity Springs, a spa that once had six hotels, meanders through Williams and on into Bedford. It is a good backroad on which to appreciate autumn colors.

# Harrodsburg
### BYPASSED BUT NOT BYGONE

Ind. 37 moved farther away from town when it was four-laned from Bloomington to Bedford, but Harrodsburg remains alive, well and prospering midway between the two cities.

Red, white and blue banners promote the upcoming festival in this unincorporated town of older homes and churches. A community center and the Burnham Auditorium are in the center of town, evidence of the pride residents take in the place where they live.

It's a town where visitors to Lake Monroe can stop at a garage or the convenience store. And where some employees can work at the Dynamic Plastic Corp.

The Starlite drive-in theater is out on old Ind. 37 to the north, one of the few outdoor theaters that remain in these days of movie rentals and cable television.

## *Trip 6*
# SOUTHWESTERN INDIANA

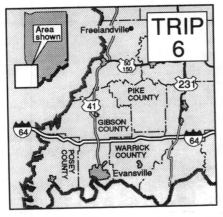

It is a late October and the fields are alive with giant harvesters reaping one of Indiana's most bountiful crops. We head to southwestern Indiana, an area blessed with fertile farms, oil wells and coal mines.

## Freelandville
### "BEST LITTLE FARM TOWN"

Freelandville, population 700, is the past, the present and the future. It has tradition, community spirit and an outlook that could be the blueprint for tomorrow.

It is a farm community, five miles west of Ind. 67 at Ind. 58 and Ind. 159, amid the rich farm land of northern Knox County.

Kixmiller's General Store is a Freelandville landmark. A yellow, red, blue and white sign on the building on a corner of the town's main intersection notes: "Oshkosh B'Gosh/The World's Best Overalls/Kixmiller's/Freelandville."

Enter the store and walk back in time, back more than 150 years to the days when Freelandville was new and Kixmiller's was erected on Lot No. 1.

Kixmiller's is more than a store. It is a living history of a family and a town. John and Julie Ritterskamp opened the first general store in 1846, then replaced it with the present building about twenty years later.

It was in the 1860s when the store sent out two huckster wagons on daily routes through the countryside, selling shoes for $1.65, overalls for 50 cents, stove polish for 5 cents, oil cloth for 30 cents and live chickens for 2 cents.

In 1890, Simon Kixmiller, son-in-law of the Ritterskamps, took over the business. When Simon died in 1943, his son, William R. Kixmiller, took over the store and worked there until he was 92. Kixmiller's daughter, Mary Kixmiller Cummings Sakel, became owner when he died in 1984.

Mrs. Sakel lives upstate at DeMotte, but she visits the store often, does most of the purchasing, supervises the staff and talks about the store when asked. She recalled in an earlier interview about being admonished by her grandfather after returning from Cincinnati where she bought what she thought were buttons by the card. She had, instead, bought them by the gross.

When the box of buttons arrived, Simon Kixmiller, exclaimed: *"Ach, mein himmel!* You have bought enough buttons to last until the year 2000."

He may have been correct. "We still have some of them for sale," she admits.

The store offers, in addition to Oshkosh B'Gosh clothing, dry goods, shoes, groceries and other items. And, those buttons.

A rolling ladder, which allows clerks to remove items from high on the wall, remains in the store which has preserved much of its decor.

Shirley Brouhard, one of the newer employees, has worked in the store part-time for ten years. She and her husband also maintain Bethel Church and its park just outside town. She is proud of the store and the town.

So is Norma Barrett, who has worked at Kixmiller's since 1984 and has been around town a lot longer. "The store was open on Saturday nights about 40 years ago. People would come into town, sit outside and visit or watch a free movie," she explains while collecting a customer's gas and electric bill, another service of the store.

She points to the cover and tear sheets from a 1988 *Farm Future* magazine which in "capturing the spirit of what made the nation great" called Freelandville "America's Best Little Farm Town."

Shirley Brouhard and Norma Barrett agree it is pride that sustains Freelandville, keeps it a prosperous, proud community in a time when other small towns are on the decline.

*Farm Future* concluded that Freelandville does face challenges, like finding community leaders to replace those nearing retirement, developing small local businesses, keeping its young people and involving them in community projects.

So far an improvement club has met those challenges. "People work together here pretty good," Norma Barrett says in what is an understatement.

When the population aged, a community organization built a 50-bed nursing home with a paid staff. Farmers still provide food to the home.

When there was no place for men to congregate, farmers and retirees opened their own Card Room, where euchre is the big game.

When the restaurant closed, a group of 19 men, including several farmers, posted $500 each to buy the building and contents and offered it to an operator rent-free. After all, a town needs a place where men can come to sip morning coffee, discuss the issues of the day, and have lunch. The incorporation called itself the "Kraut Crew."

The restaurant is across the street from Kixmiller's. The Freelandville Novelist Cafe, it is called by Michael Marx, the restaurateur and novelist.

Marx's own life reads like a novel. He was living in San Diego, engaged to a daughter of one of the restaurant owners, when they learned the place needed a new operator. "We talked it over and decided we might as well come here and run the place."

The "we" are Marx and Laverne Telligman, who is now his wife. Marx had never cooked for a restaurant, knew nothing about the business. But the results have been even better than he expected. The restaurant has done well. And he and his bride have had no trouble being accepted in town.

"I've been really happy here. All the activity keeps my brain alive," he says. "Sometimes I can't believe it. We just bought a house on a half-acre with a chicken lot in the back. We paid $15,000, less than what two cars in the driveway cost. You can't beat that."

Marx has never been busier. "I work fifty hours a week, seven days a week here, teach two English composition class at Vincennes [20 miles away] and write columns and movie reviews for the *Wabash Weekly News*.

Marx excuses himself. "I just learned ten minutes ago that we are serving a birthday luncheon for ten people," he says, hurrying off to the kitchen.

It is now 9:30 a.m. There is work to do. But Marx has had work to do most of his life.

He grew up in a small town, Waynesburg, Pennsylvania, where his father was a veterinarian. Marx went to Hobart College and studied literature and drama in Italy. He later wrote and self-published two novels, *Eric Greenfield—Middle American* and *A War Ends,* financing the costs by driving a cab in New York City.

Rather than lose much of his profit in bookstore commissions, he marketed his books door to door and says he made a profit doing it. "A publisher usually sells only 2,000 to 3,000 and I did better than that," he reports.

His efforts earned him national attention in newspapers and on television networks.

Now in his early forties, he's learning the dining habits of small-town Hoosiers, serving the food they want, adding a few surprises to the menu now and then. The cafe is open seven days a week for breakfast and lunch and for a few evening parties.

And he's attending movies for his reviews and keeping his mind alert through his commentaries written under the name, *Eric Greenfield—Middle American.*

\* \* \*

It is time to leave Freelandville. But we will return, for this is a place to renew one's belief in the goodness of a nation.

## Oaktown and Emison
### FIELDS AND ORCHARDS

We drive west on Ind. 58 from Freelandville, then take a county road toward Oaktown, past fertile farm land, landscapes topped with silos, fields occupied by livestock.

Oaktown is a community of 750 residents now bypassed by U.S. 41. Like most small towns, it has some abandoned stores, but businesses and civic pride remain. An aging, gray-haired woman in a red sweater rakes leaves, keeping her property neat and clean like most lawns are.

Oaktown is in the heart of Knox County's orchards and the town was a major commercial center for fruit and farm products back when freight was shipped on the old Evansville and Terre Haute Railroad.

The Lions Club has its own hall where it meets every other Tuesday. As long as there are service clubs there will be towns like Oaktown.

Off the U.S. 41 corridor to the south we are greeted by a "Welcome to Emison" sign. Emison is a residential community. What had been a store is closed and there is little activity on this Thursday morning.

Two dogs romp with youngsters who are off school for the day. It is difficult to tell whether the dogs or the boys are having more fun.

A park near the United Methodist Church is managed by the Emison Youth Foundation. Emison is another community which cares about its young people.

Blacktop is peeling from the county road south of Emison toward Vincennes. The terrain changes from flat to rolling and wooded. We skirt Vincennes, then notice a sign on U.S. 41 that says "St. Thomas—3 miles."

# St. Thomas
## CHURCH WORK

The land is flat as it stretches toward the Wabash River on the road to St. Thomas, a Knox County community of a few homes centered around St. Thomas Catholic Church. Stores, and gas stations would seem out of place in a setting so serene.

John Lane, a contractor, and his men are at work at the church, adjacent to a community park.

"The old rectory dates back to 1880 and we decided it would be easier to build a new one—2,200 square feet—which would be more efficient," explains Lane, a member of the parish.

The church has been at St. Thomas, which is just two miles from the Wabash, since 1830. Lane estimates about 90 percent of the members are of German descent, the other 10 percent French.

Surrounded by fertile bottoms, St. Thomas is far from the hubbub of interstate and city traffic. "Prime land," Lane calls it. It is also a quiet land. Pumps are silent as they draw oil from the ground. The stillness is broken only by the pounding of hammers and the hum of combines in distant fields.

# Patoka
## "LOG ON THE BOTTOM"

A sign off U.S. 41 boasts that Patoka is "The Oldest Town in Gibson County." Patoka, it is said, is an Indian word that meant "log on the bottom," a reference to logs that became lodged in the river.

John Severns, according to legend, settled in the Patoka area in 1789. That same year John Smith opened a store and persuaded other settlers to locate on the banks of the Patoka River.

Patoka hasn't always been Patoka. It was platted in 1813 as Columbia, but became Patoka in 1833 when the first post office was located in town and a stagecoach began stops on the Vincennes to Evansville route.

Old Patoka, population 700, remains in a scenic sitting, lined with maple trees, their leaves aglow in autumn color.

The high school, once the home of the Patoka Wrens, is now a True Value Hardware store where tractor and implement parts also are sold. The school playground has become a site for manufactured houses. High school students now attend school at Princeton.

Like other towns bypassed by major highways, much of the business has moved out where the traffic is, here along U.S. 41. It is an economic reality, for this is a day when vehicles dominate America's lifestyle.

# Lyles Station
## SETTLED BY BLACKS

Call Lyles Station the community Joshua Lyles built. It is a hamlet on Gibson County Road 500 West, a mile north of Ind. 64, founded by free Negroes before the Civil War. It was named after Joshua Lyles, one of the black men who acquired 1,200 acres and donated land for the railroad that still runs through the town.

By 1900, Lyles Station was a community of about eight hundred people, mostly black, with two churches, two general stores, a post office, railroad station and elementary school. It prospered until the flood of 1913 devastated the community, leaving damage so great it never recovered.

The school in Lyles Station is now closed, but Wayne Chapel of the African Methodist Church remains open, a gathering place for blacks as it has been since 1887.

Only four or five black families remain in the Lyles Station area. On this day black farmers like Norman Greer and David Hardiman are at work in the fields, harvesting bountiful crops.

Consolidated Grain, the only remaining business in Lyles Station, is a busy place as truck load after truck load arrive at the elevator. Evidence of a bumper crop, corn is dumped in an open pile next to the Norfolk Southern Railroad.

"Yield-wise it is good, price-wise, not so good," says Bill McBee, the manager.

A Purdue University graduate, McBee grew up at Linden south of Lafayette and was president of the Indiana chapter of the Future Farmers of America in 1984-85. He has learned to like this area of southern Indiana. "It's warmer for one thing," he says between weighing trucks in and out.

Down the road David Marvel is ready to disc fields that have been harvested. He takes time to tell visitors that it has been a good year for crops. "Dad [Ewell Marvel] says they are the best he has seen in his thirty years here."

David looks at the six big steel granaries which will hold a total of 90,000 bushels, says that won't be enough to contain all the grain the Marvels will reap. The bad news, though, is that the price today is $1.94, which may allow farmers to barely break even after the cost of production is calculated.

It is an old story for farmers: good yield, low prices; poor yields, high prices.

\* \* \*

We take Ind. 65 south of Ind. 64, to Owensville, a small commercial center in southern Gibson County surrounded by good farm land with working oil wells.

The town's Carnegie library sits on town square, amid trees whose leaves form a montage of fall colors. It is a Thursday afternoon, but this is no sleepy small town. It is a busy place, even on a delightful autumn day.

This is Halloween season and it appears towns across the state have entered a contest to see whose homes can have the best decorations. Owensville is no exception.

* * *

Ind. 65 continues south to Cynthiana where a water tower high on an elevation greets visitors entering town from the north.

# Cynthiana
## QUALITY OF LIFE

It is soon obvious Cynthiana, 880 residents, 350 households, is not just any small town. It is a small town with a lot of pride.

A sign "Welcome to Cynthiana, Ind.—Cynthiana Chamber of Commerce" greets visitors on Ind. 65 and Ind. 68.

Sandi Chaffin, clerk-treasurer, is at work in the Town Hall. She calls Cynthiana a peaceful town where hardly anyone locks his car and the only troubles are a few problems with kids.

Mrs. Chaffin has lived in town for 25 years, raised two daughters here: "I like the fact people mind their own business, but if you need help they are there. Kids can go anywhere in town and be safe."

Kenny Colbert, Town Council president, concurs. He likes small-town life and sounds like a Chamber of Commerce spokesman as he talks about Cynthiana. "We believe in the good neighbor policy and the result is a good quality of life," he says, trying to contain his enthusiasm.

He points to a bandstand in the town park which he hopes will become a national historic landmark. Built in 1915, it was dedicated "to those who served and in memory of those who died in American wars."

Cynthiana observed its 175th birthday in September, 1992, having been founded in 1817. Mount Vernon, the county seat, is a year older.

Founder William Davis named the town after Cynthiana, Kentucky. Some of his descendants still live around town, apparent proof he picked a good place to settle.

The town runs its own sewer and water utilities and law is maintained by a marshal who divides his time between the town and the Posey County sheriff's office.

The high school, once the home of the Cynthiana Annas, is now a part
of North Posey High near Poseyville. Grade school students attend the
Poseyville school.

Cynthiana, though, has managed to maintain its identity, thanks to people
like Sandi Chaffin and Kenny Colbert.

*  *  *

We drive west from Cynthiana, through the I-64 interchange into
Poseyville, a community of 1,250 residents named after Gen. Thomas Posey,
governor of the Indiana Territory. "Welcome to Poseyville—Chamber of
Commerce," a sign says.

Poseyville has lost some of its commercial activity, but it remains the
core of a farming area in northern Posey and southern Gibson Counties.

A county road leads north to Stewartsville, three miles from Poseyville.
Stewartsville has a four-way stop but not much else. A store is closed and the
only sign of activity is at an auto garage. A man who looks to be past middle
age rides a bike as he balances a cardboard box in the basket on the
handlebars. He has his hands full. The last thing he needs is to be stopped by
strangers with time on their hands.

*  *  *

South of Poseyville on Ind. 165 the fields stretch across the horizon,
further evidence agriculture is Indiana's biggest business. A rural mail box in
the heart of the farm land is decorated with a model of an old steel-wheeled
John Deere tractor.

# Wadesville
## UP AND COMING

It is mid-afternoon, Thursday, and only a few customers are in Thorn-
burg's, a restaurant and bar. Tables are set for dinner, and business will pick
up when the farmers finish their harvest for the day.

Darlene, a waitress, is friendly, like the town. No one is a stranger here
for long. She calls Wadesville a quiet place where everybody knows everyone
and no one leaves a stranger.

The bar has its own decor. Crosscut saws, draw knives, a single tree (used
to hitch a horse to an implement), a horse collar, braces and bits, pitchforks
and pulleys line the walls, reminders of an earlier time.

Darlene wishes her visitors well as they leave. It is the kind of place a
stranger will return to on his next visit.

A drive through indicates Wadesville is an up and coming town, not one that's down and going. New houses line the streets near the intersection of Ind. 165 and Ind. 66, indicating people who work in Evansville, 15 miles away, may be moving here.

# Solitude
## AND FARMERSVILLE

Ind. 165 goes south toward Ind. 69 from Wadesville toward a place called Solitude. Anyone looking for solitude will find it in a town of only a few houses and a salvage and repair shop. A farm near Solitude on Ind. 69 is listed for sale at $155,000, possibly by someone who has had enough Solitude.

Ind. 165 ends at Solitude. Farmersville, just slightly bigger than Solitude, is south on Ind. 69.

# Hovey Lake
## A DIFFERENT WORLD

Hovey Lake is off Ind. 69 southwest of Mount Vernon, down near the tip of Indiana at its deepest pocket. The lake is not as charming or as quaint as it was on an earlier visit . . . and we are a bit disappointed.

The preserve was once noted for its bald cypress trees, believed to be one of the northernmost stands in the nation. The trees rose from the waters and shoreline, giving the appearance of a southern swamp. That began to change in the 1960s when the Uniontown Locks and Dam were built, causing the water level in Hovey Lake to rise. Many of the cypress trees, their knees submerged year-round, died.

The Indiana Department of Natural Resources has planted hundreds of young cypress trees on higher ground surrounding the lake in an effort to save what should be nature's legacy.

Hovey Lake still has its charm, though, looking like a place out of a different time, a different place. Leaves are red against the water, peaceful amid the dead trees in the late afternoon sun. All is quiet here, miles away from population centers. Gulls flitter about, dipping down in the water to pluck fish for dinner, their catch greater than that of two men in a solitary boat.

Ind. 69 ends at the Union Town Locks, which opened in 1970. It is a place where visitors can watch barges pass through the locks as they are raised or lowered, usually about 18 feet, to the water level above or below the dam.

The locks are busy, for the Ohio River remains a vital link in the nation's transportation system.

The Ohio and the Wabash meet a few miles downstream in an area where no roads lead.

## Southwind Maritime
### SHIPPING OUT

Upriver from Mount Vernon, the Southwind Maritime Centre, run by the Indiana Port Commission, has opened new markets. It links southwestern Indiana to any point on the nation's inland waterways from the Great Lakes to the Gulf of Mexico, allowing grain and other items to be shipped to or from the port via rail. A grain terminal, coal transfer company, fertilizer and grain companies, timber exporter and shippers of bulk commodities have facilities at the port.

On this day, the business is agriculture. A dozen trucks loaded with corn and beans wait to unload at the center.

One of the Weinkapfels from Weinkapfels Farms up the road near Farmersville is last in line. It is his sixth trip to the terminal today—six loads, 600 bushels per load.

The yield is great, "160 to 200 bushels an acre, but the price isn't very good," he laments, affirming what other farmers have said elsewhere earlier in the day.

* * *

Twilight has arrived. A long day that has increased our appreciation of a part of Indiana is ending.

*Trip 7*

# OHIO RIVER CHARMS

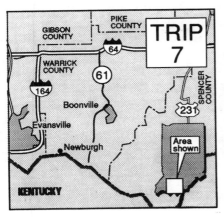

Newburgh, a Warrick County town of 2,300 residents and Ohio River charm, is too close to Evansville, too accessible, to be called part of "Backroads Indiana." But it is a good place to start another day. It is a place worth visiting for its past . . . and its present. Historic Newburgh has at least one event each season of the year to make the trip worthwhile.

Old homes and shops are near the river and the walk is easy and delightful.

Newburgh was the first town north of the Mason-Dixon line to be invaded by Confederate forces during the Civil War. Brig. Gen. Adam R. Johnson with a guerrilla band crossed the Ohio River on July 18, 1862, and confiscated supplies and ammunition.

Yankeetown, a residential community, is east from Newburgh on Ind. 66, past the giant Aluminum Co. of America's Warrick Operations. It is about 8 a.m. and the third shift is getting off work, the day shift is arriving and traffic is heavy on the highway.

Ind. 66 crosses Little Pigeon Creek, which divides Warrick and Spencer Counties and enters "the land of Lincoln."

## Hatfield
### "SMELL THE ROSES"

On this Friday morning, a lone woman dines among the men in Duffy's Diner, a little concrete block building. The woman is not intimidated.

She is, she says, on her way to get the headlights on her car straightened. "One goes this way," pointing to her left, "the other one goes this way," waving toward the ceiling and to her right.

She is a philosopher of sorts. She tells one of the men who complains about his bad luck, "You have to rise above your circumstances. I just live one day at a time. I can't see anything terrible happening, so I just plan to smell the roses."

A young man wears his philosophy on his sweat shirt: "Brew U.—Party all night and sleep all day." Another man wears a hat labeled "American" and a "Volunteer for Clinton and Gore" button. It is a friendly place. A man comes in and the diners say in unison, as if on cue, "Hi, Bob."

One of the men in bib overalls and a John Deere cap is ready to head to the fields, but not until he drains the last sip from his coffee cup.

At Duffy's Hatfield Market across the road, a sign at the cash register says, "Sorry. We cannot accept food stamps at this time." No reason is given and we do not wait to hear an explanation.

Next to the store is Duffy's Pizza Depot. Duffy is a big name in Hatfield.

About nine hundred residents live in and around Hatfield, a town that was called Fair Fight back in pioneer days before it became more civilized. Hatfield was a farming community until the E&OV Traction Line was built through town in 1907 and residents starting taking the train to jobs elsewhere.

Now it's a town with a branch bank, post office, assorted businesses and churches. And philosophers at Duffy's Diner.

# Eureka
## AND ENTERPRISE

A county road south from Hatfield leads to Eureka. It is an old town. The Eureka Pioneer Cemetery is evidence.

Eureka is a far different place now than it was back in the second half of the 19th Century when it had six doctors, a school, several stores and other businesses.

Today there are no school, no stores, only residents and the Baker's Creek Baptist Church.

(It should be pointed out that another Eureka is in Lawrence County.)

The community of Enterprise is further south, inside the bend in the Ohio. As a port on the river, it grew quickly and became a shipping point where settlers took produce to flat boats that plied the river. The boom ended and the town's importance declined when railroads that bypassed the towns replaced waterways as the chief mode of transportation.

Only a few residents now live year-round in Enterprise, but two hundred to three hundred others spend summers here on the river.

# Richland
## GOOD "OLDS" BOY

We return to Ind. 66, then drive north on Ind. 161, past farms, to Richland, population 500.

It is an old community, and the flat terrain probably explains why William Spencer bought land here in 1807. A town followed and by 1832 there were 43 votes cast in the Presidential election.

Tobacco became one of the major crops, and tobacco warehouses once were common in Richland. There were also general stores, a distillery, flour mill, print shops, a newspaper, hotel, saloon, livery stable, canning factory and millinery shops.

As in other towns, there were Saturday night movies, films projected on the side of the school and viewed from seats on the school grounds.

But automobiles arrived, allowing residents to travel to other towns to shop, causing Richland to lose some of its businesses. But it still is prosperous, with a grocery, bank, several small businesses and post office.

One of the town's businessmen wears work pants, open-neck shirt, and an implement-company cap, not a suit and tie. He is Lee Olds, "Boy," not "Lee," to the people here. "Boy" has lived in Richland 30 years, came to town because his wife grew up here.

That was after Olds had served in the Army Air Corps in World War II, spending time on Guam and Okinawa.

"See any action?" a visitor asks.

His humor shows. His eyes sharpen their gaze as he responds: "I was too far ahead to wear a necktie, too far behind to hear a shot."

Five years later, he volunteered for service during the Korean War, and served in Hawaii.

He is 76 now, but he's still busy, for farmers depend on him for things they couldn't find anywhere else. His place facing Ind. 161 could be called a junk yard. Some might call it an eyesore, but that doesn't bother "Boy."

"We've got a little bit of everything," he says—"stuff" for farmers and anyone else who needs something. If it isn't here, it probably doesn't exist.

"Old Man" Jarvis is loading his pickup with junk. "We give him a load every week or so," Olds says.

Olds appears in good health. "I work a lot," he adds, maybe to explain how well he feels. Besides running the salvage business, he does odd jobs—"plumbing, carpentry work, roofing, even drive wells."

He sees his visitor eye the political campaign signs for both Republicans and Democrats on his property. "We don't care who puts up the signs," he explains. "We don't ask their politics."

\* \* \*

Olds and his wife, Joyce, 68, have six children, and he recites their accomplishments.

He hands us his business card as we leave. He's a man whose true worth is his character, not his junkyard surroundings. We are better off for having stopped to meet him.

\* \* \*

We return to Ind. 66, then drive south to Patronville, a community at the intersection of U.S. 231 and Ind. 45. It is another town that has boomed and declined.

It once had two general stores, a post office, a blacksmith shop, a sawmill, a doctor and a veterinarian.

Blasts of music from auto tape-decks are far different from the sounds of the days when Patronville had a singing school called to order with a "tuning fork" by a man historians call Uncle Billy Winkler.

Patronville now has a grocery, truck terminal, two churches and a few residences.

We take Ind. 45 past nice suburban homes into Rockport four miles away.

# Rockport
## LINCOLN LORE

Rockport is an Ohio River town with 2,315 residents, seat of Spencer County government, scenic, historic. "City of Hospitality," the signs say.

The Courthouse square, like most county seats, is not totally surrounded by law offices, restaurants, bars and stores. There are houses across the street on the south side of the Courthouse.

A historical marker at the nearby Rockport Tavern recalls that in October, 1844, Abraham Lincoln spoke at the Spencer County Courthouse in support of Henry Clay, the Whig Presidential candidate. Lincoln was a guest of the tavern on that trip, his first to Indiana in 14 years.

A one-way drive, squeezed between the Ohio and the cliffs, winds past Rocky Side Park, which separates the town from the Ohio.

A bluff rises up to 100 feet over the river's edge where the first Rockport settlers lived. A shallow cave-like alcove formed a shelter that became a temporary home in 1808 for James Langford, the first white man to bring his family to Rockport.

There are benches in the park, but there is no one here to enjoy the beauty of this Indiana fall morning.

The smokestacks of the Indiana Michigan Power Company's plant rise up beside the river, outside town. We stand at the cave, looking at what appears to be sulfur-free smoke rising gently, and wonder what Lincoln, who knew only coal oil lamps, would think about today's electrified world.

Another plaque is at the Old River Landing where in 1828 at age 19 Abe Lincoln, accompanied by Allen Gentry, made his first flatboat trip to New Orleans. The marker claims Lincoln saw slaves sold and said: "If I ever get a chance to hit that thing, I'll hit it hard." "It might be said," the plaque concludes, "that the Emancipation Proclamation which Lincoln issued in 1863 owes its origin to the flat boat trip."

Now giant barges loaded with coal and grain ply the river. The Ohio has become a main transportation line for industry. And young men of 19 travel in fast cars on paved highways, and on luxury boats through locks on dam-controlled rivers.

Rockport long since has moved to the bluff, escaping the frequent flooding of the river side.

Sidewalks are being repaired in the business district, which stays modern while retaining its historical importance.

And family values are important here. Witness this sign at a barber shop: "It's a girl. Born to Debbie and Bill Cooper 10-4-92. I'm going to see the baby. Sorry I won't be back until November. 1, 1992. Please call again. Thanks. Halleck B. Anderson."

He is a barber who bypassed the conversation of the 1992 election campaign to visit a newborn. Halleck B. Anderson has his priorities in order.

# Grandview
## PRIDE, PECANS AND POWS

Grandview, population 700, is upriver from Rockport on Ind. 66, named, it is said, when a visitor looked across the Ohio to the Kentucky hillside and commented, "It's a grand view."

A park parallels the river and we notice a man alone in the park. His pickup truck carries a POW license plate.

"Jim Martin," he says, introducing himself. He is here in the park, he explains, to look for pecans.

"I went down to Hatfield this morning to visit a friend and decided to stop here on the way back and see what I could find. He points to a five-gallon bucket that is about a fifth full of pecans. "They aren't very big, but they sure are good," he says, explaining that townspeople get the first pick of the nuts as they fall.

Jim says he is from up the river at Cannelton, the historic town on the Ohio. We ask about the POW plate. "I was in the Air Corps in World War II. A tailgunner on a B-17. We got shot down over Europe and I was a prisoner of war for five and a half months in Luft Stalag 4D."

He returned home to Tennessee after the war and came to Cannelton to install humidifying equipment in the old cotton factory there. He liked the town and took a job in maintenance when the humidification work was done.

"I was the last worker at the cotton mill. It closed in 1954, but I stayed on until 1955," he adds. After that, he worked for a sewer-pipe company in Cannelton before retiring in 1982.

"I love the river," he says, looking out across the Ohio. "When I was younger, I used to be on the river every day. Even had a cabin on the river at one time."

Jim, a widower, says he now travels: "I've been fooling around a lot in October. Just got back from Barkley Lodge down in Kentucky on the land between the lakes. And two weeks ago, I was in Gatlinburg, Tennessee.

A visitor wishes him well. Jim takes a look around the park—and at the river—and drives away, back toward his home at Cannelton.

At the Town Hall, Carrie Claise is at work. She is office manager for town government. And it is here where residents pay their gas, water and sewer bills. She suggests we talk with Harold Schroeder, the town manager who maintains the utilities, takes care of the streets and is the town's indispensable citizen.

"He wants to retire, Mrs. Claise says of Schroeder, "but they can't find anyone to take his place." "They" are the five-member Town Council, the elected administrative body for Grandview.

We go to Schroeder's house. He is 75, has been town manager since 1952. He saw to it that the gas system was installed through town in 1963, the water lines in 1964, and took over operation of the sewage system when it went into operation in 1983.

He was born in the country eight or nine miles north of Grandview, went to one-room Agnew School in Clay Township through the eighth grade. "If one person had chicken pox, we all had chicken pox," he recalls. "If one student had measles, everyone else did."

"We got our drinking water from the same place cows drank. Everyone drank from the same cup. We'd keep our teeth together to strain out the water bugs."

Times change, he reports: "Now water has to be so pure to meet health standards no one builds up any immunity. If we go to a foreign place, we get sick from the water. It's all right to have clean water, but they are overdoing it just to meet standards. It's getting to be the same way with the sewer system. It is getting tougher and tougher all the time to meet standards. And now, gas systems workers will have to be certified, too."

Schroeder came to Grandview to high school in 1932, the first year a school bus picked up country kids and brought them to town. Schroeder and his family moved into Grandview in 1943. "I felt my wife and four children would be safer here when I went into the Navy during World War II," he explains.

He is asked about pecan trees. "We don't cut pecan trees," he says. When we have to thin out trees, the pecans stay. The squirrels—we have a lot of white ones here—get most of the pecans before we can pick them up. We used to get a bushel from under one tree."

He calls Grandview "a nice country town. We're close enough to Evansville and Owensville, which is a big shopping town, even Louisville. Of course Rockport is a nice town. The location [Grandview] is nice, which is why people like to locate here."

As town manager, he has "pretty well" done it all: "We're working hard to get someone I can train to take my place. The common-sense part of the job can come from me, the rest can come out of books." He believes forty years is long enough for one person to serve the town.

So what does this man who has spent his lifetime working long days and long hours plan for his retirement? He started thinking about that several years ago when his doctor advised him—since there was no one to take his place—to try to slow down, to get a hobby to take his mind off his responsibilities.

He takes us to a 26-by-32-addition to his house filled with what has become his hobby. It is a room filled with hundreds, make that thousands, of models of almost every farm tractor ever made—models of farm implements, of construction equipment, of trucks of every make, of rare cars including a John Deere his guests never knew had existed.

"Want to see the trains run?" he asks. It's a question that needs no answer. He turns on a few switches and a Southern Pacific passenger train rolls around the track, its sound like those of steam engines of the past. When that train stops, he sends a Great Northern diesel on its way. Again the sound is authentic. Lights shine in some of the cars, the horns and whistles blow—sounds out of the past when America traveled by rail.

He isn't through. He sets out an aquarium rail car, turns a switch, and model fish move realistically as if in a glass tank. He places another car on the track. This one has hoboes moving about on a flat car.

Schroeder isn't finished with his hobby. Likely he won't ever be. There are more train lines to lay out. "I've got a lot of work to do," he says as he turns out the lights and closes the door.

After all, he is a man who has found that life is best when lived to its fullest.

# Newtonville
## THE TOWNSHIP TRUSTEE

Darla Reynolds, the Hammond Township (Spencer County) trustee, lives in Newtonville, a wide spot on Ind. 70. Mrs. Reynolds's office, a room in her home, is open, officially, 15 hours a week. She works more than that, though, she says: "I don't work at another job, so I'm available whenever I'm needed."

Her budget is small. The total township tax rate is 15 cents per $100 of assessed valuation, and that's divided among the general fund, poor relief, and fire protection, which is contracted through the town of Grandview.

As trustee, she also is the tax assessor. "Now, that's a job," she says, explaining the difficulty of keeping property owners happy when real estate taxes are involved.

Most of the township is rural. "We have a lot of big farmers. And farms are getting bigger. Little farmers are becoming a thing of the past," she explains.

That doesn't mean there isn't a need for poor relief. "I had 33 cases in 1991, three times as many as the previous trustee had in 1990," she says.

"If residents who get utility disconnect notices have kids, we have to help." She also provides vouchers to poor families in case of fires or other disasters. "But it has to be an emergency. Whatever the case, we want them [the recipients] to actively seek employment."

*   *   *

It is a perfect fall day, far too nice to discuss work and worry. Her husband, Steve, points to a pond in a ravine just north of their house. "That used to be a strip mine," he says, "before the land was reclaimed." It now is a grassy area, and the fish population is growing after a stocking by neighbors.

Mrs. Reynolds looks out across the pond and the rolling hills to the trees, decked out in their autumn glory, and offers, "You couldn't paint a picture as pretty as that is."

Chances are that the few residents who live in Newtonville aren't concerned that the community no longer has a trading post and several businesses, as it did in the late 1800s. It still has its churches, and good roads lead to busier communities not too far away.

It is time to visit other Spencer County towns.

# Chrisney
## BUFFALOVILLE AND GENTRYVILLE

Chrisney, population 550, streets tree-lined, is on U.S. 231 just north of the Ind. 60 junction. It is a nice town, its homes well-maintained, a hardware store, two taverns, a liquor store, grain elevator, five churches, a town hall and volunteer fire department among its features.

The elementary school is still here; the high school, pride of Chrisney from 1911 to 1972, is now a part of Heritage Hills High with Dale and Gentryville.

A park has two shelter houses, a community building, ball diamond, a nine-hole golf course—indications that Chrisney didn't wilt when the high school left.

Gentryville, at Ind. 162 and Ind. 62, was named for the James Gentry who in 1818 bought the land where the town now stands. Abraham Lincoln grew up not far from here, and returned in 1844 to make a political speech at the home of William Jones, who operated a trading post.

The town grew and, after the Civil War, had stores, blacksmiths, cabinet shops, a hotel, tobacco warehouses, a cigar factory and a grist mill.

Now there is a gas station, antique and craft shops, two churches and a few other businesses, including at least two bed-and-breakfasts.

* * *

Buffaloville, a town of a few houses but no businesses, is south of Ind. 162 between Santa Claus and Gentryville. It is far different than it was in an earlier time when the town had a feed mill, a tobacco barn, and a post office, a time when A.B. Burkhart taught school, ran the funeral home and operated the general store.

* * *

It is time for lunch at the Lincoln Inn at the U.S. 231 and Ind. 62 intersection. We greet the waitress with a "Nice day."

"Too bad I'm stuck in here," she replies.

A young man waits for lunch to take to his father in the field. "He'll probably keep combining corn while he eats," he says.

The place is open night and day, but the day belongs to the farmers and to the drivers of big coal trucks. Food is good, plentiful, more for active farmers than for travelers.

Ind. 62 west crosses over Little Pigeon Creek back into Warrick County, then passes through some wasteland, past the Warrick County Coon Club, into good farmland. Hogs behind an electric fence glean corn the harvester missed.

# Tennyson
## It's Quiet, Usually

Tennyson, a town on Ind. 161 north of Ind. 62, appears to be Ross Perot country. His signs are in front of mobile homes and big houses and in vacant lots.

Berniece Capehart is at work at the Tennyson Hardware, owned by Dorris Downing, an engineer at the ALCOA plant in Yankeetown. Mrs. Capehart came to town ten years ago from Otwell and has found Tennyson to be a friendly town. "It's quiet . . . except on Friday nights when the kids make noise and young drivers squeal their tires."

She ticks off the other businesses in town: McBride's grocery, the gas station, Bob and Carol's family restaurant, a hair salon, pool hall, post office and a place with tanning beds, a necessity for every town it seems, big or small.

Tennyson no longer has a high school. Athletes who would have been Tigers now perform for the Boonville Pioneers.

# Folsomville
## "Closed at Sundown"

A county road west toward Folsomville eases over rolling land past small fields, two shocks of fodder, and old strip mines.

The post office, a concrete block building about 10 by 12 feet, is closed. "Open 8 a.m. to noon. Mail dropped after 12 will be dispatched the next day," a sign says.

Another sign at the town cemetery reads, "Closed at Sundown." A visitor wonders if the residents there need their rest.

Folsomville, like Tennyson, lost its high school to Boonville during the consolidations of the 1960s.

Back on Ind. 161, the road winds over hills that need to be bulldozed for mobile homes, which still have to be leveled on concrete blocks.

A place on the map called Heilman turns out to be a bend in the road.

# Selvin
## Hall of the Future

We leave Ind. 161 at Ind. 68 and are greeted by a sign, "Selvin— Founded 1839." We stop at the Selvin Market and walk into the store through an old screen door with printing that reads, "You can depend on Dr. Caldwell's syrup pepsin, the family laxative."

Two youngsters, out of school for the day, are buying cigarette bubble gum, hands full of it.

"It's been a store for 100 years," employees Donna Winge and Darlena Kolley explain. They work for Sandra Robinson, who owns the place.

"That picture on the wall was how it looked in 1922," Donna explains. "Louie Zollman, a welder and artist, painted it from an old picture."

She calls attention to the town's "Future Hall of Fame," a gallery of the town's young people—pictures of babies, toddlers, preschoolers. "Parents and grandparents bring in the pictures and post them there," Donna explains. A quick count shows there are more than thirty pictures in the exhibit.

Business is good. People keep coming and going. It's even busier each morning, especially on Saturdays and Sundays when men congregate to smoke, talk, drink coffee and argue. The old pot-bellied stove was removed about five years ago, but an ancient bench remains where the men can talk about old times.

Chances are they talk about the days when Selvin still had a high school where the Wildcats played basketball. And about the season ahead for Tecumseh, which absorbed the school in a consolidation three decades ago.

A liars' bench, purported to be 100 years old, is out in front of the store. It is time to sit a spell . . . and think of the history it would have recorded had if it had eyes and ears.

\* \* \*

We are headed for Stendal, but can't find the road marked on the map that purportedly leads there. It turns out there is no highway.

"Just a gravel road," a woman at the Yellow Bank pottery shop outside Selvin says. "Go about five miles, and don't go off on any of the side roads, or you'll really get lost. Keep going until you hit the blacktop, turn left and you'll soon be in Sten-*dal,*" she said, putting the accent on *dal.*

There is no traffic, none, just dust on the road . . . a narrow lane past trees, hardscrabble land and hardly any houses as it crosses from Warrick into Pike County.

This is real "backroads Indiana."

# Stendal

### LOVE AT FIRST SIGHT

The directions are exact. We reach Stendal, our destination, where we find Ind. 257 begins. A state road never looked so good.

Stendal, the hometown of former Sen. Vance Hartke, D-Ind., turns out to be a surprise, a gem at the end of a gravel road.

L'Louise (pronounced Eloise) Childress, is at work at the Stendal Store she bought a year ago. It was a case of love at first sight, she explains.

"We were living in Bloomfield when my husband, Wayne, got a new job in the area. We saw a vacant trailer near here and came to Stendal to find out who owned it. As we came into town, I got this feeling of going back in time. We drove by this store, saw the 'For Sale' sign and stopped in. No one had heard of the owner of the trailer, but it didn't matter. I fell in love with the store. We thought about it for two weeks, and decided to buy it."

Mrs. Childress had lived in Anderson, Cincinnati and Indianapolis, but the change to village life came easy.

"We didn't know how we'd be accepted, but the people seem to have taken to us. I can talk about anything. If they talk about farming, I know what they are talking about."

Now, a year later, they know everyone in town, all 100-plus of them, and a lot of other folks from around the community.

"I really enjoy the store. It's different here," she explains. The general store has become a community gathering spot. The places at the round table in the back are often filled mornings and evenings with men who, when they aren't talking, sip coffee or soft drinks.

Most of the men are farmers who talk about their work, about sports— this is Indiana University Country—and about politics.

Ralph Steineker is a frequent visitor now that he's retired, even though he is a Purdue Boilermaker fan. "Two of my boys went there," he explains. He likes general stores, has ever since he was a boy and his grandfather ran a store at nearby Velpen.

Mary Rademacher, who spends her summers in Indianapolis and winters in Naples, Florida, enters the store. It has been 59 years since she left town, but she remembers the store and its "gossip bench." And Saturday nights in the summers when she came to town from out on the old McCallister place to socialize and watch silent movies shown outdoors.

Like all towns, Stendal has changed, but it has maintained its pride. A community club now runs the old gym, once the home of the Stendal Aces. The school closed when it merged with Otwell, Petersburg, Spurgeon, Union, Velpen and Winslow to form Pike Central.

And it has also maintained its friendliness. Deer hunters from around Indiana and from Michigan and Wisconsin will come as strangers, leave as friends. L'Louise and Wayne Childress will see to that.

*  *  *

We take Ind. 257 north out of Stendal and drive through Pikeville and into Velpen, which has a convenience store, a post office and a few house. Up ahead, Ind. 257 meets Ind. 56 at Otwell, an active and prosperous community of five hundred residents. It's in the center of a good farming area, which explains why its athletic teams were called the Millers before the high school consolidated with other county schools to form Pike Central.

The sun is setting. It has been a good day, worth remembering for the places and the people.

*Trip 8*
# FALLS OF THE OHIO

The Falls of the Ohio are on the back streets of Clarksville, on Riverside Drive off Exit O at the north edge of the I-65 bridge between Indiana and Kentucky.

It's not on the back roads of Indiana. No matter. We have time on this Friday morning to stop at the park which delights geologists and historians but may cause some visitors to yawn and move on.

A swift current races over a limestone shelf several miles long for much of the year. Early shippers, traders and travelers found it necessary to portage around the impassable section of the river, stops that caused the region to be settled.

The falls contain an estimated 600 species of 350-million-year-old Devonian fossils. "Devonian" designates the geologic era characterized by the appearance of forests and amphibians.

It is late autumn, a good time for a visit, because there is little water along the falls. September, October and November usually are the best time to see the rocks, which are covered by water other months of the year.

About a hundred school children are coming over from Louisville this day to observe the rock formations and the ancient fossils. "We tell them about the history of the falls. We talk about the natural history. We go down on the fossil beds and let them explore the rocks," a tour guide from Louisville explains.

Tom Risinger lives in Clarksville, has most of his life. He is down at the falls, as he is almost every day. "I've been around a long time, have studied the falls, and I know a little of their history," he says. "If anyone has a question, I try to answer it. I just help out however I can."

# Magnet
## A CLIFF HANGER

It is time to visit Magnet, a Crawford County hamlet a mile or so east off Ind. 66, all but hidden between the cliffs and the Ohio River. Like a magnet on the refrigerator, it clings to the bluff, high enough to escape high waters.

On a good day, Magnet's population may reach 40, too few to support a post office, the government decided, closing down the operation when Postmaster Mary Jean Cassidy retired in October, 1992. Mary Jean had run the post office, a Magnet institution since 1848, from the corner of the town's general store.

Now, weeks after the post office closed, residents still depend on Mary Jean. "All my old customers told the postal driver that they wanted their mail picked up and delivered here to the store," she laughs.

With the post office gone, the general store and Hooter's Bar & Grill across the road are about all that's left of the town. Neal Cassidy owns Hooter's, bought it a little over a year ago. He's the son of the retired postmaster.

It is a rainy morning in late October, a good time to stop at Hooter's. Betty Scheler is at work, awaiting the arrival of farmers and other workers who will be off work because of the rain.

"This is the busiest little place I've ever seen," says Betty, a slim brunette who has lived in the area all her life. It is Friday and crowds are always big on weekends when customers crowd Hooter's for drinks and chicken and catfish dinners.

"People come from everywhere, all over Crawford County, and from Jasper, Ferdinand and other places. I wonder how they find the place," she says, speaking of Magnet's isolated location.

"Any entertainment?" she repeats a question, then answers with a laugh, "Just ourselves."

Bruce Miller has stopped in at Hooter's for coffee on this damp morning. His wife, Elaine, their daughter, Kayla, 3, and son, Garrett, three months old, are with him. It is too wet for Miller to finish his harvest. "Twenty-five acres of soybeans are still in the field," he reports, but he already has harvested his 160 acres of corn and 175 acres of beans.

"Best crop I've ever had," he says. "Corn averaged 160 bushels an acre." That's a good yield for the area.

Miller is just 29 and he's far from the fertile fields of northern Indiana, but he's as up-to-date as farmers in more productive counties. He sold almost all his crops on the futures market, getting prices above the going market rate during the bumper harvest.

He also operates a seed business, selling Pioneer seed corn among other things. "In bad years, the seed business kept food on our table," he says, sipping a second cup of coffee.

His personal computer is tied into the Pioneer Seed Co. system, allowing him to place orders quickly, to exchange information, to learn what is going on.

"I miss the post office," he says. "I mail a lot of packages and it was convenient to drop them off here when the post office was open." He now has to take them to Derby or Tell City.

Bruce was born here and has lived nowhere else. He graduated from Perry Central High School and took over the farm operation at age 20 when his father died in 1983.

"I just kept the farm going," he explains. Like all farmers, he has been through "some pretty tough" times in the last decade. We haven't always made a good living, but we've kept going," he adds, adjusting his Stihl chainsaw cap. He is also wearing a plaid shirt and jeans.

Weather has always been a factor in farming, as it is on this day. Now farmers face a new threat. The deer population is on the increase and Miller has noted some damage from the animals: "One farmer told me he estimated the deer had reduced his soybean yield by five bushels to the acre. That's enough to make the difference between profit and loss."

Unlike Miller, his wife, Elaine, was a city girl back in Owensboro, Kentucky. She was a student at an Owensboro business college when she met Bruce through some friends at a Christmas party. The relationship developed from there.

After eight years, Elaine has grown to like the peaceful area around Magnet. "It took some getting used to," she admits. "It takes 33 minutes to get to town [Tell City, the county seat], so I just go once a week. I had been accustomed to a five-minute drive to get whatever I wanted. Now I go home and find there is so much chaos in the city, I'm ready to return to Magnet."

Bruce is accustomed to long drives. He was graduated from Perry Central High School, which was an hour-long ride from his farm home. In an earlier time before consolidation, he would have gone down the road to school at Dexter.

Cable television has not yet reached the area. This is Indiana University country, and Miller says fans have been known to drive fifty miles to watch a game when the Hoosiers are on ESPN. "Either that or they go to someone's home where there is a satellite dish," he adds.

We ask the route to Buzzard Roost, a scenic overlook up river from Magnet. Miller gives us directions ("take the road up the hill, turn right at the blacktop"), then explains that the forestry service and the county plan to widen the road to make it more accessible to visitors.

Betty Scheler offers to refill our coffee cups a fourth time, but it is time to go, even though we are reluctant to leave.

# Buzzard Roost
## IT'S NOT FOR THE BIRDS

Although it is not marked, we find Buzzard Roost at an overlook 875 feet above sea level, 400-500 feet over the river below. It is a vista almost isolated from the world, an area where the only sound this day is a small plane that follows the river as it skims below the bluff, 200-300 feet above the water.

Across the Ohio, not too many feet above the water, are wide fields in the Kentucky bottom lands, sharp contrasts to the bluffs on the Indiana side that

magnify our respect for whatever, whomever, created the land.

We walk along the top of the bluff, enjoying the view, looking up river, wondering if somehow it knows the impact it has had on lives and on history.

We imagine the scene that gave Buzzard Roost its name, try to visualize the slaughterhouse that was down on the river, see in our minds hundreds of buzzards at roost, waiting for the day's work to end before gliding down to pick up the refuse that remains. The slaughterhouse is gone and the buzzards have left, but Buzzard Roost remains as magnificent as it was then.

We think about the stakes that have been placed to widen the road up to Buzzard Roost. We wonder if the people who drive here over an improved road will come to marvel at the site, to appreciate what they see, or to litter it with soft-drink cans and fast-food wrappers.

We drive on, the road following the river, stopping occasionally to observe nature's splendor. We leave the river bank for a time, driving over more broken asphalt and crushed stone until we cross from Perry to Crawford County.

# Artist Point
## Out on Oxbow Bend

A county road meanders through Alton, angles northeast, like the river, then goes north to Cape Sandy, a community of a half-dozen homes. We drive north to Artist Point, which offers another view, this one almost unlimited, of the river below. A county road rounds Oxbow Bend, passing the few farms that are out on the tip of the bow that gouges eastward into Kentucky.

It is another contrast in Indiana's geography. We return to Artist Point, take another long look at the river, and continue along its banks to Fredonia.

Fredonia is quiet on this day, unlike back on the first weekend in October when the Fall Foliage Festival was held. And unlike the time from 1822 to 1843 when it was a shipping center and the Crawford County seat.

# Leavenworth
## ONE NAME, TWO TOWNS

Leavenworth is two towns in one—the old still down on the river, down to First Street, down to the boat ramp; the new Leavenworth on Ind. 62, high above the river.

Blame the river! The Ohio's worst flood ever inundated all of what was then Leavenworth in 1937, destroying 111 homes and 21 businesses.

The Stephenson "Old Time" General Store has been in both towns. It was rebuilt on the high ground after the disaster and celebrated its 75th year in 1992. Stephenson's may be a tourist lure for some travelers, but it is a visit back into the past for people who remember when every town had a general store.

A man who is in the store to buy stove pipe appreciates the wide variety of merchandise. "Cold weather is coming on," he says as he carries the pipe from the store.

Tin and copper wares, quilts and rags, handcrafted wood items, sleigh bells, stone ware and pottery and country crafts and antiques are just some of the items available.

Higher on the hill, the Overlook Restaurant offers a panoramic view of a sweeping turn in the river . . . if you can get a seat by a window. It is here you can watch a barge ease up or down the river or see the sun set behind the hills to the west.

# El Bethel, Pilot Knob
## AND FROMAN'S GROVE

We go north out of Leavenworth on roller-coaster Ind. 66, past places called El Bethel and Pilot Knob. The road levels out. So does the terrain and suddenly we are in some of the best farm country in Crawford County.

We stop at a wide spot in the road where a few cars are in front of a convenience store called T-Mart. "What's this place called?" we ask. A couple of the men shake their heads, unknowing. Another replies, "All I ever heard it called was Froman's Grove. Old Man Froman had a grove back there," he says pointing to the east.

Whatever, it is now a gathering spot for farmers, who order coffee or soft drinks and have lunch.

We pass Crawford County High School, a consolidation of all the high schools in the county. Marengo Cavemen, Milltown Millers, English Red Raiders and Leavenworth Rivermen joined to become the Wolfpack back in the early 1970s.

Like many consolidations, Crawford County High is out in the country, four miles south of Marengo. It is far enough away from any town so none of the old rivals can claim it for their own.

# Marengo
## BEYOND THE CAVE MEN

It is soon obvious Milltown, north on Ind. 66, is rustic and colorful, which might be expected of a town where creeks called Whiskey Run and Brandywine Fork meet. Marengo's population is just 850, but it is the second biggest town in Crawford County.

Marengo Cave is nearby, bringing visitors to town who might not overwise come. The 112-acre Marengo Cave Park offers horseback rides and has picnic grounds and camping, a swimming pool, nature trails, restaurant and gift shops.

As in other small towns, some businesses here have closed, but there still is commerce in this quaint town with narrow streets. The Marengo Farm & Home Supply store is busy. Customers stop, chuckle at the sign that's posted: "Children! Tired of being harassed by your parents? ACT NOW! Move out, get a job, pay your own bills while you still know everything." It is a sign indicative of a town where the values of the past are still good enough for today.

Ron Newton grew up west of Marengo near Eckerty, goes to church at Birdseye and has lived all his life in Crawford County. He works at the store, likes the job, likes the area.

Crawford County changes little, but some of the people do. Newton cites a case in point: "An Amish settlement [14-15 families with 70 members] has gone modern. The young people are buying tractors, adopting new ways." It started, he explains, when young people began to ask why they should continue to use horses when tractors were available.

The change, he explains, has caused some of the older Amish to return to Michigan, from which the settlement came.

We drive on Ind. 66 through Marengo out to the four-way stop at Ind. 64. and go southeast to Milltown.

# Milltown
## FLOATING

Were it not for a few clues, a motorist might think he has driven back in time as he leaves Ind. 64 and enters Milltown. Only video satellite dishes, video rentals, late-model cars and a directional sign to a karate camp reflect the 1990s.

Milltown is the biggest town in Crawford County, according to the 1990 census, its 917 residents living on the hills and along Blue River.

Chances are the town was named for the old mill that was on the river, down near the old one-lane iron bridge that remains. A 10-by-30 foot mural shows the mill as it once was. Signed "Thomas J. Crecelius," the mural adorns a two-story building on a main corner of town.

It is the river that supports one of the community's biggest businesses, Cave Country Canoe, which has about 275 rental canoes for float trips on Blue River. The float trips offer a chance to see the beauty of the region, which will remain if visitors heed the sign at Cave Country Canoe:

"Blue River is patrolled regularly by DNR [Department of Natural Resources] enforcement officers so that everyone may enjoy the river and so it will remain in a natural state. Cave Country recommends that no alcohol be taken on the river."

Like the river, Milltown seeks to retain its charm. The Town Hall is in the old First National Bank, an architectural reminder of decades gone by. The Old [Mille] Food Store is now a pizza shop offering the "best pizza by a dam site." The "Must Stop" sells liquor, wine and beer.

Christine VanLaningham is at work at Maxine's Market, which is owned by Maxine Archibald. It is a convenience store and it is busy on this Friday afternoon.

Carl Mackey pauses to talk as he leaves the store. He appears in vigorous health for a man of 76. Maybe that's because he enjoys his summers relaxing in Milltown, his winters fishing at Okeechobee.

"Fish five days a week in Florida," he says. "Quite a few of us [from around town] go south each winter. There's not much going on in Milltown in the winter." He pauses, then adds, "And not a whole lot in summer for people like me."

He doesn't fish at all when he's back home. "We do set up a booth at craft shows now and then," he explains, without saying what kind of crafts he sells.

You get the idea he likes the town, even though it may be out of the mainstream. Except for those winters in Florida, he has lived all his life around Milltown, driving as far as 55 miles each way daily to jobs in Louisville (Navy Ordinance) and at Charlestown (Indiana Arsenal). "I drove out of town to work for 37 years before retiring 17 years ago," he says.

He has earned summers in Milltown, winters in Florida. Chances are other residents who drive out of town to work, find Milltown a good place to drive home to.

## Trip 9
# MINING COUNTRY

Ind. 63 angles southwest of Terre Haute from the Federal Prison into rural western Indiana, through Prairieton and Prairie Creek, past big farms not far from the Wabash River. We notice a "roaster hogs for sale" sign. Pig roasts are big on these cool October evenings.

This is Vigo County, and we notice a place marked Vigo on the map. We follow a road west from Prairie Creek, fail to find Vigo, if it still exists. We see no traffic on the rural road, only a lone rooster strutting proudly on the pavement.

Prairie Creek is a town with a post office, a community building, a "Crafter's Junction" in an old brick building. Gone is Prairie Creek High School, once the home of the Gophers. Students now attend Terre Haute South.

South of Prairie Creek, a historical marker notes the "Fairbanks Massacre" which occurred three miles to the southwest in September, 1812. It was there where Sgt. Nathan Fairbanks and about a dozen soldiers were ambushed and killed by Indians as they escorted supplies from Fort Knox, near Vincennes, to Fort Harrison, at Terre Haute.

## Fairbanks
### "NO JOBS FOR YOUNG"

For a small town, Fairbanks is busy on this Tuesday morning. Customers enter and leave the Fairbanks branch of the Sullivan People's Bank.

Alice Flesher drives up to the post office. She is in a hurry to deliver the mail, but she takes time to talk. She says she has been a rural carrier for 12 years, driving 85 miles a day, making about four hundred stops, two hundred each from routes out of Farmersburg and Fairbanks.

"Takes two hours to sort the mail, four hours to deliver it," she explains.

She grew up at Farmersburg and knows the area and the people. A grocery and a gasoline station/restaurant have closed, the town has changed. Fairbanks High School, its athletes known as Trojans, closed years earlier when North Central of Sullivan County was built. And now the nearby Breed Power Plant, where some residents work, may be abandoned in a few years.

"Young people, who don't stay on the farms, go elsewhere for jobs," she says, adding that despite changes, residents have remained the same. "If you have a problem, there are people around to help." It is people like the Drakes, Halberstadts and other families who have been around for decades, who give Fairbanks the stability small towns need.

# Graysville
## "A VILLAGE," SHE SAYS

The towering smokestack at the Merom Power Plant is still miles to the south, but it is visible, the exhaust fumes feeling their way into the blue sky above.

At Graysville, Ind. 63 traffic stops, giving east-west vehicles on Ind. 154 between Sullivan and Illinois the right of way. It is a beautiful October day and a work crew spreads gravel on the driveway at the Graysville grade school, where kids romp on the playground at morning recess.

(Graysville's high school closed and students were sent to Sullivan after the 1961 class of 11 seniors was graduated.)

A fading sign hints the Padgett grocery hasn't been open for years.

Postmaster Marcy Kennett calls Graysville "a nice little town. There are about a hundred people in the village, as I call it. We don't have any crime. No one even soaps windows on Halloween.

"The people are hard-working. It is a community of older people, a nice farm community where everybody pulls together. Last week, for example, volunteer firemen took time off from their regular jobs—some came out of the fields—to talk to kids at school about fire protection."

The post office is in an antique store owned by Jeannette Watson, a retired teacher. Customers who come in to check their mail boxes—or visitors who stop to talk—can examine the old books and other reminders of the past.

Mrs. Kennett calls the post office a community meeting place, more for women than for men. "The fellows go to Ralph Ham's filling station," she explains.

Mrs. Kennett wants it known that the late Will Turman, an artist of some note, did most of his painting in the area. Turman is a proud name in Graysville; the township is called Turman. Pioneer Benjamin Turman built a blockhouse for protection in 1810 and Gov. William Henry Harrison acquired Turman's land the following year, ordering the blockhouse expanded into a fortress which helped maintain communications between Harrison's army in northern Ohio and Vincennes.

# Ham-ing It Up

We enter Ralph's Marathon and are greeted by Ralph Ham, Lester Crooks and cigar smoke. It is a nice day and the farmers are busy with the harvest. On bad days Ralph's is packed with farmers in search of a place to loaf.

"You won't hear much gossip here," Crooks says, a smile on his face and a tongue in his cheek. Ralph has owned the station for years. "Way the hell too long," he says. "Forty three years. Since 1949." We get the feeling he'd leave if he didn't like it so much.

He no longer does mechanical work at the garage. "I have arthritis. Can't stand on my feet too long. And if I sit too long I get stiff. Can't win," he says.

When Ralph got out of the service after World War II, he worked for a time at a garage at Sullivan. "That's when I decided to go into business for myself," he says. "If I had it to do over again, I'd be a preacher. All I'd have to do would be eat fried chicken and talk."

Ralph is small-town America, open and candid, a man without pretense. Lester Crooks prods Ralph into talking about himself. Gov. Evan Bayh made Ralph a "Sagamore of the Wabash" back in 1990. It was an honor Ralph earned for having driven a school bus for 35 accident-free years without ever missing a day.

Ralph is still driving, now in his 38th year. Still no days missed, and no accidents, either. "I want to drive two more years. Bought a new Chevrolet bus so I have to drive long enough to get it dirty."

Ralph knows about young people. "Kids have lost all possible respect for anything and anybody. Parents just raise them that way today. They get a lot less supervision in the home. And that's where it starts." Then he hastens to add, lest someone think he's bitter, "There are still some good kids, just like there has always been."

Ralph was one of the first drivers in the state to install a Camcorder on his bus and let it run from the time he picks up his first student until the last leaves. "I've used it twice to show parents why I disciplined their children. Both times, the tape showed their kids had done what I'd said they had done. One father said his son wouldn't do anything like that. I ran the tape and he said, 'By George, he did do it.'"

Change can be good and bad. "When the high school closed," Ham says, "it hurt the town sports-wise, it hurt everybody. High school students still get involved in activities at Sullivan, but probably not as much as they would if the school was still here. Every available boy played basketball here [for the Graysville High Greyhounds], every girl took home economics. It's not like that at Sullivan."

Lester Crooks is dressed in coveralls, says he works nearby at the Breed Power Plant and admits his pending retirement probably is coming at a good time. Environmental Protection Agency regulations have made the future of the old plant uncertain.

It is time to leave and let Ralph and Lester get on with some serious loafing.

# Merom

## DAYS OF CHAUTAUQUAS

Ind. 63 ends at Merom as does Ind. 58. So does Indiana, for the town sits high above the Wabash River, which here separates the state from Illinois.

It is just after 11 a.m. but several men already are having lunch at Roop's Merom Mart and Cafe. The special for the day is kraut and sausage, fried potatoes, cottage cheese or apple sauce and a drink, all for $3.99. Coffee is still a quarter.

The restaurant section is to the rear. The general store is out front—groceries, stove pipes, nuts and bolts, a bit of everything. Edmond Roop owns the store and cafe, one of the last businesses left in town. The feed store next door is for sale.

Roop is an adopted Hoosier who moved from Montgomery, Alabama, to Merom, where his son works at the power plant. He bought the store in April, 1991, entering business for the first time.

He has found Merom to be "a pretty, quiet little town with a lot of nice people. We enjoy it. It's a new experience. We have knocked down a lot of rough edges but we still have a few things to learn." Life, he is finding, is a never-ending learning process.

Richard "Smitty" Smith, eating alone, invites us to share his table. He's a tool pusher for the M&E Drilling Co. out of Casey, Illinois, has been in "the business of roughnecking off and on for thirty years" and is on his way to Oaktown, south in Knox County.

"We moved a rig into Oaktown a few days ago. We drill on con-tract—some wells for big corporations, others for individual prospectors," he says, answering questions about the business. "We usually have to go down 2,100 to 2,200 feet to find oil, if it is there. It depends on a lot of factors."

There are no certainties in this search for black gold, he reports. "Our chances of finding oil? You just never know. I'd say 60 percent in producing areas [where wells already exist], 10 percent in nonproducing areas. But again, you just never know."

M&E operates its rigs 24 hours a day, and it is Smith's job to keep them running. "Some of my work days are 30 hours long," he says, "others six to eight. In this business, anything can and will happen."

He has seen so many wells come in, he has lost track. "I'm glad for people when a well comes in, but for us it is a contract job," he says. "If we get a good well, of course, we get more business. But as far as a new strike turning me on, it doesn't faze me much anymore. That [success or failure] is all a part of it."

He finishes his lunch and is off, expecting the unexpected.

Merom may be small, but there always seems to be something to do. A handbill in the store calls attention to a wiener roast and hayride at Merom Bluff. Another flyer promotes a "Harvest Festival," also at Merom Bluff.

At Merom Bluff, a historical marker recalls the days of the Merom Bluff chautauquas held each year from 1905-1935. They were ten-day religious and educational events—concerts, debates, plays and lectures, designed to bring culture to Merom. Carrie Nation, William Jennings Bryan, William Howard Taft, Warren Harding and Billy Sunday were among the speakers who came to town.

The town still has its Chautauqua Days, now annual three-day events that bring hundreds of visitors to the giant shelter house, picnic grounds and benches along a wall on the bluff, 150 feet above the Wabash River.

It is quiet here in this scenic setting. We listen in the stillness and imagine those sermons Billy Sunday preached, those speeches Williams Jennings Bryan orated, the pleadings of Carrie Nation.

Out across the vast bottom land of Illinois, giant grain elevators, silos and water towers rise from out of the horizon. Only the barks of a dog across the river, the lonesome call of a crow in the valley break the stillness.

Time stands still here above the river. It is a good place to forget the time of day, or the day of the week, or the year of the calendar . . . at least for a while.

There is still more to see in Merom. Across town is the Merom Conference Center, once Union Christian College, which served as a preparatory school and college from 1862 until 1924. In 1936 it became Merom Institute, a rural enrichment center, and is now a camp, conference center and recreational area operated by the United Church of Christ.

\* \* \*

Southeast of Merom, hundreds of turkeys eat feed in giant turkey barns, unsuspecting that they, too, will be eaten in a few weeks.

# New Lebanon
STOVE PIPE HATS

Walk into the store at New Lebanon and meet Diane and Kenneth Wence. She's the postmaster, he's the self-proclaimed "old grouch."

The post office is in a corner of the store, which Diane says "has a little bit of everything for sale." The post office has about sixty boxes where residents like the Bridges, the McCammons and the Shorters can pick up their mail, buy stamps, mail packages.

It is the post office that preserves the name New Lebanon. "If we lose the post office, we'd just be known as rural Sullivan," Diane explains. New Lebanon no longer is near a state highway since Ind. 54 was closed when the Merom power plant opened.

The post office is a community center for women, a place to talk while the men congregate at the coffee shop up on the corner.

The Wences have lived in Sullivan County most of their lives. They bought the store June 1, 1992, just before Diane, who had experience in business, became postmaster.

"We live, eat and sleep in Sullivan County and spend eighty percent of our money here," Kenneth says.

He is a coal miner, working at a Sullivan County mine. He has worked the second shift most of his laboring life. "I'd like to have a good day-shift job, but I'm more worried about keeping a job," he says. "The coal business is not good and, for the last ten years we haven't known whether we'd have a job one month to the next, one day to the next."

Coal once was king here, but EPA regulations and debates about sulfur content have made its future less certain.

Up at Pirtle's coffee shop, a lone customer waits for his soup to heat. A few hours earlier, the place had been filled with farmers sipping coffee before a day in the fields. They left before 8 a.m. on this date, but on rainy or winter days they may linger until noon, talking politics, crops and basketball. Three weeks before the election, political discussions have turned into political arguments, Pirtle says.

New Lebanon has been home to Johnny Pirtle for more than sixty years. He owns the coffee shop which is surrounded by evidence of a general store that no longer is in operation.

A sign on the blackboard facing the stools says, "Happy Birthday Gary." In small towns, everyone knows each other's birth date, and anyone with a secret is likely a stranger.

Another customer comes in and John asks about the man's family. The other customer has his soup. He says between bites, "You could leave money on the counter all day, and nobody would take it. We even make our own change from the cash register."

Pirtle has seen the town change from a time when there were "four or five stores, a grain elevator, implement dealership and other businesses. The number of houses hasn't changed much, though. I'd say there has been a net gain of two homes since 1945."

"We don't have many problems here," Pirtle says. "We have water and natural gas, but no decent sewage system." It is not a complaint, just a comment.

He's the unofficial town historian. "The first high school in the county was here," he says, riffling through a Sullivan County history. He finds the page, shows it to a visitor. The New Lebanon Academy opened in 1853 and, like he said, it was the first high school in the area.

Pirtle graduated from New Lebanon in 1945, one of 12 seniors. The school, whose teams were called the Tigers, merged with archrival Merom, the Beavers, to form Gill Township in 1949. Students from both Merom and New Lebanon now attend Sullivan High.

Pirtle wants it known that New Lebanon once had a role in a Presidential inauguration. The Brock Hat Factory, which operated in New Lebanon from 1832 to 1850, gave one of its stove pipe hats to John W. Davis to wear to Washington, where he was speaker of the House in 1844. James K. Polk is said to have admired the hat, had one ordered, and wore it in his inaugural parade on March 4, 1845.

# Hymera
## MINING ITS BUSINESS

Hymera, on Ind. 48 in northeastern Sullivan County, is a town that owes its existence to coal. It is believed the name is derived from the ancient Sicilian city of Himera, for it was men from Italy and its island of Sicily, as well as elsewhere in southern Europe, who came to work the mines and first settled here.

In 1904, John Mitchell, president of the United Mine Workers of America, called Hymera the neatest and most progressive coal-mining town in America. The town is still neat, except for some four-letter graffiti on the water tower. The grade and junior high school is manicured, well-maintained. (The high school, whose athletic teams were known as the Shakamaks, now is part of North Central High School at Farmersburg.)

Two men pitch horseshoes in the town park, just as men have done there for decades. Meanwhile, too busy to be disturbed, three men are at work on a frame church.

Time is growing short, and we need to stop at Coalmont.

# Coalmont
## NO MORE MINE WHISTLES

Kenny Summers is turning the service station he bought in Coalmont in 1991 into an old-fashioned emporium. "Shakamak General Store," he calls it, Shakamak State Park being down the road a ways. He points to antique coffee cans, milk bottles, soap boxes, bottles for beer brands that are no longer made. And to an old hand rocker type washing machine with a crank ringer and a 1902 date.

This isn't the first time Summers has been in the store business. He had stores near Indianapolis and in Brooklyn in Morgan County until four years ago, when he sold out, expecting to go into another line of work. When he didn't find what he wanted, he moved to Coalmont, where a farm has been in the family since 1845, and re-entered the grocery business. His wife, who once had a flower shop, has craft items for sale in the store.

A sign out front says: "Good luck Cindi on Hoosier Lottery." The Summers' daughter, Cindi, will be on the televised Hoosier Lotto the next Saturday where she will have a chance to win $1 million. (She won a few thousand dollars, but not the million.)

Across Ind. 159, Joe West and his son are trying out a new mechanized wood-splitter. It works fine, and Joe is reluctant to take time out to talk about Coalmont. He does, though, for he knows a lot about the town.

"Lived here all my life," he says, "except for the time I was in the Army. I came back and worked in the strip mines, then ran a garage in the place where Kenny Summers now has his store.

"This once was a busy town. There were five mines and you could hear the whistles from each. Now there are no mines and the small coal companies have been taken over by big ones like Peabody and Ayrshire. There are few, if any, small operations."

The furniture store "there on the corner," he says, is now a sale barn, and there is little commerce in what once was a thriving community.

West drove a school bus "thirty-some years" before his wife, Marjorie, replaced him 12 years ago. Together, they have driven the same 38-mile route for 47 years. Marjorie's passengers are grandchildren of some of the students that rode on Joe's bus.

"Kids have changed over the last 12 years. We are not allowed to discipline them now. The kids need it but they [school authorities] don't want us to."

Coalmont High School, home of the Cardinals, closed at the end of the 1963-64 school year and students now attend Shakamak High outside Jasonville. The grade school closed later, leaving the playground operated by the Clay County parks system as a center for the community's young.

We hear no mine whistles, only the sounds of Joe West's wood-splitter, as we leave town at quitting time.

*Trip 10*
# WEST ON 40

Abandoned motels now line U.S. 40, once the National Road linking America's East and West. Traffic is sparse now that cars and trucks use Interstate 70, bypassing towns that helped build America.

## Reelsville
### AND/OR PLEASANT GARDENS

The Putnam County town is marked Pleasant Gardens, but indications are that it is Reelsville. Off to the south of U. S. 40 is the Reelsville school, where buses unload students at 8 a.m. The Reelsville post office is also here. So is the giant "Cook Lumber Co. of Reelsville," dealer in Indiana hardwood, maker of pallets and skids.

A block north of U.S. 40, a few cars are parked at the combination grocery and cafe. We are greeted by a waitress wearing a red apron advertising "R & D Grocery and Lunch."

A man at one of the tables introduces himself. "Al Thompson," he says extending his hand. "Al Thompson Logging," the label on his cap says. He is in the lumber business, buying and selling veneer logs, domestically and overseas. "White oak, actually all oak, is in demand," he adds. "So is walnut, although customers are preferring lighter furniture," he explains.

Thompson, a big, friendly man, grew up in neighboring Clay County, went to school at Van Buren, and unlike most Hoosiers, says he didn't care much for basketball. "I had other interests," he says, a twinkle in his eyes. One of those nocturnal interests was raccoon hunting. "I didn't do it for the kill or to sell the fur. I just liked to hunt and train the dogs. Don't do much anymore. The body won't support working and hunting," he says. He looks in good health, on the younger fringes of middle age.

It is now just after 8 a.m. and the restaurant is becoming busier. Like Thompson, most customers are ordering biscuits and gravy, a stick-to-the-ribs country breakfast.

Thompson doesn't pretend to be an expert on the town. But he says some men who stop at R & D claim Reelsville was once the most prosperous small town in America. He looks across the street at an abandoned red tile two-story building the late "Hub" Chew owned. An old Chevrolet sedan sits in front, rust beginning to appear on the hood.

"I've been told it once was the busiest Chevrolet dealership in Indiana," Thompson relates. "It was a booming place at one time, probably in the '30s and '40s."

Now, R & D is the only business, the post office the only other gathering place in town. "We have to go to Brazil or Greencastle to buy gasoline," Thompson adds.

Times are changing for the timber business, too. A lot of trees remain in the area, but the quality, he says, isn't as good as it once was.

"Time to go to work," he explains.

James Williams, a stubby field of whiskers covering his face, is finishing his biscuits and gravy at a nearby table. "Lived here 43 years," he says, subtracting the 11 years he spent elsewhere. He says he is self-employed, explaining, "I'm into recycling. Most people don't want to hire a man with one kidney."

Williams seems to have a vast knowledge of the area. We mention Reelsville. "You're in Pleasant Gardens," Williams corrects us. Pleasant Gardens, Williams says, supposedly was named by President Lincoln—or perhaps some other President—who stayed overnight as he traveled along the National Road in late spring. When Lincoln, or whoever, awoke the next morning he was greeted by the beauty of flowers, trees and terrain.

"This place should be called Pleasant Gardens," the President suggested, or so legend has it. Whatever the case, Williams does know the difference between Pleasant Gardens and Reelsville, even though the Reelsville post office is in Pleasant Gardens.

"They are twin towns. Reelsville is down over the hill along the old Pennsylvania Railroad. The National Road made Pleasant Gardens, the railroad made Reelsville," he explains. Now neither is a commercial center.

A visitor asks about a portrait on the wall. "That's Edith Davis," Williams explains. She ran the place from 1936 to 1987, the last ten years after her husband died.

The real Reelsville is where Williams says it will be, down a steep decline in the Big Walnut Creek valley, beyond the one-lane bridge on a county road. A Methodist Church on the opposite hill sits watch over the morning stillness. Wood smoke eases from some chimneys. A canoe is grounded above the creek. Another day of peace and serenity has begun.

# Lena
## A DUSTY DRIVE

Further west on U.S. 40, a sign invites motorists to the Lena Church of Christ. "Five miles," an arrow points to the north. We accept the challenge. It is not an easy journey, for the roads turn to gravel, the curves and twists creating doubt about where they may lead.

A long "five miles" leads to a hamlet at the northeastern corner of Clay County where it is touched by Putnam and Parke counties. A one-lane humpback bridge with steel poles for railings crosses double railroad tracks and leads into Lena, a town of fifteen or twenty houses and mobile homes without post office or business.

A large concrete building is closed, the pumps removed from the Texaco sign overhead. An outdated sign promises "Auction—Nov. 28."

There is competition in Lena, though. The Methodist Church is within a block of the Church of Christ, whose sign brought a visitor to this place on this day.

This is a Thursday and there are no saints or sinners to be seen. On Sunday, perhaps, motorists will stir up the dust on the unpaved roads as they come to worship.

The roads out of Lena in the opposite direction aren't any better, still crushed stone with no directional markers. A sense of direction takes us south and west. Eventually we arrive at Ind. 59 north of Brazil and notice a big, well-painted road sign suggesting motorists "Visit Historic Bridgeton."

We follow that advice and enter Parke County. The roads are paved and an occasional pot hole now and then is no problem after miles of dust and crushed stone.

# Bridgeton
## BACK IN TIME

The road eases by Big Raccoon Creek, where a sign reads "Remember When!" Another sign reveals we have reached Bridgeton. Up ahead is a covered bridge, just south of a new modern span over Big Raccoon. The old Weise Mill sits on the bank, a reminder of days when farmers saw their wheat become flour, their grain become livestock feed. Water from heavy rains cascades over the dam, the sound breaking the silence in this place that seems lost in time.

It was the 245-foot-long two-span Burr arch bridge that allowed farmers and travelers to enter the town from the west for a hundred years. It is the bridge, built in 1868, replaced in 1968, and now a National Historic Landmark, that is the town's major attraction. That and the picturesque, quaint peace and serenity the town projects.

Mostly closed on this day, shops line the streets. A law office and "Ye Ole Town Hall" are all but lost in an almost continuous row of antique stores and craft shops along Main Street, the town's commercial spine.

There are few cars around, except for an occasional merchant coming and leaving the stores. It will be different in the three days ahead, the first weekend in December. Then, Parke County will observe the last of a year-long series of events. It will be Christmas Shopping Days in Bridgeton and other towns like Mansfield and Rockville.

After that, Bridgeton will return to its peacefulness until the Maple Syrup Festival the last weekend in February and the first weekend in March. The

Covered Bridge Festival, of course, will come again the second Friday in October, turning Bridgeton into a tourist mecca for ten days.

This is a town, though, that needs no added attractions to be worth visiting. On a quiet day it is far from rush-hour traffic, far from blaring horns, factory whistles, smoke stack emissions, urbanization.

Colleen ("everyone calls me Kay") Bratcher is alone in the post office. She has been postmaster seven years, has lived around Bridgeton since 1952 when her parents decided to leave Indianapolis for the serenity of rural Indiana. She attended Bridgeton High School, which she says has been bought by a young couple who plan to turn it into apartments.

Grade school students now attend classes at Rosedale, high school students at Riverton Parke. There are no groceries, no gasoline stations, no convenience stores.

"We have to drive ten miles to buy gas to mow our grass," Mrs Bratcher says. But it is not a complaint, more of a fact of life in small-town Indiana in the late 1900s.

Give the Bridgeton Heritage Foundation much of the credit for keeping Bridgeton alive and well. It is the foundation that has sponsored fund-raising efforts like raffles to raise money to maintain the town's legacy and its place in history.

It is outsiders, people from as far away as Chicago, who come to town during festivals, sell their wares and leave with money in their pockets.

It is the residents who remain who have saved Bridgeton, who work to keep it a place worth visiting even when no festivals, no Christmas sales, no special events are scheduled.

# Carbon
## PAUL'S PLACE

Back on Ind. 59, we head south toward Carbon, which is just over the Parke County line in Clay County. Carbon is east of Ind. 59, past the giant Pike Lumber Co.'s Carbon mill, past the water tower, there to the north after a stop at the railroad to allow a Conrail train to rumble east through town.

There is no activity at the Clay County Park system's recreation area, in the heart of town, on this sunny winter day. The shelter house and playground are vacant. It is quiet, too, at the Town Hall, a building that once was the town's grade school.

Paul's Place, the town tavern, is open. Two men are at the bar at 10:15 a.m. One empties the last drop from a beer can, orders another. The other asks to have his Coke glass refilled. A third man they call "Clifford" enters and orders a Sprite.

The men talk about the alleged hazards of "sidesaddle" fuel tanks on some GMC pickup trucks, allege automakers sometimes would rather face lawsuits than recall vehicles to eliminate any perils they might have. They are basing their comments on an NBC report.

(A few weeks later, NBC apologized for the way tests on the safety of the truck were conducted.)

Pat VanDeventer is working as the bartender. "I work part-time for Gina Black, the owner," she explains. Pat grew up in Carbon, lived for a time in Las Vegas, where she worked at an Air Force base and for the school system. She seems to have mixed emotions about life in Carbon versus Las Vegas.

A visitor notes that beer is still a dollar, compared to $1.50 or more at most bars.

"We try to keep the prices reasonable to accommodate the people of the community," Mrs. VanDeventer explains. Paul's Place is a community center, a place adults can go to relax. That appears to supersede the desire for big profit.

# Cardonia
## POINT THE WAY

It is not easy to find Cardonia, not even when it's there on the official Indiana road map, just east of Ind. 59, south of Carbon. No signs point off Ind. 59 toward Cardonia. We see an improved road, head east, drive a mile or so to a four-way stop. A few houses are behind, a few to the right, a few to the left, one or two straight ahead.

Cardonia, a four-way stop on Clay County roads, is a town without a post office, without identification.

Perk's Country Store is open for business, but there is none at the 11 o'clock hour. Evelyn Perkins, wearing a sweater that says "Mom," is alone in the store, stocked with assorted items that keep Cardonians from taking trips to Brazil or elsewhere.

"This must be Cardonia," a visitor remarks. "It is," Mrs. Perkins confirms. The visitor scans the store. There is a little of everything. "My husband likes to buy and trade," Mrs. Perkins explains. Her husband is Marvin, who still works in Brazil, where he is superintendent of the water treatment plant.

The Perkinses bought the store 12 years ago, moving from Saline City south of Brazil. "We were looking for a place and found Cardonia," she explains.

It is a friendly place, she says. "We like it pretty well, although it does get hectic here in the store at times." It is a community center of sorts, there being no other place for residents to gather.

Cardonia, she agrees, is off the beaten path, unknown to most people, nonexistent as far as the state highway department is concerned. "Carbon has a sign on Ind. 59," Mrs. Perkins says. "I don't know why there can't be one pointing to Cardonia," she wonders. It probably is a question asked by other motorists who have tried to find Cardonia.

* * *

We drive back west on what he have learned is Rio Grande Road, cross Ind. 59, pass a mailbox topped by a model of a John Deere tractor. This is farm country, and the map says Fontanet is up ahead. The road turns slightly to the north, past a row of houses, past a convenience store.

"This must be Fontanet," we tell a clerk in Fran's General Store, as if we are experts on geography. "It's not called anything," she adds, not eager to strike up a conversation with a visitor who isn't going to buy anything except a cup of coffee.

She does gives directions to Fontanet. "First road to the right."

# Fontanet
## No Beans About It

Fontanet is where the clerk said it would be, right there in the northeast corner of Vigo County. It is almost noon, and there are a few cars outside the "Keg and Cod," a tavern and restaurant across the street from the town's new post office. A dumpster is filled with empty beer cartons, an indication of a busy community gathering spot.

In the tavern, idle Hoosiers do what they do best—play euchre. Two men kibitz, their chairs queued between open spots on the round table. Three of the players make fun of the fourth. "I'm going up on the hill, but I'll be back before you finish dealing," one of them taunts. The dealer continues to shuffle the deck slowly, ignoring his antagonists.

A woman tending bar explains the "Keg and Cod" thus: "We sell a lot of beer and cod fish."

Mike Goda, wearing Oshkosh B'Gosh bib overalls, is sipping beer at the bar. He talks about how the town has changed over the 41 years he has observed it from his home less than a mile away. Goda is friendly, eager to talk. Towns change. Down-home people like Mike Goda stay the same.

A road out of town to the north passes the fire department, past Bob's Auto Parks, a giant junkyard where old cars have gone to be stripped before death.

A park on the left is marked with a sign: "Home of Fontanet Bean Dinner." The visitor makes the connection, confirms it later. The old high school athletic teams were called the Beantowners. Boston couldn't be prouder.

(High school students from Fontanet now attend Terre Haute North High School, as they have for three decades).

\* \* \*

We drive north of Fontanet, angle left where the road splits and see a giant tree in the middle of the pavement. It's huge, a yellow ribbon ringing its circumference, its branches reaching out over the two lanes it divides. It is a living testimonial that nature sometimes survives in its perpetual struggle with progress.

# Rosedale
## PRIDE IN ITSELF

We drive on to Rosedale, a little commercial oasis in the agricultural Big Raccoon valley. It is a nice tree-lined town with a drug store, hardware, bank, IGA Foodliner and other businesses like the Schopmeyer Farm Supply elevator.

The chili at the Harvest House restaurant ("breakfast, lunch and carry out") is good on this cool, sunny day. The place is busy and so is the town.

A town of eight hundred off a highway, it has lost its high school and its basketball team, the "Hot Shots," to consolidation at Riverton Parke, but has managed to survive and keep its identity. And its heart at Middle and Main streets. That's the intersection where the old brick Florida Township Civic Center is located, a place that still gives the town pride in itself.

# Mansfield
## LURE OF THE DOLLAR

On this day before the start of Parke County Shopping Days, Mansfield is abuzz with stand-holders setting up for business. Commercialism has taken over what once was a quaint town with a grist mill, started around 1820.

The mill that was the focal point of the community is still open, except for a historical sign the only indication of those pioneer days.

We drive away, disappointed that tourism and heritage seem to conflict, the lure for the dollar more important than natural beauty.

*Trip 11*
# WEST-CENTRAL INDIANA

Call this a one-day detour from the backroads of southern Indiana to the small towns of west-central Indiana.

## Russellville
SAD BUT TRUE

Signs on Ind. 236 welcome visitors to Russellville, a farm community to the north. A smiling face decorates a "Midland Co-op welcomes you to Russellville" sign. Another marker offers a "Welcome to Our City—Russell-ville" sign.

The annual "Russler's Roundup" festival is over, but the town still is decorated. Small corn shocks hug posts in the once-thriving business district, now almost void of stores.

Ron Higgins, 41, is still in business. He owns Ron's 66 Service, has for 23 years, ever since he was one of ten seniors to graduate in 1969, Russellville High School's last class.

The town has aged more than Higgins. "When I was in high school, there was a business in every building on Main Street. Now not much is left and that's sad," he says. The change has been slow, first one store, then another: "I remember when we had four filling stations, two banks, two grocery stores, two hardware stores, two restaurants, two barber shops, a shoe cobbler and a variety store. Now there is just me and the grocery."

The high school is gone, and students are taken 15.5 miles to the big North Putnam consolidation. "I wore out two cars taking my two sons to and from extracurricular events," Higgins says.

A customer walks in and wonders why there is no light in the station office. "Bulb burned out. I'll have to go to Waveland to get one," Ron answers. Waveland is six miles away.

His garage is heated and it's a winter gathering spot for farmers, who have no restaurant in town to visit.

# Annapolis
### Ghosts from the Past

Annapolis, a Parke County hamlet off U.S. 41 just north of the Ind. 236 junction, is a town bypassed by time. Only a historical marker recalls the decades in the mid-1800s when Annapolis was "a thriving town with many factories, stores and potteries."

Its days of glory are now gone.

# Bloomingdale
### Past and Present

Bloomingdale is off the beaten path, its last grocery closed, but it's neither down nor out. It is a tree-lined community on a Parke County road a few miles off U.S. 41. It is an old town where a Friends meeting house (church) was established in 1827 and where a Quaker school educated students from 1846 to 1916.

Just to the west of the site of the old Bloomingdale High School, where the Bulldogs played before they joined with the Bloomingdale Academy Immortals, the Marshall Bobcats and the Tangier Tigers to form Turkey Run High three decades ago.

The stone entrance to the school remains. So does a plaque of Lincoln's Gettysburg Address which was awarded in 1954 when the school won a Rockville American Legion Post oratorical contest.

The last grocery has closed, but the town does have a restaurant, an insurance agency, a volunteer fire department, a tool and die firm and two related plastic plants. And it has its own telephone company, Bloomingdale Home Telephone, which also serves Marshall and Kingman. "It provides good service," says Janice Watts, the postmaster.    Janice Watts misses the grocery. "Women used to come across the street from the grocery and talk after shopping, but that's changed, too."

# Dana
### ERNIE'S HOME

Visitors to Dana on Ind. 71 need not check the phone book or ask for information about businesses in town. They are right there, in colorful art work on the entire exterior south wall of a vacant building erected in 1874, in a montage that is a directory of town businesses.

Dana, a farm town of 625 residents a mile north of U.S. 36, was named after Charles Dana, a stockholder in the Indianapolis, Decatur and Western Railroad which ran through town. It is more famous, though, for Ernie Pyle, the World War II correspondent whose stories about average GIs earned a Pulitzer Prize in 1944, a year before he was killed by a Japanese sniper on the island of Ie Shima. Pyle's home was moved to Dana from out in Helt Township, and now is a state memorial.

There are few visitors this day, but the grain elevators next to the railroad are busy, for Dana is just a couple of basketball bounces from Illinois in the fertile prairie of America's breadbasket.

* * *

We head down Ind. 71 south toward St. Bernice, through expansive farm land crossed by electric-transmission lines on steel towers that look like robot frames with arms bent downward to clutch the wires. The terrain begins to turn from flat to rolling.

# St. Bernice
## COMEBACK FROM DISASTER

St. Bernice, population 950, is so close to Illinois a whisper could be heard across the state line. A tavern is open, so is the post office. Chances are as much gossip can be heard at one place as the other.

No matter. We opt to visit the library. Librarian Pam McDonald is at work as she is each Monday, Thursday and Saturday morning.

Mrs. McDonald grew up in Oliver, Illinois, but her husband Jim was born here and works at the Eli Lilly & Co. plant in Clinton. "It's a friendly place," says Mrs. McDonald of St. Bernice. "We had a bad tornado here two years ago and everyone pitched in to help each other. A lot of the town was destroyed, but except for the school about everything has been restored."

St. Bernice is a farming community and workers not involved in agriculture have jobs in Clinton or Terre Haute. The biggest event of the year comes July 4 when the town has its annual celebration at Miller's Park south of town, an event marked by fireworks, games, free beans. It's an informal occasion, befitting a farming community.

The old school, circa 1927, is a mess. Twisted metal, collapsed bricks, ripped roofing remain as stark reminders of the awesome power of the tornado. The mangled structure once was the home of the St. Bernice Hornets, but the school already had become part of South Vermillion near Clinton. Grade school students attend the Ernie Pyle elementary school up the road toward Dana.

# Blanford
## AND UNIVERSAL

We stay on the highway as it nudges south along the Illinois border to Blanford, a town that has developed where north-south Ind. 71 terminates at Ind. 163. A store and coin laundry are open, but it is the community park that impresses a visitor. A sign notes the park—ball diamond, tennis courts, swing sets, playground equipment—is named in honor of James Perona. Perona must be proud, wherever he is.

* * *

We go east, then south, on Ind. 163 and over a Vermillion County road, past a car-crushing operation to Universal, a town marked by its name on the water tower. The terrain is rough around the old coal-mining town, were some residents still complain about the blasting and the environment. Scattered slag mounds remain.

Jo Jo's Bar and Grill is open, but the post office has closed, as it does after 1 p.m. each day. The basketball court is idle.

Peabody Coal's giant Universal Mine is at the south edge of town. Coal is big in Universal, as it has been for decades.

* * *

Road 00 goes south of Universal to New Goshen, where we turn northwest on U.S. 150 toward Shirkieville. There the terrain flattens into vast fields stretching west into Illinois.

# Shirkieville
## BAYH COUNTRY

It's time for lunch, and the Midway Bar in Shirkieville turns out to be an old-type restaurant with a long bar and a friendly bartender. A sign says the place is owned by Bob and Joan Hallett.

This, too, is mining-farming country, and a sign on the beer cooler stresses, "Why Not Coal/United Mine Workers of America." Coal is still abundant, still cheap, and thousands of Hoosiers still depend on it for jobs. Another sign says "Union Yes."

This is a tavern for ordinary folks, like the two men at the bar. One says he started a job last week and is off today because of the rain.

An older couple comes in for an afternoon break. He sits at the bar, she crawls onto a stool beside him. They talk with the bartender about the weather. The man says, "Waiting for winter is like being on death row. You know it's coming, you just aren't sure when."

Chances are these folks will be back the next week, if not before, for Wednesday is euchre night and euchre is Indiana's favorite card game.

The Bayh—as in Gov. Evan Bayh—family farm is out on the prairie land near Shirkieville, but politics and governors are not topics for conversation at the Midway Bar on this afternoon.

## *Trip 12*
# TOWARD VINCENNES

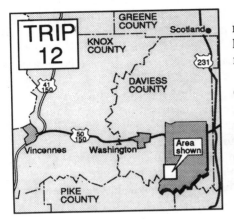

The holiday season is over and a new year has begun. It is time for our holiday hiatus to end, our travels to resume.

Winter has changed the landscape of backroads Indiana. Frost coats grass browned by freezes, driving cattle to dinner at round bales of hay. Wood smoke rises like tiny clouds from rural homes as bundled youngsters wait at the road for yellow school buses to arrive.

## Scotland
### A PLACE TO GO

Robert Minks, decked out in new Oshkosh B'Gosh overalls and a plaid shirt, is the lone customer at 9 a.m. at Tootie's Cafe in Scotland, a town about a mile off Ind. 54/58 at the south edge of Greene County. Harold and Edna Manis, the owners, already are preparing for the lunch bunch, expecting the usual crowd that fills the booths under assorted antiques that hang from the walls.

"Every town needs a place like this to loaf," Minks explains. "Otherwise they'd just be dead. If it wasn't for this place, we wouldn't have anywhere to go."

Minks has lived around Scotland since 1947. "Married a girl from down here," he explains, then adds softly, "I lost her five years ago."

Minks is friendly, like most men and women in small towns where faces change but little else does. "In Scotland," he says, "people die. New ones come and pretty soon you don't know anyone in town. The town, though, hasn't changed much."

Oh, a few businesses have closed. The nearest gasoline stations are at Bloomfield, seven miles away, or Newberry, a little farther. The high school where the "Scotties" basketball team played is no more, its students now part of Bloomfield High.

Minks is retired after working 35 years at the Crane Naval Surface Warfare Center. "I drove a truck back and forth to Indianapolis every day for years, then worked on the base. It was a good place to work," he says.

He now raises Black Angus calves on a farm near Scotland and sells them at the feeder auction at Springville. His farm truck is outside. He's on his way this morning to Bloomfield to buy feed. "Need to be going," he says a couple of times, adjusting the ICC Seeds cap. He repeats himself, either to convince himself he should be on his way or not to seem rude to the stranger who invited himself to sit at the Minks' booth.

Mrs. Manis walks from the kitchen, refilling the cups with fresh coffee. The service and the coffee are better than at fast-food or chain restaurants.

She leaves the talking to Harold. Harold and Edna have operated the store 22 years, ever since Harold returned to town after 22 years in the U.S. Air Force. Harold grew up four miles from Scotland, proof you can take the boy out of the country—even for years—but chances are he'll be back.

Minks pays his bill and leaves. Chances are he will be back for lunch. "This place has the best hamburgers around," he wants us to know in case we can return on another day.

Tootie's will remain quiet until noon when farmers and workers from Crane arrive for those hamburgers.

We follow as Minks out as he drives his truck out of town onto Ind. 54/58. There are no other cars on the road.

# Raglesville
## COUNTRY COMMUNITY

"Entering Daviess County," the sign on the highway says. Daviess, it should be pointed out, is pronounced Davis not Dayvees by its residents, and anyone who does call it Dayvees can be spotted right off as an outsider.

* * *

A buggy with a fringe on top is parked behind a motorized truck, linking the past and the present. Giant draft horses are in barnlots. Clothing hangs from lines outside neat homes.

There are Amish families around Raglesville, a farm community without a store, business or post office. What had been a store is now a residence.

No town-limit signs define the town which is south of Ind. 58 on Daviess County Road 1100 East. Only a "Lions Club—1st and 3rd Mondays 7:30—Evans Park Building" sign greets visitors. It is service clubs that create pride in small communities, generates funds for improvement, give a sense of fellowship.

A number of cars are in the parking lot at the Mt. Joy Fellowship Church.

"Raglesville Rockets" reads a sign on the scoreboard at a baseball diamond west of the Van Buren Township grade school. It is the site of the old Raglesville High School which closed in 1939 when students were sent to Odon (now a part of North Daviess High).

# Odon
## COMPLIMENTARY COFFEE

A horse hitched to a buggy is tethered in the business district near the intersection that is Odon's business district. On the corners of that four-way stop are The Malt Shop ("home cooked meals"), the Odon Tavern called "Main Spring," First National Bank ("Uptown Branch") and Lodge 303 F&AM. Next to the bank is the Odon Clothing Company, a business that lures customers, license plates indicate, from distant counties.

On this morning, coffee is free at The Malt Shop, compliments of the Wilson Agency, an insurance firm. An old-fashioned pharmacy is next door, a reminder of the days before local boy John Poindexter grew up to become President Bush's national security adviser.

Listen closely and chances are you may hear old timers talk about the Odon basketball team that went to the final eight of the state tournament in 1959 before losing to big-city New Albany, 70-68, in double-overtime at Evansville.

On this day, though, the talk is about the North Daviess High School (which absorbed Odon in consolidation) Cougars, for this is a town for the present as well as for the past.

We are reminded, eight months early, that Odon's annual Old Settlers Picnic, "the oldest continuous festival in Indiana," will start the second Tuesday in August. Visitors are welcome, we are told, just as they are here at any other time of the year.

\* \* \*

Out west of Odon on Ind. 58, in mid-country, is North Daviess High School, home of the Cougars, a consolidation of the Odon Bulldogs, Epsom Salts, Plainville Midgets, Elnora Owls and Raglesville Rockets.

# Epsom
### SALT OF THE EARTH

Any town that had a high school whose teams were the Salts deserves a visit. It is not easy to find Epsom, even if you take the road south at the Epsom sign on Ind. 58. The roads are rough—crushed stone, freshly graded, muddy from the rain.

They are roads used by heavy machinery at the giant Black Beauty Coal Co. mines, for this is an area blessed with good farms, where coal is near the surface and oil down deeper. Signs advise "Warning/Mine Explosives in Use."

We take a wrong turn and end up in Plainville. It's a rural business center astraddle Ind. 57, too big, too busy to be considered "Backroads Indiana."

We see a sign on Ind. 57 that points toward Epsom. We drive, and drive, then drive some more. It is obvious we again have missed Epsom. We flag down a repair truck and its two occupants provide directions. We retrace our route, turn at the crossroads as indicated, finally see a few houses off to the left.

"This Epsom?" we asked a man driving an oversize Silverado pickup with a fifth wheel, a livestock trailer in tow.

A grin on his face, the driver replies, "What there is of it. Wagler, Henry M. Wagler," he says identifying himself without being asked. "What's your name?" he wants to know. Wagler is proof Hoosiers know no strangers.

We tell him, explaining we are in search of "Backroads Indiana." "You've found it," he says. "This is as backroads as you can get."

Wagler has lived around Epsom all his life. Has seen, he says, the school closed, then torn down. Has seen the grocery closed. Points to the place Chet Shandley ran up on the corner where an old broken bench and a rusting clothes dryer now sit under the porch roof.

"Once the school closed, the town went to nothing," Wagler says.

Wagler has grown too old to farm. Now he drives the livestock rig when someone needs animals moved or taken to market. "I do a little hauling for some extra money. Social Security doesn't quite make it," he adds.

We find the old school grounds. It is now a garden plot. The death of old Epsom High is marked with a tombstone. It's a short epitaph: "Epsom School 1909-1968."

As Wagler said, the tombstone could have been for the town as well as the school. When the students moved on to North Daviess, the town, in a way, died.

*  *  *

We drive cross-country, past the oil wells, coal mines and huge farms, resources that are a boon to Daviess County. Only instinct plus occasional road signs keep us from losing our way.

We enter Montgomery from the north and are reminded that this is the home of the Daviess County Turkey Trot, an annual September event featuring "turkey racing at its finest." And they call the Indianapolis 500 the greatest spectacle in racing!

# Alfordsville

### IT BEATS BOSTON

We walk into the little service station in Alfordsville (pronounced All-fordsville) and feel as if we have stepped into a Norman Rockwell painting.

Inside are Norman Cole, Sr., his son Norman, Jr., and Junior's father-in-law, John Phinney. They're talking about American troops in Somalia and Saddam Hussein in Iraq and have no shortage of opinions about either.

Some people call the younger Cole "Junior." Others call him "Mr. Station Man."

The older Cole looks down at the oiled wooden tongue-and-groove floor, and says, "He runs the place." "He" is Buster, a dog asleep next to the wood stove that's warm on a cold day. Buster doesn't care about Somalia, Iraq or even the stranger who just entered the store. It's a dog's life and he's making the most of it.

Actually it's the younger Cole who owns the place, has for the last three years. The station, though, has been a fixture in Alfordsville for more than a half-century. "I've been loafing here, off and on, since 1940," Norman, Sr., says.

It is still the community center, especially for men. A pool table is in the back. A hand-printed sign offers "Cold Pop 50 cents/Sandwiches $1.50."

Junior traded "a good job" in a plant at nearby Jasper for a chance to be his own boss: "I wouldn't go back [to factory work] for a million dollars. I work longer hours, don't make as much, but I'm happier here."

Happier, too, is his father-in-law, Phinney. Phinney talks with an accent that's alien to Alfordsville. It's obvious he isn't a Hoosier and hasn't been around long enough to pick up the southern Indiana dialect.

"You can't be from here," we observe.

"I'm not," he says. "I'm from Rockland, which is south of Boston." That's Boston as in Massachusetts. The accent is New England.

"So how did you happen to arrive in Alfordsville?" he is asked.

"He married my daughter, brought her here, and I followed later," he explains, looking at the younger Cole. "You could give me Boston, put me on a pedestal on the highest tower, and I wouldn't take it. I can sit here and listen to the coyotes, hear the grass grow, see cows from my porch. I don't care if I ever go to town." He sounds convincing.

"It's nice here," he adds. "I'm just waiting for spring when my neighbor can plow my garden."

Cole the elder agrees. "We've been all over the U.S. and Canada and seen lots of nice places with great scenery. But when we get within twenty miles of home we know it's the best place there is. There's a lot more to look at than in the cities. I like it here," he adds, accentuating Phinney's opinion.

Cole, Jr., goes into the back room, returns with a mounted fish. "Two-and-one-half-pound blue gill. Caught it in a pond at the edge of town." The fish is his proof that Alfordsville is home.

Cole, Jr., was in the Army, back from Vietnam where he was a crew chief and a gunner on a helicopter, when he met Debrah Phinney. "I did what I had to do," he says of his 18 months in Vietnam. "I didn't like getting shot at, but that was part of it."

He and Debrah returned to Alfordsville in August, 1972, and stayed. "The change in geography . . . and life style . . . didn't come easy for Debrah. It took her a while to adjust."

She wasn't accustomed to herds of dairy cows meandering along the sides of roads coming from pastures to barns and back to pastures. Or seeing livestock at the edge of her yard. She, too, grew to love Alfordsville, just like her dad did when he came to visit.

Like Cole, Jr., the two older men served their country in war. The elder Cole served 37 months with the U.S. Army in World War II, seeing action in the North African campaign, later moving to the Orient to serve under Gen. "Vinegar Joe" Stilwell in Burma and India. "I missed being home, but I never let it bother me," he recalls.

Phinney served a four-year hitch in the U.S. Air Force (1947-51), two years of it in Alaska. "Didn't get frostbitten until I got back to Great Falls, Montana. I did a lot of flying, weather missions over the North Pole in a B-29 Flying Fortress. Best plane ever made," he boasts.

The younger Cole tosses another stick of wood in the stove. Buster looks up, then drops his head back on the floor.

The elder Cole talks about an earlier time when Alfordsville was a boom town. "We were on the main road between Loogootee and Jasper and there was a lot of traffic, a lot of business. Two grain elevators, five service stations, a drug store, hardware store, funeral parlor, two blacksmith shops, three groceries, two doctors and a hotel.

"The population wasn't much bigger than it is now [about a hundred residents], but folks came in from out in the country to trade and learn all the gossip.

"The town started dying when U.S. 231 opened a more direct route between Loogootee and Jasper to the east. But in my opinion, what really killed the town was when the school closed," he adds.

Alfordsville High closed after the class of 1965 was graduated. Students in the community now are bused 12 miles to Montgomery to attend Barr-Reeve High School.

The old school, now privately owned, still stands a blocks or two away, surrounded by junk. A limestone marker set in the brick wall is a tribute to the townspeople who formed a holding company to build it in 1953.

Athletes who would have once been Alfordsville Yellow Jackets are now Barr-Reeve Vikings. A team picture with a calendar of games hangs on the wall of Junior's store. "This is Viking country now," says the younger Cole, accepting the consolidation that hometown pride could not deter.

The fire in the stove is growing warmer. It is a friendly haven on a cool day. We leave, knowing there will always be an Alfordsville as long as there are such warm places to loaf.

## *Trip 13*
# BACK TO CUMBACK

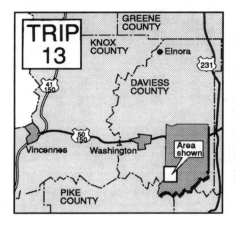

It is another day, and we are returning to Daviess County. The cold weather has warmed enough for a few garage sales. A sign promoting one of those sales hangs on an eye-catching scarecrow tied to a rural mailbox post in northeastern Knox County.

We enter Elnora from the west where flood-control levees line the banks of the West Fork of White River.

## Elnora
### WORTH A HOOT

An old one-lane bridge spans White River at the edge of Elnora and we wait for a pickup before crossing into Daviess County. The river is up after heavy rains, but it is far from threatening.

Elnora was called Owl Town when the first settlers came in the mid-1800s and noted the different varieties of owls that roosted in the area they called Owl Prairie. That changed when William Griffith, a merchant who helped plat the town, called it Elnora for his wife.

No matter. The Elnora High School athletic squads were known as Owls until the merger with North Daviess.

Elnora grew up around the Evansville and Indianapolis Railroad line which brought commerce and customers. Most of the commerce now is carried on trucks that arrive on Ind. 57, which crosses Ind. 58 at the edge of town.

Elnora now is a town 750 residents call home. It has retained some of its businesses and held onto its identity, melding its past with its future.

# Cornettsville
## Circuit Riding

A sign south of Plainville points to "Cornettsville—3 miles." We take the Daviess County road and find Cornettsville amid fertile fields, strip mines and oil wells.

Cornettsville is seven houses, two mobile homes and the United Methodist Church. Except for some German Catholic towns, we have found a Methodist church in almost every hamlet of southern Indiana, a reminder of the days of the church's active circuit-riding ministers.

\* \* \*

Ind. 257 southeast out of Washington seems to have been laid out by a snake as it twists and slithers and roller coasters through cattle farms.

Piped water is available from the Daviess County rural water system and building sites are available, the "For Sale" signs luring home builders to the serenity of rural life.

# Glendale
## Baiting Visitors

We head east into the morning sun from Ind. 257 toward the Glendale State Fish and Wildlife Area and Dogwood Lake. Warmer weather will bring more visitors in the days to come.

Glendale, the hamlet, is quiet on this day, except at two bait shops which are open for business. One sells groceries and beer as well as bait. Another advertises coffee and sandwiches.

There is no sign of the old Glendale High School where the Golden Bears played until about 1948, when the school closed and students were sent to Montgomery (now Barr-Reeve).

A giant bell sits in front of the brick Glendale Masonic Lodge. A basketball goal hangs on a tree near a decaying barn. A church no longer is in use. A burned mobile home which may have been used for training firefighters is near the Harrison Township volunteer fire department.

# Cumback
## Okay, We Will

We return to Ind. 257, then go west on another Daviess County road that appears to lead to Cumback. We stop at Aikman Creek Baptist Church, which is at a T in the road. An old bell—"Moshane Foundry, Baltimore, Md.,

1889"—rests on a brick stand. A marker from an even older church is dated 1844-1896. It is a church that has seen the joys and sadness of the area for almost 150 years.

There are nice houses, an A-frame, and four newer houses in a row on the road that meanders to the west. Another new home is built into the side of a hill. We decide this conclave of homes in the center of a farming area in southwestern Daviess County must be Cumback.

We are told later we did not go far enough to the west—that Cumback is farther out the road, its store with gas pumps out front no longer in operation, the baseball diamond out back no longer there. About all that remains, we learn, is the Mt. Gilead Church.

We make a note to come back some time to see Cumback.

\* \* \*

We have better luck finding Hudsonville. It is three miles off Ind. 257 to the east, out County Road 700 South, past an outhouse behind a farm home, a reminder of the days when water didn't run in houses and plumbing was a slop jar.

At Road 500 East a sign at Barber Equipment Sales claims it is "first in farm supplies." To the south, is the Dogwood Coon Hunters Club.

# Hudsonville
## COUNTRY MORNING

Glenna's Country Diner, a tile building painted white, offers "food, gas, bait." Three pickup trucks are parked out front, which means it must be a good place for breakfast. A German shepherd greets visitors, friendly like, outside the door.

Glenna Barber owns Glenna's Diner, a clean little place she redecorated before opening for business in 1992. It is early Saturday and Glenna is at work in the kitchen, ready to fix whatever anyone wants to order from a full menu.

Her customers are three farmers, two travelers. The farmers know each other, exchange their plans for the day. "Andy" has just walked in. It's obvious he's a regular customer.

"No rush," he tells Glenna, who has sat down to rest a spell. Glenna takes him at his word, waits a minute or two, then asks, "What'll it be, Andy?"

"French toast," he orders.

"Whatta ya have on today?" A customer asks Andy. Andy's a farmer and there is work to do today, even when fields are too wet to plow.

"There's always something," Andy says. "We've got some fence to roll up, I have to fix a flat, then haul some manure."

The other farmer nods, knowingly: "Seems like I've been building fence for the last five years."

Another customer, more interested in stock-car racing than farm work, talks about the Brickyard 400, the first NASCAR race planned at the Indianapolis Motor Speedway, 15 months away in August 1994.

This is a friendly oasis, an unexpected gem, a place where the conversation is endless, the coffee always hot, the food good enough to make a person delay his work, except on Mondays and Tuesdays when Glenna closes the doors and takes two days off.

Except for the restaurant, the Hudsonville United Methodist Church and the nearby Miller's Getaway From It All Campgrounds, there isn't much to Hudsonville.

Hudsonville, like the hamlet of Glendale, is near the Glendale recreation area. Sooner or later, fishermen and campers will hear about those breakfasts at Glenna Country Diner.

# Iva and Algiers

## BUCKTOWN AND ALFORD

We drive south on Ind. 257 over White River from Daviess into Pike County and turn northwest at Ind. 356. Iva is two miles north of Ind. 356 on a narrow, pothole-littered, poorly-drained road. A squirrel runs along the road, for there are not enough cars to teach it not to play in traffic.

A home is abandoned, perhaps another farmstead sold by a small operator to another farmer who has learned that only the big survive in today's

agriculture. Only the Iva Union Church, built in 1902, marks the town. A house across the way appears to be just as old.

If Iva ever was, it isn't now.

\* \* \*

Ind. 356 goes northeast toward Algiers, past Pike County farms with well-kept houses and out buildings. Power lines on steel towers cut across fields on their way from the Indianapolis Power & Light Co. plant at Petersburg.

There are no businesses in Algiers, no post offices. What stores there were are closed, perhaps surrendering to the competition up the pike at Petersburg.

Pike County, too, has coon hunters, and their club is near Algiers. A homemade sign points north off Ind. 356 to "Bucktown," a row of houses along a well-paved county road. Two drag lines on the horizon remind us we are back in coal country.

\* \* \*

Flags fly at homes in Alford (pronounced All-ford), a neat, orderly community which almost touches Petersburg on Ind. 356. New houses line the highway and there appear to be no other streets on either side of the road.

## *Trip 14*
# SOUTH OF COLUMBUS

Rain has fallen and the fog has settled in on a warm winter morning. It is not a good day for outside work, so farmers and other men with outdoors jobs should be at their favorite hangouts in small towns.

## Jonesville
### "THE BRICK"

A white dog, his skin darkened by rain, doesn't move from his resting place in the center of a Jonesville street. It is *his* street and any visitor can avoid him. Other dogs race out of their yard to greet cars.

The Jonesville post office is in a house trailer. There is no pretense in this village off Ind. 11 south of Columbus.

Cars and pickups are parked around an unmarked building. "You must be 21 to enter," a note on the door warns, a clue it is the town tavern. Inside are men in caps with seed-corn and construction-firm labels. It is 9:30 a.m. but a few have already ordered beers. Others are drinking coffee, having breakfast.

We are in "The Brick," a tavern for most of the century, before Prohibition, then again when it ended. The Brick was a garage back in those days in the late '20s, early '30s when only bootleggers sold beer and liquor.

We sit at the bar next to Bob Piercefield. The Brick, he says, is noted for the coldest beer and the best hamburgers in Indiana. A sign at the bar offers "Hamburgers $1.50. Cheeseburgers $1.85." Another notice warns: "Please be patient. I have two speeds and if this one isn't fast enough then I'm sure you won't like the other."

Piercefield answers questions about himself. "Retired from Reliance Electric in Columbus," he explains. "Been retired five years on the 29th of January [1993]," he adds. "I missed being at work the first three or four months. Don't miss it much now."

"Times aren't so good for some people around Columbus," he adds. "Quite a few people are laid off."

The Brick is a neighborhood bar, a good place for men like Piercefield to meet friends, a community center of sorts. "A lot of retirees come in here," he says, "and it is really packed when fans are here to watch Indiana University basketball games."

We are taking notes. A customer approaches and says, "If you are writing checks, make me out one."

"Name's Fred Meyer," he says. Meyer is wearing a plaid shirt and a jacket with a "Beck's Hybrid" seed-corn patch. Meyer farms near town. "I still have some corn in the field," he says, confessing, "I like to fish more than farm." It's an exaggeration. The moisture content of the corn was too high in the fall, then rain and winter weather delayed the harvest.

Meyer is as friendly as Piercefield. He talks about vacations in places like Alaska, about newspaper cartoonists and about The Brick's hamburger while watching one sizzle under a two-inch blanket of onions. "They call the hamburgers 'bricks' but I've never heard anyone complain about one," he adds.

It is too wet to resume the corn harvest, but Meyer has other things to accomplish. He leaves. We turn to talk again with Piercefield, but he has left.

Chances are both Piercefield and Meyer will be back later in the day, or tomorrow morning for sure. The Brick is the kind of place that can become habit-forming.

# Hayden
## MAKING HAY

Motorists who ignore the "Hayden" sign on U.S. 50 between Seymour and North Vernon miss a bit of Indiana history. Two county roads lead north from the highway into town. One road goes through a "decorated" viaduct under the railroad that helped give Hayden a place on the map. "Welcome to Hayden" and "Go Perot! No More Gridlock" are lettered in red, white and blue on the viaduct's walls. The election is three months past, a new President is in office, but the sign remains.

Hayden hasn't always been Hayden. The community at the crossing of a Jennings County Road and the Ohio and Mississippi Railroad (later the Baltimore & Ohio) was first called Hardenburg.

The rolling land around the community was ideal for forage crops, and tons of hay were shipped from town on the railroad. It was for that reason that Hardenburg became Hayden in 1890. The high school basketball team became the Haymakers, a nickname the grade school retained when the high school became part of consolidated Jennings County High School.

Ed Whitcomb, Governor of Indiana from 1969 to 1973, grew up in Hayden, played on the Haymakers basketball teams, and was graduated in 1935. He still owns the house where he grew up in Hayden.

Roger Ruddick, who has written the *History of Spencer Township,* cares about the town and the community. And he's making sure young people are aware of their heritage through his work with the Hayden Chapter of Little Hoosier Historians at Hayden Elementary School.

Ruddick says J.P. Swarthout came to town as the railroad station manager in 1854, building the first house and the first store. That store Swarthout built still stand, believed to be the oldest public building in the township. It is now "Eder's Hayden Market"—a 134-year-old brick with a cupola on top that makes the store look like an old church or a school. The cupola, Ruddick explains, was added to cover a leak in the roof that had become difficult to repair.

Except for a delivery man making his weekly stop to refill the potato chip display, only the storekeeper is in the store. A customer comes in later to return a movie. Videotapes are big business for stores in areas where cable TV is not available.

The post office, across the way in a building that looks to be about 12 by 15 feet, is busier. It is a place for residents to come each day to pick up their mail and swap information.

Hayden is off the highway, but it is not out of touch.

# Brewersville
### NO LONGER A GRIND

Adam Keller didn't have a road map, but chances are he found where he wanted to go more easily than we did.

Keller settled on Sand Creek in 1823 where he built a water mill and began grinding corn. Jacob Brewer arrived in 1837 picked another spot on Sand Creek, named it Brewersville, and turned it into a Jennings County milling center. There are no mills in Brewersville now, only a few homes along the north-south county road.

It is not easy to find Brewersville. No signs point off Ind. 3 to the community, which is east on a county road, then south toward Sand Creek.

# Alert
### WEST OF SARDINIA

To find Alert, look first for Sardinia on Ind. 3 in southern Decatur County, then drive three miles west to a crossroads surrounded by farms and clean, clear air.

Alert, a four-way stop where Decatur County Road 1200 South crosses Road 1050 West, is quiet on this Thursday morning. A few houses line the roads for a few hundred feet to the west and south, but no one has stepped outdoors.

What appears to have been a general store is closed, its windows covered. An "Alert State Bank" etched on a limestone block among brick in an abandoned building hints of the days when Alert was a busier place.

# Westport
### ALIVE AND WELL

Westport is no backroads village, not with 1,500 residents and a business center with banks, hardware store, law offices, restaurants and bars. It is a prosperous town just off Ind. 3, a shopping center for residents in southern Decatur County. A Baptist church here has four stone columns out front, and the Methodist church is also impressive.

We are surprised. Westport, which was platted in 1836, has managed to survive—without a high school—in an era when many small towns have withered.

\* \* \*

South Decatur High, off Ind. 3 in the center of farm fields, lets motorists know that its football team won its division in the 1990 state football playoffs.

South Decatur combined part of Burney and Jackson and Sandcreek townships during the school consolidations of the 1960s. Westport and Letts had merged to form Sandcreek years earlier.

# Letts
### MEMORY LANE

Letts, an unincorporated community along Decatur County Road 700 South just east of Ind. 3, has a few houses, two churches, the Sandcreek Township Park and the Community Volunteer Fire Department, which is housed in the biggest building in town.

An old store is closed; so is a garage. The old Letts High School, once the home of the Bearcats, joined with Westport to form Sandcreek Township before it became part of South Decatur.

The town, laid out in 1882, was named after Allen Lett, the first postmaster. The post office, like Lett, now lives only in histories of the community.

# Millhousen
### HIDDEN TREASURE

Gems are difficult to find. Call Millhousen a jewel—remote, picturesque, hidden inside a rural area away from any major highway.

A pencil-thin line stretches on the map east from Letts across southern Decatur Township. We aren't sure we are on the right route until a church spire rises in the distance, a beacon to travelers. It stands, as it has for exactly 100 years, about 175 feet high, over St. Mary's Catholic Church at the edge of town.

German Catholics came out of Cincinnati and Madison to form the community in the 1830s, making it a religious center for southeastern Indiana, and naming it after the German town that had been the home of Maximilian Schneider, one of the leaders of the settlement.

Streets in town rise, fall and wind. Millhousen is a town laid out, it seems, to fit the terrain rather than straight lines on a plat book.

Most of the luncheon crowd has dined and left Stone's Restaurant and Lounge. At 1:20 p.m. all is quiet. A waitress and the woman bartender are watching the soap opera on CBS. So is a woman at the bar.

A man at the bar ignores the show. He's more interested in his tenderloin sandwich than what appears to be "The Young and the Restless."

The show ends. The women who have remained silent, glued to every word, now discuss the show.

"She really has a messed-up marriage," one says.

Another agrees, then adds, "She'd be smart to put out a contract on him right now."

The third adds, "The marriage would break up on its own, if he [the father of the wife involved] would give it time."

The first woman, still caught up in the drama, asserts, "She really laid it on the line to him [her father], though."

A young couple enters. The husband asks if there are any athletic events on TV. There is no cable in Millhousen, and he settles on a fishing show he finds on a Cincinnati station.

The soap operas are over for the day. It is time to tour Millhousen.

Around one of the corners in town is the Smith Brothers Feed Mill, a reminder of an earlier time. Larry Smith is the owner. There is no brother involved. The name remains from a day back in 1947 when Smith's father and uncle took over the business. Larry's dad bought out the brother in the 1950s and Larry took over the operation after he was graduated from Indiana University in 1974.

The mill is a reminder of a time when every community had a feed mill where wheat could be turned into flour, grain ground for livestock, where men could meet to argue basketball, politics and news of the day.

Most such operations have closed, having surrendered to competitors who are bigger and better-financed.

Larry Smith explains that the number of customers is down as farms get bigger, which increases competition among suppliers for those farmers who remain. That means he needs to cut his margin of profit to be competitive.

He has two full-time employees, one part-time worker. He knows the day may come when he has to lay off an employe, or worse yet, sell or close down the operation.

It is uncertain whether the mill will be a place where his sons, now students at South Decatur High School, can give new meaning to Smith Brothers Feed Mill.

Closing the mill would mean the loss of Smith's individuality. "I've never worked for anyone, but I've always had bosses. Every farmer who does business here tells me what he wants and when he wants it done."

It is that way, too, for a new business Larry Smith has started. He bought a limousine in August, 1992, and already has bookings eight months in advance. There are reservations for weddings, school proms, corporate trips and other events. He is seeking contracts with corporations in the area——especially Japanese-owned firms—to drive executives to airports in Indianapolis and Cincinnati. And to do that, he enrolled in a Japanese language class at Indiana University-Purdue University in Indianapolis.

Smith talks about crime, homicides including multiple killings—that have occurred in the serenity of rural Decatur County. But on this day, in the beauty of the rolling terrain, the quietness of a mid-afternoon January day, crime seems far away.

Millhousen has turned out to be a pleasant surprise, a delight to the traveler who finds it.

\* \* \*

We return west across Decatur County and find Waynesburg, a rural community clustered around the Waynesburg Christian Church. There appears to be no commercial business, just a few houses. It, like dozens of other similar communities, is surrounded by farms that stretch out almost endlessly.

\* \* \*

It is January and the sun, which has chased away the rain and fog, is setting early. We think about the day, record to memory pictures of narrow bridges with iron rails, beauty shops far back into the country, away from towns, rural tanning salons, old brick homes well-maintained even after a hundred years, neat lawns, junk-filled yards, cars and farm equipment left to rust without decent burials, hand pumps and outdoor toilets kept as reminders of decades past.

It is an Indiana that travelers on interstates seldom see.

# FAITH, HOPE, AND CORTLAND

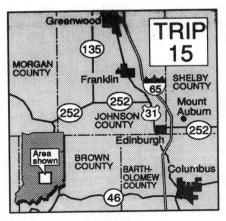

January's dreariness has broken. The sun is out and there is no snow in the forecast. It is a good day to travel. We begin our journey by turning off U.S. 31 at Edinburgh and heading east past horse farms on Ind. 252.

## Mount Auburn
### AMAZING GRACE

St. George English Lutheran Church dominates the intersection where Mount Auburn Road meets Ind. 252. The church is a landmark that has endured for generations. Two miles to the north is Mount Auburn, a Shelby County town built around a four-way stop where an old gas station sits abandoned.

Cars are parked around Niebel Engines, proof that as long as there are cars there will be engines in need of repairs. Playground, slides, swings and a basketball court are in a wooded area next to the Christian Church. Men, generations past their youth, can watch the games and recall the days when old Mount Auburn High School had teams sometimes called the Rangers, sometimes the Blackhawks. The high school is gone and students now attend consolidated Southwestern High.

Like most towns, Mount Auburn has a mixture of neat, large homes, some not so big or so well-kept. A yard at one house is filled with ceramic animals, with no indication whether they are for sale.

Mount Auburn has not yet awakened to greet a new day.

## Flat Rock
### CHANGING TIMES

Maurice Tennell is proof you can take a boy out of a small town, but you can't always keep him out. He grew up in Bengal, a rural hamlet, lived in Shelbyville where he worked at Pittsburgh Plate Glass, then moved to Flat Rock in 1969.

He likes small towns, and Flat Rock, seven miles east of Edinburgh, is one where 350 residents can be counted on days when no one is out of town.

Tennell is at work at Tennell's Hardware on this Wednesday morning. It's a friendly place, where a stranger is given a cup of coffee and all the time he wants to ask questions.

Tennell operated the hardware business in a store across Ind. 252 until 1975 when he moved into "this place," which had been a grocery store. "That's where I have my mower and small-engine repair shop now," he says, pointing across the street.

"This place," as Tennell calls it, is big and old. He walks outside, gray sweater over plaid shirt, onto Ind. 252 and points to "1892" chiseled into a limestone block set in the brick gables. "The top part, I'm told," Tennell explains, "wasn't built until five years after the first floor, so part of the store must date back to 1887."

The building is a monument to craftsmanship. It's 150 feet long, 30 feet wide, almost as sturdy as a century ago. A roller with a cutter blade, loaded with heavy brown wrapping paper of a half-century ago, is still in place. So is the spool from which the twine can be unwound to tie the packages.

The Detroit scales, with the oil float, sits nearby, still as accurate as the day it was installed 75 years or so ago. "An inspector who checked it called it the most accurate scale in the state," Tennell says. When a customer orders five pounds of nails at Tennell's Hardware, he knows he's getting five pounds of nails.

"I like it out here," Tennell says. "It's a quiet town. I make a living and that's about it. But that's about all you can do anywhere."

Arts and crafts were added to the store's merchandise last summer, because, as Tennell explains, "The hardware business wasn't getting it done." The center of the store and one wall are filled with arts and crafts, most of which have been left on consignment by craft makers from nearby towns. "We have one man from Kentucky who left some of his work," the storekeeper adds.

Women who seldom stopped in the store for hardware now come to see the crafts on display. Business is growing as more people learn what's on sale. Customers, some from out of state, are finding their way to Flat Rock in search of crafts and antiques. What was once a male domain is slowly becoming a center for both men and women.

Chances are, though, the "Flat Rock Loafers Club" will continue to gather on Saturday mornings to talk about basketball and whatever topic may arise. It's a club for men whose pictures are mounted on three-foot-square cardboard under a "Loafers Club" sign. The officers are identified, as are the "bouncers" and the "non-active" members. (The latter category, for a loafer's club, gives one pause.)

A voice comes from a speaker. Tennell stops talking and listens. He's a member of the Flat Rock Volunteer Fire Department. Even in a quiet town, a person has to be alert.

This is not a fire alarm, though. It's just an announcement that one of the fire engines will be out of service for the day.

Flat Rock remains quiet . . . at least for a while.

\* \* \*

Ind. 252 ends at Flat Rock, but a county road continues east to Norristown, a hamlet just off Ind. 9. It's a farm community with a few houses, the Community Church and a well-maintained brick building marked "Farmers Lodge."

Another hamlet, Geneva, north and east on the Flat Rock River, is named for the city in Switzerland.

# Hope

## A GOLDEN NUGGET

A sign at the north entrance on Ind. 9 reads "Hope . . . Surprising Little Town." It is an understatement, for Hope is, indeed, a surprise, a small town that not only has survived, but has prospered.

A manicured square, a park in the heart of town, is surrounded by businesses, including a supermarket, travel agency and the Golden Nugget pawn shop.

And there is the Yellow Trail Museum, a storage place for artifacts of local historical significance. "Yellow Trail," according to *Indiana: A New Historic Guide,* originated with a filling-station owner who marked telephone poles with yellow paint, creating a trail which led to his business.

It is not the only museum in the Bartholomew County town. The Indiana Rural Letter Carriers Museum also is on the square. The state's first successful Rural Free Delivery—the nation's second—began in Hope in 1896.

Up at the Owl Nest Restaurant, customers are waking up with coffee and reading the January 31, 1993, edition of *The Star-Journal,* "Hope's Weekly Newspaper Since 1912," the nameplate boasts.

Two businessmen discuss a letter to the editor. A waitress and a female customer are engrossed in the paper's six pages of hometown news and advertisements.

Readers get their say in Column One, Page One. "Not that you are going to do anything about it, but this business about gays in the military makes me sick," one reader has written. Another reader observes, "The Hope police must not be doing their jobs. No one is complaining about them any more." The editor responds, "Good question. We guess the gripers are hibernating for the winter."

A news item lets the people of Hope know that 1993 dog and cat tags are for sale at the Utility Office from Town Administrator Delight Adams. The honor roll for Hope Elementary takes up much of Page 3. It's printed, not in agate, but in 10 point type. The School lunch menu for Monday is hot dogs with tater tots; for Tuesday pizza, corn and applesauce.

Names and meals make news in Hope.

Dogs also made news in Hope on Jan. 20, according to the police blotter printed in the *Star-Journal*. Police received a dog complaint call at 8:47 a.m from Hitchcock Drive and again at 7:40 p.m. from Jackson Street. The only other calls to police that day regarded vandalism to a vehicle parked at Hope Elementary School, a possible intoxicated driver and a call to assist emergency medical technicians.

Crime sometimes takes a holiday in towns like Hope.

# St. Louis Crossing
## CHURCHES ITS SALVATION

A Bartholomew County road leads off Ind. 9 to St. Louis Crossing, a rural town in the heart of rich Bartholomew County farm land.

Its railroad (the old Penn Central) gone, St. Louis Crossing has seen better days. Closed are:

—A building that once housed a business. An old soft drink dispenser is rusting out front.

—A filling station, rust slowly corroding a lone gasoline pump.

—A store that appears to have just closed. A "For Sale" sign is on the window. So is "Closed For the Reason." We wonder what the reason is, but there is no one to ask. An old church pew sits out front, next to the new soft-drink dispensers.

Grass has surrendered to winter, won't reappear until spring, leaving a horse on a lot in town to stand in the thawing mud. It is a sharp contrast to the fertile fields that stretch out in all directions.

St. Louis Crossing is a town of houses and two churches, the big brick Independent Methodist Church with its paved parking lot, next to the smaller, frame Baptist church.

Residents may go elsewhere to shop, but they do not leave town to worship.

* * *

We drive across northern Bartholomew County to Taylorsville, a community at the I-65 interchange with U.S. 31, then south to Clifford, four miles to the east.

# Clifford
### RED, WHITE AND BLUE

Fields flat, even and endless meet County Road 550 North, the landscape broken only by an occasional fence row and irrigation sprinklers. Columbus Municipal Airport is just a couple of miles south, on land ideal for aviation. The city of Columbus has reached north toward Clifford, which is becoming more of a suburb than an isolated rural hamlet.

American flags, just as at the Clifford post office, flutter over many of the houses. Some mailboxes are painted red, white and blue. A young man walks down the street from the post office, reading mail, oblivious to a stranger who drives by.

The old Clifford depot that sat along railroad tracks, long removed, is now a residence. The high school is gone, now joined with Hope's to form Hauser High School.

Less than a mile to the north is Armuth Acres, a housing development on land that once was farm fields. Now a bedroom community where residents live in clusters, Clifford is a town far different from the one of decades earlier.

* * *

South of Columbus, we take Ind. 58 southwest and are slowed by speed bumps. On a state highway yet! The bumps are a warning for a four-way stop to allow traffic from Bartholomew County Road 500 to safely enter Ind. 58.

# Ogilville
### LUNCH IS SERVED

Meyer's Grocery is the hub of activity in Ogilville, a wide spot on Ind. 58 three miles west of I-65. Ed Meyer, the owner, isn't there, but Bonnie Brooks is, just as she has been for 17 years.

It is noon and she is busy making sandwiches. Two businessmen from the big industrial park out on I-65 order "tenderloins, with mayonnaise."

"I have chicken breasts and turkey today, too," Mrs. Brooks tells them in case they want to change their orders. The men stick with tenderloins. Other customers come and go—men in bib overalls, flannel shirts and vest jackets; men in suits.

"The deer hunting is extra good around here," she explains, "so a lot more men will be here when the season opens. And when the weather is nice, we get a lot of sightseers who stop in for snacks."

Meyer's Grocery also is a place to buy beer and wine, ice, groceries, hardware, gasoline, hunting and fishing licenses and bait. "Red worms, African night crawlers, crickets," a sign says.

And where customers can post sell or buy notices, advertise items, promote events. One sign offers "Free Puppies."

Bonnie Brooks has a chance to relax. She talks about the store. It has been here for years, she says, understating its age, which could be measured in decades. The ceiling is metal, standard in most general stores of the '20s and '30s. The pot-bellied stove is gone, replaced by central heat.

"You ought to talk to my dad," she says. "He has lived around here all his life and he likes to talk about Ogilville." Her dad is Irvin McCord, 81. He grew up here, has lived in the Ogilville-Waymansville area all his life. He recalls when Ogilville was called Sawmill, when his father worked at Charlie Taylor's flour mill, when the community had a blacksmith shop and other business.

Those were the days when the community had a post office with a "Moore's Vineyard" postmark. "The name Ogilville came later, probably because some Ogilvies used to live around here," McCord says.

He attended School No. 4, "the only place I ever went to school," then worked 44 years at factories in Columbus. He says, "I've seen a lot of changes," both at Ogilville and at Waymansville, where he now lives.

"I recall going with my dad to Waymansville to sell butter my mother had molded," he adds. "Back then there were blacksmith shops, a hardware store, groceries and other businesses in town."

As long as there are men like McCord, there will be Ogilvilles and Waymansvilles, stored deep in the recesses of men's memory banks.

*  *  *

We drive southwest on Ind. 58, past Mt. Healthy School, a modern brick school with indoor plumbing, a far different place than the one-room school Irvin McCord attended.

# Waymansville
## POSTSCRIPT TO A DREAM

There was a simple, practical reason Alan and Margaret Crossland went into business in Waymansville. They had been laid off after 18 years at diesel-maker Cummins Engine Co. in Columbus.

"We had to do something or sink," Mrs. Crossland explains about their decision to buy the store in Waymansville in 1991 and rename it Crossland Market. They knew there was competition up the road at Ogilville, down the road at Spraytown, that theirs would be the third store along a stretch of Ind. 58.

Whatever the competition, Mrs. Crossland is busy this noon, fixing sandwiches for men who drift in and out.

Alan, black-bearded with a Cadillac agency cap on, keeps the conversation going at the round table where some of the men stop to eat the old-fashioned sandwiches Margaret has fixed. Alan has some opinions and doesn't hesitate to express them. Neither do the men who join him. There are no lulls in conversations at Crossland.

It is obvious the men don't like government red-tape. They complain about a license branch. "The people are so slow, fleas won't even land on them," Alan says of some of the workers. And they are bitter about the idea of homosexuals in military service and wonder if Bill Clinton will ever get on track after a slow start as President.

Mrs. Crossland ignores the debate. "Oh, yeah. I like it out here in the country. It's the only place I'd live," she insists, mentioning that she grew up near Glasgow, Kentucky.

She and Alan went into business without any experience. "The store was somewhat run down. It has taken a while to get business built back up, especially since we are new at it." If she is disillusioned, she doesn't show it.

A TV is on in the corner of the store, but no one seems to be watching. There is no cable in Waymansville. "That's why we rent so many movies," she says.

Young people who stay at Lutheran Lake, a church camp west of town, look forward to trips into Waymansville to visit Crossland Market. "Many of them are from big cities, so they have a ball here in the store," Mrs. Crossland says. "We handle some of the old-fashioned small Coke bottles, which they have never seen. And we try to find things they wouldn't see in town," she adds.

The Lutheran Christian School (grades one through eight) is near town, and it is obvious there is a German influence here. "People wondered how I'd fit in since I'm not Lutheran," Margaret Crossland says. "I do have some German in my family background. Maybe that's why I don't feel like a stranger."

Two construction workers enter the store and order sandwiches. "Pete," the older of the two, removes a quart of milk from the cooler and drinks from the carton.

He sits down next to Alan. "How are things today?" he asks.

Alan responds, "Not too well. I got the day off in the wrong way by talking politics." He switches the conversation to fishing. "I'm waiting for some good old-fashioned fishing weather," he says.

It is a warm January day. There hasn't been enough cold weather for ice-fishing and it appears doubtful Alan will be able to move his fishing shack out on the lake at all this winter.

It may be just as well. His wife, he says, has threatened to get a stick of dynamite and throw it at him if he spends too much time fishing.

Margaret just smiles. She likely has heard the comment before.

"Pete" puts down his carton. It's hard to laugh with a mouthful of milk.

POSTSCRIPT: *Less than six months later, Alan Crossland died in the outdoors he loved, the victim of an all-terrain vehicle accident near his Waymansville home. Police said the vehicle was believed to have flipped backwards as he rode over a hill in a wooded area.    It was one weekend when few people laughed and joked in Waymansville.*

# Spraytown
## TENDERLOIN, BREADED

Spraytown isn't much more than a wide stop in the road, but you can't drive through town without pausing. That's because there's a stop sign where a county road enters Ind. 58 on a 90-degree turn.

Spraytown, at the north edge of Jackson County, could be called Rucker instead. "Rucker" means business in Spraytown—Rucker's upholstery, Rucker's groceries and hardware and Rucker's restaurant.

The restaurant section of the store isn't busy and it seems like a good time for a tenderloin sandwich. "They're good, $2.50," the waitress says. It arrives, breaded, hanging like a roof from an oversized bun that is as big as a dinner plate.

"This would be $5 anywhere else," the customer says. The waitress has heard that comment before.

Outside, Gene Thompson sits in his old Chevy pickup truck. The waitress brings him a sandwich.

"Didn't know you had curb service," a customer observes.

"Just for some people," the waitress says, smiling.

Gene explains why: "Lost my leg twenty years ago." The other customer sees the crutches in the truck, is embarrassed by his indiscretion.

Thompson is wearing a seed-corn cap and a jacket that shows wear. "I do some stock hauling he says. Take livestock to Columbus and Seymour mostly," he says, adding, "Times are getting so hard, a man can hardly make it."

We wish each other good luck. Chances are Thompson will be all right. People in towns like Spraytown have a way of watching out for each other.

* * *

Ind. 58 turns and twists past small farms, the speed limit varying from 35 to 45 mph between Ind. 58 and Ind. 258.

# Surprise
## EXPECT THE UNEXPECTED

Surprise! We have found Surprise, east on Ind. 258, a few twists of the road beyond Easyville, out by a place called Acme.

A sign points south to Surprise, just down a county road, close enough to Acme to be one community. "Railroad," a lone street sign in Surprise, is a reminder of the days when trains on the Milwaukee Railroad linked Surprise with Bedford and Seymour.

The railroad is gone, the post office is gone, the general store is gone. The old brick grade school, its windows broken, is now only a faint chapter in Surprise's fading history. Not much remains, just a few houses, two churches across the road from each other, and a lot of memories.

Millicent Eudy has a mindful of those memories, stored over 80 years, which she can recall at the sound of a question. She has stepped outside on this bright winter day, a sock cap on her head, a sweater over her thin shoulders, brown work gloves on her hands. She's a wisp of a woman, quick of wit and sharp of mind.

She grew up nearby, spent almost all her life in the area, except when she was following her late husband, Robert, from post to post during his 22-year army career.

"My name was Findley, some spell it Finley, before I was married," she volunteers. It is obvious she is proud of the Findley name as she relates stories of her family background.

Her most poignant ancestral recollection is about a great-grandmother who saw her boyfriend—"Johnson was his name"—off to the Civil War, thought he had been killed in battle when she didn't hear from him, and later married a man who became a judge.

Mrs. Eudy recalls, from stories she has been told, that decades later, very much alive, Johnson returned to the area to visit, and told his story: "I was a prisoner of the South for a long time. That's why people thought I had been killed. I came back to Jackson County after the war and heard she [his former sweetheart] had married. I decided then to move on, settled in Pennsylvania and married."

It wasn't until his return to Jackson County that he learned he had not been betrayed in love, but by the reasonable assumption that he had been killed. When he learned that, Mrs. Eudy relates, "he cried and cried and cried."

Mrs. Eudy lives alone in a small frame house. "We bought it when we were back on leave. I moved here in 1958 when my husband was sent to Germany," she explains, "and he joined me when he retired in 1961.

She's an old-fashioned woman who didn't demand to know everything her husband did. She reports her husband "was stationed in Germany when the Berlin wall was built and I'm sure he helped a lot of people cross over before it was finished.

"I didn't ask him no questions. I knew he had a high security clearance, and that was all I needed to know. He spoke German and he always said he would tell me all about it sometime, but he never did."

Surprise is miles away from a town with a store, but Mrs. Eudy makes do even though she has no car, never learned to drive. Neighbors see that she gets what she needs, is driven where she needs to go.

"I always told my husband he could do the driving and I'd do the praying," she says. "That worked pretty well when we were stationed in San Francisco and he had to drive across the Golden Gate bridge.

"He is dead now. Died back in 1981, buried in the Acme Cemetery, up the road there in Acme. There's just me and my sister, who lives over there," Mrs. Eudy says, pointing to another house.

She looks over her glasses again, into the present, and says, "We used to have a rural route address, but the politicians changed it." It is obvious she doesn't like change for change's sake. "Now my address is Douglas Avenue. But I know it's Railroad Street because it runs along the old railroad. I guess I'm on Douglas Avenue because a man named Billy Douglas surveyed the town."

"How about Surprise?" we asked. "I was told it was named because people were surprised the town was even here," Mrs. Eudy replies.

An old Ford Granada turns onto the narrow, one-block-long Douglas Avenue. The woman driver asks, "Do you remember me?" and Mrs. Eudy calls her by name, without hesitation.

The visitor is Lillian Claycamp, who has her own version of the naming of Surprise. "After the railroad came through, the town got a post office. People were so surprised, they just called the town Surprise," she relates.

We leave the two women to reminisce. Sometimes a visitor can be a lonely woman's best friend.

# Cortland

## BIG VS. BETTER

Carl Tinder walks across a street in Cortland to get his afternoon *Seymour Tribune*. He stops and talks.

"Lived here all my life," he says. He's retired, rents his farm out now. The farm business has changed, he says. "It's rough now if you are small. A man who farms two hundred acres or so can't make it. You have to be a big wheel to survive. Any small farmers that are left have jobs in town to make ends meet."

Cortland is surrounded by the fertile valley that stretches east from White River. The farms grow larger each year.

"I don't miss the farm work," Tinder says, explaining he keeps busy, even in retirement. He looks at his house, a big two-story frame that's well-maintained, its lawn clean and neat. "I have a big garden and big yard. That and my berries keep me busy when the weather is nice. The old house gives me something to do in the winter."

He laments the death of small high schools in the 1960s when consolidation swept the state. The town still has a grade school, but high school students, once the Cortland Eagles, now are among the 1,300 students at Seymour.

"A lot of people were hurt when we lost the school. It was a mistake when schools went big. Kids don't learn a damned thing anymore," he insists.

And he fears the town may lose its post office. "It's just a matter of time," he says. "The politicians already have taken the two rural routes away from the Cortland post office and given them to Seymour."

A grocery, Stahl's, is open, but a sign out front indicates it is for sale. The owner has found a job in town where, chances are, the hours are shorter and the income steadier.

In the midst of Cortland's decline, the grain elevator has grown, Tinder says. Just like the farms. Small is not a word in the computer thesauruses and spell-checking programs farmers use today.

*Trip 16*
# PUNKIN CENTER

A trip through the heart of southern Indiana is more than a drive. It's like an adventure movie, the pictures changing as rapidly as they can be recorded by the camera of the mind.

An Amish farmer plows with two horses on a sunny, warm February afternoon. A man in a black hat with a wide brim rides in a topless buggy pulled by a trotting horse.

There are landscapes: old barns, round bales of hay lining fences, mailboxes on wooden barrels, private graveyards, cars abandoned on hillsides and in valleys or resting on concrete blocks, neat farm homes, others surrounded by junk.

And country churches, far from towns, and churches in competition with each others in towns too small for stores.

It is the diversities that gives the land its character.

## Punkin Center
### NOT AT ANY PRICE

Don't believe the signs and road maps that say Pumpkin Center. That's a citified name. This is *Punkin* Center, on Tater Road in eastern Orange County, standing still in the backwash of the 20th Century.

Punkin Center isn't a town, unless two households can make a hamlet. It is, instead, a dot on the map where travelers can step into the past as if they are traveling in a time machine.

You can't visit Punkin Center if Mabel Gray isn't home. She owns the Punkin Center store, which is more like a museum of antiques, "keepers" Mrs. Gray has helped collect over parts of eight decades.

"Come In! We'll know you are here," a sign advises visitors at the gate to the barn-like addition to the store. Another reminds visitors, "Gossip doesn't start here. It just walks in."

Inside, Mrs. Gray sways back and forth in the chair that hangs from the ceiling. "There's a bit of history behind every item in here," she says.

There are thousands of items, some a century or more old, and there is a story with each. You can buy a soft drink here, or a Punkin Center cap, either left- or right-handed pencils, other items. Don't even ask about buying the antiques, though. They are for conversation, not for sale.

"My husband, Add, always said this was a place where a man could bring his wife and go away happy," jokes Mrs. Gray.

Like the antiques, Tater Road comes with a story. So does Punkin Center.

"Add opened the store here on January 25, 1922," Mrs. Gray explains. "A bunch of boys who lived up the creek talked about a pile of pumpkins that was here at one time. They threatened to tear up the place if it wasn't called punkin. Add, who of course didn't want the place torn up, said, 'We'll just call it Punkin Center, then.'"

"Tater Road" comes from the potatoes farmers once grew. It's still Tater Road as far as Mrs. Gray is concerned even though the road marker says it is County Road 500 East and the post office lists it as 2197 N. 500 East.

A sign at the store says, "Punkin Center, Population 5 1/3rd." Mabel explains that, too: "Add put that up before he died. The 1/3 comes from the fact that my mother lived with us one-third of the time. My mother's in a nursing home, Add is gone and so is one other person. So Punkin Center is down to 3."

Punkin Center *is* Gray's country store, except for a single house across the road, which is a business of sorts, too. A sign there advertises White's, a place that weaves rag rugs.

Punkin Center has been home to Mabel Gray since June 9, 1934, the year she married Add and moved in to start their 54 childless years together. Add died in 1988, but he's still in her heart and in her words.

He was just 21 when he opened the store with $325 worth of groceries. There were already stores at Bromer and Syria, which folks around here call "Sorry." Add built between the two towns and, Mabel recalls, "People doubted he could make a go of it."

He not only made "a go of it," he developed it into an institution. By August, 1922, he had bought a truck and was hauling for farmers, taking cattle and hogs to stockyards and pumpkins to Austin.

Business improved despite the Great Depression. In 1933, using logs from trees he was given by a customer who had run up credit, he built an addition to the store. "Cost came to $69, because he had to have some extra help," Mrs. Gray says, her memory sharp.

Add proved to be a good businessman for a fellow who had earned a teacher's license at Central Normal College at Danville, Indiana. "Politics wasn't right back then [before he opened the store in 1922], so he didn't get a school. He never did teach, except as a substitute for a day or two," Mabel says.

It was an old-fashioned romance that brought Add and Mabel together. "Add's sister married my uncle, who died of ptomaine poisoning. When his property was sold at an auction in August, 1929, Add furnished food at the sale. I helped him that day and we started seeing each other after that."

When they married almost five years later, Mabel moved with him into part of the store. "I've lived in the store all my married life," she says. She points to a kitchen area and says: "We ate downstairs so we could attend to any customers who came in. Sometimes Add would have to get up seven times during dinner to wait on people."

He didn't mind. Neither did Mabel. "Sometimes the customers would sit down at the table and talk while we ate," she remembers.

Time passed. Eventually the couple was selling groceries to the grandchildren of their earlier customers. The Grays discontinued the grocery in 1970. Now, it is the relics, the antiques, the unlimited miscellaneous items, that bring visitors.

Of these items Mrs. Gray says, "We had the store for 45 years. When we got something, it would be an item we could talk about, something that came with a story or with a bit of history.

There is a 1922 automobile, for example. It's a "Gray," an item that was kept because it carries the family name.

There is a forked stick. "It was the first washing machine," Mabel laughs. "A neighbor used it to lift clothes from a boiling kettle." There is a collection of canes: "Add used some of them. Some customers brought in some." There are buggies in the shed, a story about each.

Mabel has never counted the items. A quick glance shows they run into the thousands, items more than a hundred years old, items that could be called junk, items that are priceless, now worth 100 times their cost.

"We never threw anything away. They say if you save something for seven years, it will come back in use." But, she adds, "I try not to get anything else. I really need to know what to do with what I already have."

Mrs. Gray closes the place at least one day a week to visit her mother, who is 104, at a nursing home in Salem. "If people want to be sure I'm here they call first. Some of them say they have to call for an appointment," she laughs.

Appointment or not, she has had visitors from Germany, Switzerland, South America, exchange students from other countries, and curiosity-seekers from almost every state. And film makers from Indiana University who want to preserve the history the place represents.

Mrs. Gray walks past her late model Oldsmobile, then across the road to remove her afternoon *Bedford Times-Mail* from the box. A daily paper and a nice car are necessities for a woman who wants to keep up with the present while living amid the past.

# On the Road

We drive south from Punkin Center to U.S. 150, then southeast into Washington County through Hardinsburg and into Fredericksburg, its residents observing the world pass by from their vantage point along the road.

Further southeast in Harrison County, at U.S. 150 and Ind. 135, is Palmyra, a town of seven hundred residents that has long been an important crossroads. U.S. 150 was the old New Albany-to-Vincennes highway. Ind. 135 followed the north-south Mauckport Road that stretched from the Ohio River north toward Indianapolis.

Historians believe Palmyra was named after King Solomon's fortified city in the Syrian desert.

\* \* \*

Central Barren is four miles south of Palmyra on Ind. 135. It is a wide spot in the road, little known except for the fact that the famed Buffalo Trace, often called Indiana's first highway, ran through town on its way from Clarksville to Vincennes.

# Bradford
## AND CRANDALL

It is late afternoon, the day shift has ended, and cars crowd the parking lot outside the tavern in Bradford, a Harrison County town east off Ind. 135. Bradford has churches, a post office, a deer-dressing business and the Gettelfinger Popcorn Co., an operation that is involved in both domestic and international sales.

\* \* \*

Crandall is to the south, three winding miles east off Ind. 135. An old depot, once a stopping spot for trains out of New Albany, still stands, the rails that ran alongside removed.

It is a town built on the side of a hill, its streets, like Walnut and Oak, named for trees. A street is blocked by a construction truck and there is a small traffic jam.

Only a junky area at the entrance to town detracts from the quaintness of this quiet, scenic place.

# CRADLE OF INDIANA

We remain in Harrison County, which has forty miles of frontage along the Ohio River. Sometimes called the cradle of Indiana, it is historic, hilly, cavernous, but big enough for good farms on the high ground.

A new day dawns and we are in no hurry. We turn west off Ind. 135 south of Corydon, following a sign that points to "Lickford." There is no Lickford on our maps, but we feel adventurous. We go west, the only car on the rolling, blacktop Lickford Bridge Road, dogs coming out to meet us at almost every house we pass.

Pastures where horses gnaw on frosted grass are potted with sinkholes. A sign at a farm offers "Buffalo Meat for Sale," but no buffalo are in sight.

Farm land ends, woodland begins, huge grapevines squeeze gnarled trees. Shored up with crushed-stone "rip-rap" in places, the road dips down into a hollow, past three mobile homes, and continues to an old green steel bridge with a wood floor, a monument in early road construction.

We find no town. The only Lickford we can find, other than the bridge, is the Lickford Valley Camp Ground, along the creek that flows under the bridge.

Not every treasure hunt unveils a jewel.

# Central
### AMONG THE SURVIVORS

Central is high on a rise that provides a panorama of southern Harrison County. Wood smoke rises in puffs from chimneys in the distance. Ind. 135, once Central's main street, has been relocated a half-mile or so to the west, leaving the streets to local traffic.

An old cemetery is on one side of the old road, a new one on the other, the gravestones telling the history of the community. Two churches, Methodist and Christian, are nearby. A post office is in a private home.

Like other small towns, Central has seen businesses come and go, like Reed's Garage, which once advertised, "We Doze, but Never Close." But, it's closed now, apparently for good.

A survivor, however, is Longbottom and Hardsaw, remaining one of Central's major businesses, just as it has been since 1929 when Longbottom started the business. The Hardsaw part came later. It is a firm that has outlived two competitors that also were in the grocery business.

Clark Hardsaw runs the business now, has since 1977. He was Longbottom's grandson, Hardsaw's son. He's busy in the general store this morning, answering phone calls.

A sled hangs on a wall, waiting for a snowfall to encourage a youngster to ask his parents to buy it. Sandwiches are available, as are groceries and other items.

Longbottom and Hardsaw is more than a general store, though. It's a six-employee market serving farmers, offering lumber, metal siding, roofing, fertilizer and seed.

Hardsaw talks about plans for a complete computer system to handle all business transactions. Longbottom and Hardsaw has been in business for more than sixty years, and Clark Hardsaw wants to make sure it continues to be successful. That's why he is considering moving part of the business out on Ind. 135 to attract customers who use the road but do not drive into Central.

At the edge of town cows congregate around a round bale of hay, their community gathering place, just like Longbottom and Hardsaw is for area farmers.

* * *

We drive west out of Central over a Harrison County road that winds through wasteland and woods, over a hill where a cow steadies herself on an incline as she reaches out for a sprig of grass.

New Amsterdam is ahead, around two 90-degree turns, in a secluded area of the state on the Ohio River.

# New Amsterdam
## THE SMALLEST SURVIVES

New Amsterdam is isolated, far from any highway, the river smoother than its few streets. Not many strangers come to New Amsterdam. That's obvious when a woman looks through the panes of the window at the New Amsterdam General Store, observing a car that has driven up. A young boy then stares out the window, then a man.

They are curious, not unfriendly. James Shaffer owns the store. He introduces his wife, Christine, their son, Christopher, 4, and his pup, "Terminator," who isn't as mean as the name indicates. Daughter Jacqueline, 7, Shaffer says, is in class at Heth Washington Grade School.

Students once went through all 12 grades at a school in New Amsterdam, but that was long ago, back when the high school's basketball teams were known as Rivermen and Indians. Junior high and high school students now go to Corydon, fifteen or so miles away.

The Shaffers bought the store in October, 1992, after it had been closed three or four months.

"Business ain't all that good," James says. "We just carry a few things that might keep folks from having to make a special trip out of town." The store also has given residents a place to gather, a meeting place for men to tell lies and stretch stories far beyond the truth.

On this day, James and Christine count 38 residents of New Amsterdam. "Smallest town in Indiana with a town council," James said. The council doesn't have much to do, except maintain the street lights and keep what streets there are paved, mostly with gravel.

"Mom and dad, Waneta and Richard, are on the council," James says. "Dad" is Brent Shaffer, the council president. "Mom" is Mary Faye Shaffer, the clerk treasurer. Waneta McCarty and Richard Brown, Jr., are the other two members.

Christine says Mary Faye is concerned about how the town can find $400 to conduct the 1944 municipal election. Tax money isn't needed, though, when the town holds its annual pitch-in picnic, the biggest event of the year, each June. Chicken is barbecued and residents, former residents and their guests gather for a day of fun.

James says he has other businesses besides the store. "I sell firewood—$25 a rick, delivered—help a farmer in the summer with his tobacco crop, and have started a scavenger service. So far I have 12 customers, but I'm approved by the Indiana Department of Environmental Management, and expect to get more."

Today, Howard Phillips is the lone customer in the little store, a small white frame building trimmed in red. Howard is there more to talk than to buy anything.

If James has his way, before the next school year he'll buy Howard's school bus route, which covers 38 miles twice a day. Phillips gives no indication he's ready to sell out, though.

We leave the store, noting the street lights and gravel on the streets. Without them, New Amsterdam wouldn't be much different than it was when it was a pioneer river town.

\* \* \*

There are but two exits out of New Amsterdam. We can retrace our route and return to Ind. 135, or drive south along the Ohio to Mauckport. We take the river road and cross a bridge a resident built at the edge of town when the county neglected to replace one that no longer could be used.

\* \* \*

It is with reluctance that we here publicize the river drive between New Amsterdam and Mauckport. We are told that the beauty of the road is that nobody knows about it.

It is narrow, and we stop twice to let road workers rake out asphalt being used to fill potholes. It is no matter for this is not a place for the impatient, not an area where time is of much essence.

Residents recommend two seasons to make the drive. One is in the spring when the wildflowers bloom, beauty best observed when the sun is behind the car. The other is when the leaves change, which usually is later than in other areas because of the warmth of the river.

# Mauckport
## GO WITH THE FLOW

Mauckport is a town that lives and dies with the Ohio River. Laid out on the river in 1827, Mauckport grew quickly and soon became a busy river port.

Postmaster Linnea Dean Breeden, who grew up in Mauckport, knows its history. And what she doesn't know, she can find in a book called *Recollections of Mauckport and Central.*

That book offers some insight into the Mauckport of the past, a place where David Bell built a large home and used it for the first underground railroad station in Indiana before the Civil War. It was his home that provided safe harbor for slaves escaping their Southern masters.

That could be why Gen. John Morgan and his raiders lobbed a shot through the house from across the river at Brandenburg, Kentucky, before their incursion into Indiana during the Civil War.

It was the great Ohio River flood of 1937 that almost eliminated Mauckport as a town. It never totally recovered from that disaster. Its population, Mrs. Breeden says, is now 118, pending any moves in or departures. It may grow, again because of the river, if a marina is developed as expected near the Ind. 135 bridge into Kentucky.

The Old Town Liquor and Tavern is expanding, getting ready for a possible business upturn. Not much else is new in town, where some old buildings are vacant, some of the bricks removed. Clothes are on the lines outside house trailers.

Back at the post office, Armand Roach has stopped by for his daily morning visit. He calls up every morning to see what mail he has, then drives on into town. He entertains customers with his wit and impresses strangers with his knowledge of Mauckport.

Roach, who has lived in places like Harlingen, Texas, and Acapulco, Mexico, now calls the Mauckport area his home. He's a history buff, a man who has studied Indiana's past and doesn't hesitate to talk about what he has learned.

He mentions the nearby Squire Boone Caverns, which was home to Squire Boone, brother of Daniel, from 1804 to 1815, when he died and was buried in one of the small caves, now open to the public in warm weather. There are tours of the major cave.

The area, Roach says, was important to Indians who found geodes implanted in limestone contained flint which they used for arrowheads and other purposes.

Some customers pause and listen to Roach, who doesn't mind being ribbed for his enthusiasm about this adopted home. The post office is Mauckport's center, a place to talk, listen and learn.

The postmaster's job has been a family affair for six decades. Linnea Breeden succeeded her father, Welton Dean, who was postmaster for ten years (1945 to 1956) before he drowned in a Sunday afternoon boating accident on the Ohio. Her mother, Kathryn Dean Timberlake, then was postmaster for almost thirty years before Linnea took the job.

Mrs. Breeden posts mail in 325 rural-route boxes and in 45 boxes rented by customers who pick up their own mail.

Down at the proposed marina site, a sign on the river edge says, "Future site of yacht club, loading dock, swimming pool, tennis court, fuel dock, club house. Buy now and save."

Mauckport may be born again.

* * *

Ind. 135 has become a more heavily traveled road since the Matthew Welsh (a former Indiana governor) Bridge across the Ohio opened in 1966. Ind. 11 begins at Ind. 135 at the edge of Mauckport and continues along the river before turning north at Laconia.

# Laconia
## To Their Credit

Laconia is a crossroads community and its business center, if it can be called that, is at the intersection of North Tobacco Landing Road and East Laconia Road.

Many roads in Harrison County have names, not mundane numbers like 200 E. 200 S. in other counties.

A sign puts Laconia's population at 60, big enough for a post office, two churches, the United Presbyterian and Grace Tabernacle. The Grace Christian School is here, but another old school is for sale. Laconia High School, home of the Aces, was here until it joined with Elizabeth to became part of South Central.

Five men are having lunch around a table at the Laconia General Store, watching noon-time TV when the conversation drags. Some of the men have bought their sandwiches at the store, others have brought their lunch in boxes from home.

Russ and Jane Parker have owned the store for three years. It is obvious Parker is a hunter and fisherman. Mounted deer heads are on the back wall. So is a king mackerel "caught by Russ Parker, 1979." It is a good catch, worth letting customers know about.

It also is wise to let customers know company policy. "Credit limited to $50—some restrictions may apply," a sign warns.

"Tobacco seed for sale," another sign proclaims. Laconia is in the heart of some of the best tobacco land in the state and in a matter of days it will be time for farmers to seed hot beds and raise plants.

## Dogwood
### THE NAME'S THE THING

We can't pass up a chance to visit a town called Dogwood. We find it on Ind. 337, not far off Ind. 11, its only employer a lumber business.

We count ten houses, notice that Jack Frederick is the Agri-gold salesman, Henry Withers the Pioneer seed dealer.

If there are any dogwoods, it is too early to see their blossoms.

\* \* \*

"Buena Vista," a sign says. We take the three-mile drive south off Ind. 11 and find it, a secluded area, without road signs, void of stores. What few houses we see are in the woods in a nice scenic area, isolated and quiet.

\* \* \*

South Central Junior-Senior High School is four miles southwest of Elizabeth. Despite the consolidation of Elizabeth and Laconia, it still has but 220 students in all four grades.

## Elizabeth
### SMALL BUT BUSY

Towns are few and far between in southeastern Harrison County, and Elizabeth has become an oasis for customers who don't want to make the drive into Corydon or New Albany.

Among the businesses are Wilson's general store, a food mart, Pop's Place which offers hot sandwiches, an auto parts outlet and a liquor store.

It is an old town, built partly on a hill, some houses built out near the streets.

Basketball season is nearing an end, and South Central has one of its best teams in years. A poster at the general store promotes the South Central-Corydon game at Corydon. "Be There," the sign tells South Central fans. (A few days later we check the scores. Corydon's talented underclassmen have defeated the South Central Rebels, 71-42.)

* * *

Ind. 11 continues its snake-like crawl north toward I-64. We do not mind, for we are in no hurry to return to the noise and traffic of busier highways.

*Trip 18*

# MORGAN COUNTY BACKROADS

Another siege of winter has abated; the itch to travel has returned. We drive into western Morgan County, past flat fields, their owners waiting for the frost to leave the ground so they can commence another season. Sun glistens on galvanized storage bins and silos, evidence of the productivity of the land.

The spirits of Hoosiers, dulled by the weather, are revived. It is a good afternoon to visit some backroad towns.

## Hall
### OLD AND NEW

Hall may be off a main highway, but it is not isolated. A sign on the "Hall Grocery and Post Office" suggests that residents "Mail Your Packages Here—UPS and Federal Express."

It is an outdated sign. There is no post office inside. The sign's just a reminder of when Hall was a postmark and not a rural route out of Monrovia. The post office closed in the 1970s, but the postal boxes remain, unused, in a corner of the store.

They are not the only hint of the past. Kerosene lamps, steel pulleys, advertising signs from the 1930s and '40s, other antiques and collectibles line shelves along the walls.

A loafers' bench is at the rear of the store. An old Florence wood stove warms the store on this day when the temperature is in the low 40s.

The store is stocked with a full line of groceries and there's even a jar or two of penny candy. "We want the store to be as country as possible," says Paula Smith, the store manager.

The store may be as old as yesterday, but it's as new as today. A deli features daily specials, which please farmers during planting and harvesting when time is money and a quick sandwich replaces an hour's stop for lunch or dinner.

Movie videotapes are available for rental, a contrast to the reminders of the past. Cable has not yet reached into Hall or the surrounding countryside, where granaries outnumber houses.

Bill McCarns owns the store, has for four years, Paula says. McCarns, an Indianapolis pipefitter who once lived in Delaware, bought the business in 1989.

Paula Smith worked at the IGA in Martinsville before taking the job at Hall when McCarns bought the store. "I love it here," she says. She must for she is at the store by 5:30 a.m. to prepare food each day.

"The store and the granary [Dorsett's feed mill]," Mrs. Smith says, are the community gathering spots, unless it's on Sunday when the congregation meets at the Mount Pleasant Christian Church.

"We have loafers from ages 3 to 80," said Mrs. Smith. "They get a pop, sit and talk, and hear all the local gossip."

Marshall Hurt is the lone customer on this afternoon. Truth is, he's not really shopping. He's just here to smoke, sip a Coca Cola from a can and scratch off some Indiana lottery tickets with Paula.

"We haven't had any big lottery winners," Paula says, "except for one person who won $1,000." Hurt's luck isn't too good on this day, either. He wins only an "entry," a remote possibility for a TV appearance and an even more distant chance to win $1 million.

Another regular customer enters the store. "Have an entry here you can buy for 50 cents," Marshall says. The ticket has cost him $1. But he figures it's better to settle for a half-dollar than take a chance on the ticket being drawn for a chance on a television show where he probably wouldn't be comfortable anyhow.

"I'll take it," the man says, selecting a candy bar.

Marshall Hurt, 78, has lived around Hall all his life. "I like it, I reckon," he says. "Besides, I've been too poor to move away." And it is here where many of his relatives still live.

He is a rural humorist. And a farmer. "Still mess around," he says of his farm work.

Has the town changed? "A right smart," he replies. He recalls the days, "must have been back in the '20s," when Hall had two groceries, a bank, doctor's office, filling station, blacksmith shop and a drug store.

Now folks have to go "four or five" miles (Paula and Marshall can't agree on the distance) to Monrovia to buy gasoline. That's okay. Hall still has something bigger towns don't have. That's the Hall Store, offering a wood stove, hospitality, friendly banter and the ability to turn chance acquaintances into friendships.

# Lewisville
## CURE FOR THE BLUES

Call this Morgan County hamlet Little Lewisville. A bigger Lewisville is over in Henry County on U.S. 40. It has more people and is easier to find.

This Lewisville is unincorporated, has no post office, no state highway through town, and what residents there are don't have the same rural route. In what could be called a triplication of services, mail is dropped off by rural carriers from Paragon, Cloverdale and Quincy.

The town is south of Eminence, well off Ind. 42, nestled near a corner of Owen County, its few households on either Wilson Road or Lewisville Road. Its focal point is the Lewisville General Store, just as it has been since 1880.

Youthful Mark Stierwalt now owns the store. His mother, Darlene Stierwalt, operates it for him. Mark bought the store in July, 1989, when he was in his late teens. It was a challenge he considered for some time before deciding he'd never know if he could operate a business if he didn't try.

So far things have worked out well. Mark continues to work some for the nearby Eminence school system and finds time to be an Ashland-Adams volunteer fireman.

His mother's experience has been helpful. She had worked five years at an IGA store and found she liked "this kind of business."

Actually, it is more than a business. The store is a day-brightener for customers. "If someone comes in with a crabby attitude, we make sure they are smiling when they leave," Mrs. Stierwalt explains.

It's no wonder the store is a place for residents and nearby farmers to gather. They come in for coffee, sit around the table and talk.

"I bring in the Martinsville paper and they talk about what's in it and whatever else comes up," Mrs. Stierwalt says. "The older men like to talk about things way back when. You hear a lot of strange stories."

Jim Jessup, a former Morgan County commissioner, enters the store and heads straight for one of two candy barrels. He picks out a pack of old-fashioned horehound candy, holds it up and says, "Better than cough drops."

Another customer arrives. He stacks up a number of coins and trades them for bills. It is mid-afternoon. Business is more brisk at noon when farmers and road workers stop in for a quick lunch at the deli. Mrs.

Stierwalt's sandwiches have become famous beyond the fields around Lewisville.

"I make and sell an awful lot of ham salad," she explains. "A woman from Mooresville [25 miles or so away], calls to see if I have any, then drives down and picks up a supply."

Once a person visits Lewisville, however, he doesn't need a reason to return.

# Plano
## PLAIN AND SIMPLE

Towns get their names in different ways . . . but few stories are stranger than the way Plano was given its identification. Stories passed down over the decades say Morgan County's "Plano" came from the name on the first binder that was used to bundle wheat.

Plano was a thriving little community back in those days when Harrison Shields had that binder. It was a time when houses lined the roads where Plano and Arend roads cross.

A post office served the community from 1889 to 1964. Now it has a Martinsville (17 miles away) address, and delivery trucks often go there mistakenly in search of Plano addresses.

Shirley Campbell owns the Plano general store, has since 1961. It's the only business in town, a place for farmers and other workers to order sandwiches at lunch.

It's a place a stranger will likely be asked if he is lost, for few outsiders find their way into the community.

It's a place where customers can open an old-fashioned soft-drink cooler, remove a bottle, flip off the water, remove the cap and pay the store owner.

It's also a place that's a lot busier from late spring to early fall when campers retreat to this rural serenity to spend their leisure hours at nearby Lake Melissa, a private campground.

Shirley Campbell keeps the store open from 7:30 a.m. to 7 p.m. daily, except Sunday. A store operator needs a day to rest after 80-85-hour weeks.

As long as there's a store, there likely will be a Plano, which already has outlived the binder by six decades.

## Trip 19
# LITTLE TOWNS OF BETHLEHEM AND CANAAN

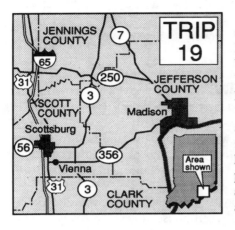

There is sadness on this day in southern Indiana. Indiana University lost to Kansas in the NCAA basketball tournament a few days ago, and I.U. flags fly at half-staff outside homes of fans.

Warm weather is only a wish, but a man in the town of Vienna on Ind. 356 near Scottsburg looks over his hot bed, eager for seeds to become plants. A lawn-service worker sprays a yard with fertilizer and insecticides, a prelude to the green season.

Vienna has its own water tower, a volunteer fire department, an elementary school, and several houses, mostly modest, and Spring Valley Farm at the edge of town.

Ind. 356 rolls like waves across southern Scott County, past streams muddy after heavy spring rains. Small American flags, about 9 by 12 inches, flitter in the morning wind over graves in a cemetery where Easter flowers are eager to burst into bloom.

## Lexington
### CAN'T STOP WORKING

It is soon obvious Lexington is an old town. Rustic-looking "Welcome to Lexington, A Pioneer Town" signs greet visitors at Ind. 356 and Ind. 203.

"Settled in 1804, Platted in 1813," another marker boasts. A historical plaque notes that *The Western Eagle,* the second newspaper in the Indiana Territory, was printed in Lexington from 1815 to 1816. Yet another sign recalls the incursion by Gen. John Hunt Morgan's Confederate raiders, who stayed overnight in Lexington on July 10, 1863, before leaving for Vernon. A wooden street sign marks the corner of Mulberry and Main. Old houses are built near the streets, a reminder of an earlier time.

A food mart, a minute mart, a service station, a few other businesses and the post office are open. So is the barber shop where Earl Milles awaits customers.

Milles was 92 a few day ago (March 25, 1993) but he doesn't look a day over 70. Except for three years when he barbered in Henryville, he has been around Lexington his entire life, 72 of those years as a barber. Five generations of Lexington men have been his customers.

"I cut hair for quite a few women when I first started, but almost all of them go to beauty parlors now. Oh, I still cut a few," he says.

He charged 25 cents for a haircut back in the 1920s, then raised the price to 50 cents later despite protests of some men. "They got over it," he says. And no one complains about the $4 he now charges. It's about half what they'd pay at other shops.

"The days of a shave and a haircut are about over. I don't average over five or six shaves a week, and I'm glad of it," he confesses.

Milles went to high school in Lexington, "two years, all they had back then. I would have had to go to Charlestown if I wanted to graduate.

"Rather than that, I attended a barber school in Indianapolis and took up the barber trade when I was 19. I came back here, I guess, because it was my hometown. I used to know everyone here, but not anymore. Most of the old-timers are gone. I'm about the oldest one left.

"My doctor tells me to keep on working, because that's what keeps me going. Oh, I have a little trouble, but nothing serious."

He doesn't mind that he isn't as busy as he once was: "I just give the old-time haircuts and the young people don't like those. I don't mess with haircuts with initials and other designs."

He is at the shop six days a week, except some Wednesdays. "I close then, if I have anything to do," he says.

Lexington, like barbering, has changed. "I recall when there were five grocery stores here and they all did a good business. That street over there was solid with buildings," he says.

"What's the name of that street?" he repeats a question. "I'm not sure. When you are here 92 years, you don't need to know the street names."

He recalls when the town had a canning factory, a sawmill, a hardware store, a bank. Farm people would bring their eggs and chickens to town and go around to see which store would pay the most for them.

"Back then, people would drive into town in horse-drawn buggies and the streets would be so muddy they'd have to throw boards onto the street to keep them from going knee deep in mud."

He thinks for a while. "Nobody had any money then, but it seemed like everyone got along well," he observes.

Even the barbershop conversations have changed. "There used to be a lot of talk about hunting and fishing," he reports. "Now it's mostly politics. I don't get mixed up in it. I got friends on both sides, so I can't say much."

He does get involved in community service, giving haircuts at the retirement center. "There used to be 21 men there. Now there are only two, so I guess my haircuts killed them all off," he says, a twinkle in his eye.

"An old fellow who has been there for 24 years thought I deserved a birthday party, and he made them give me one," Milles said, showing a clipping of a story from the *Scott County Journal* about the occasion.

Milles' wife, Aletha Muriel, died in 1991, two months short of their 70th anniversary. Their two daughters, Earlene Kleopfer and Flora Jean Kleopfer, married brothers. Flora Jean, who lives just outside Lexington, checks on him once a day and Earlene calls from down in Louisiana about once a week.

And James E. Kleopfer, Jr., the Scott County circuit court judge who is Earlene's son, lives with his grandfather. "He never married. I reckon he's had so many divorce cases, he knows better," Milles laughs.

Age hasn't stopped Milles from driving. He reports, "I was at the license branch getting plates earlier this year when the examiner heard me say that I would have to wait for new glasses [after a cataract operation]. He asked me to read the fifth line on the letter chart. I read it right off. He says, 'Let's go for your driving test.' I drove for a few blocks and he says, 'Go on back to the branch and I'll give you your new license.'

"He did tell me to wear my new glasses to drive when I got them. Anyhow, I can drive for three more years, but I don't drive at night.

"I told the examiner that I don't drive much, just to go to the grocery store and doctor. He said, 'You stop at the most expensive places you can find,'" Milles recalls, laughing at the remark. "He was right."

Earl Milles is worth a longer visit, but it is time to go. Outside, a slight drizzle is falling. It does not dampen the enthusiasm of students romping during recess at the grade school. Earl Milles can look out his window and wonder what Lexington will be like when they are 92.

* * *

Nabb is south of Lexington on the Scott-Clark county line on Ind. 362. An old grain elevator is closed, replaced by a new operation, evidence that the surrounding land is flat, the ground productive. An abandoned store with imitation brick siding has a "no trespassing sign" out front. What appears to have been a store is closed.

An American flag flies in front of a house trailer, evidence that patriotism is not measured by wealth.

Nabb is another town that grew up with the railroad, then withered when the train traffic dwindled.

* * *

Marysville is just off Ind. 3 at the northern tip of Clark County. It's a clean, neat town with big homes and a community center in an abandoned school. A consignment shop, despite a sign promising a "one-half-off sale," is closed.

A big farm operation is at the edge of town. The Double D Trading Post is open now. "For Sale/Inquire Within," a sign says.

# Otisco
## RIGHT DIRECTION

H&B Groceries at Otisco, a wide spot on Ind. 3 in Clark County, is busy at midday. It's a business that offers more than groceries. A sign out front calls attention to "Onion sets, seed potatoes, bulk garden seed. And Bread—2/99c."

It also proves to be a place to get a good cup of coffee and excellent directions to New Washington. A friendly clerk says, "Go north on Ind. 3 to the first road, that's New Market Road. Turn right and go to second road, that's Michigan Road. Turn left, go to the stop sign at the T. Turn right and that'll take you right into New Washington."

It's obvious people here are helpful. A garage has mileages to about twenty different cities painted on its front. It gets attention, creates conversation and provides information motorists on the highway appreciate.

* * *

We cut cross-country, past farms with white wooden fences, along streams, filled with water from the spring rains, meandering through low areas.

The roads lead to New Washington, just as the clerk at the grocery in Otisco said.

# New Washington
## ON THE BALL

New Washington is the business center of northeast Clark County, an old community at Ind. 62, where a restaurant posts daily grain market prices for the benefit of farmers who dine there. It is a town with a number of businesses, but it has been the high school's basketball team that has made Hoosiers aware of New Washington.

It's where Jim Matthews coaches. It's where his twin sons, Jamie and Scott, teamed up with Shannon Arthur and two role players to win two basketball sectionals. All three played college ball and Jamie was the most valuable player on Ball State's 1993 NCAA tournament team.

\* \* \*

We are en route over a paved Clark County road to Bethlehem, a village on the Ohio River seven miles east of New Washington. Smoke rises cloud-like from a power plant along the Ohio River. Easter lilies grow wild on a bank of the road and in fields, a prelude to Good Friday and to Easter. Trees are beginning to leaf, grass is born again.

The road dips sharply down a mile-long hill, the pavement turning back on curves, almost meeting itself, following what appears to be a cowpath of least resistance. Guard rails protect motorists from the bluff along the edges.

The Ohio is in the distance. Bethlehem is a mile or so from the bottom of the hill, remote, isolated, a picture for a postcard.

# Bethlehem
### THERE'S ROOM AT THE INN

It is a quiet April morning at the post office, far different from December days past and those yet to come. Dorothy Selmier, postmaster here for 18 years, has seen as many as 30,000 Christmas cards arrive each December to be hand-stamped with the Bethlehem postmark and the Star of Bethlehem.

"I think each year that I've never seen so many cards, but we manage to get them all posted," she says.

"People in town come in and ask about their cards. I tell them they are in that pile there, that they shouldn't worry, that we'd get them all out. And we do.

"We even get a lot of mail from overseas."

The U.S. Postal Service does provide Mrs. Selmier. some help for the December avalanche. The rest of the year she is alone in the little building that's not much bigger than a mini barn on a suburban yard.

A rural carrier out of Marysville drops mail at the post office and Mrs. Selmier places it in forty boxes and hands it out to about ten residents who don't rent boxes.

Mrs. Selmier has "a hearing problem" and says she has some difficulty seeing, but she is friendly, eager to talk, enthusiastic about the town.

Her late husband, Angus, brought her to Bethlehem as a bride in 1941. They had met in Charlestown when she was a high school student.

"We were married 46 years and were already talking about our 50th anniversary when he died at age 76," she says, softly, sadly. About Angus, she says, "You would have liked him. He could have told you everything about this town.

"I lost him in a tragic way, February 6, 1987. We owned a farm down the road. It was a pretty day and he wanted to finish cleaning a fence row before we left on vacation for the Smoky Mountains.

"One of our grandchildren, who was staying with us for the day, looked out the window and said, 'Grandma, I see smoke.' I said, 'Oh, no, no, no.' We jumped in the car and flew down to that field, which was totally black. My husband had burned to death. Over nine hundred people signed the book when they called at the funeral home."

Bethlehem had changed before Mrs. Selmier arrived in 1941, has continued to change since. The town was once a busy trading post, with riverside shanties, fish markets and a button industry that used mussels from the Ohio.

"Bethlehem," Mrs. Selmier recalls, "used to be full of people. When school would let out there would be so many kids heading for Matthews' store for pop and candy, cars would have to creep along."

Bethlehem is still a busy village at times. "Church members from throughout the area come to town for a Christmas carol sing in December. We have a good turnout at Easter for a sunrise service and, then, for breakfast at the church. And in September we have an annual homecoming with a big pitch-in dinner," Mrs. Selmier explains.

Bethlehem's past may be its future, if Mrs. Selmier and others are successful. "We've started a historical association and we are going to make the school into a community building for parties, suppers and other events," she says.

We make a mental note to revisit her, but not in December when those Christmas cards await the Bethlehem postmark.

\* \* \*

There are no stores in Bethlehem now, and residents must drive to New Washington, Charlestown, or even further, to shop. That doesn't bother Bill Haddix, who likes the leisurely pace in Bethlehem compared to Indianapolis, where he lived almost forty years.

He enjoyed Bethlehem in 1984 when he bought a lot near the post office, cleared it off and parked a trailer for weekend visits. The solitude led him to buy a riverfront lot and incorporate the remains of an old ice-house into a permanent residence.

He found 18-inch-thick walls in the ice house, yellow poplar boards up to 22 inches wide, 20 to 25 feet long. It was lumber from native trees, gems of timbers no longer available. And he kept the framework as part of the new addition he added.

Haddix retired from the Ford Motor Company plant in Indianapolis and moved to Bethlehem to stay in January, 1991. He likes the quietude, enjoys being away from urban life, as he sits in his kitchen and watches the Ohio. The house is above the high-water mark, safe should waters rise as high as the devastating flood of 1937.

A tombstone for the 1833 burial of a New Jersey regimental veteran is in his front yard. "There may not be a grave there," Haddix says, "but I'm not going to check to see.

"It's super, nice and peaceful," he says again of his new surroundings. Even quieter than his native home back in Jackson, a southeastern Kentucky town of about three thousand people.

\* \* \*

The Inn at Bethlehem is in a restored two-story brick Federal-style home, "stately and secluded," its brochure claims. It is that, indeed, with six rooms for bed and breakfast, at river's edge.

Chester and Jeanne Brown, who live in Indianapolis, restored the inn, believed to have been built about 1830, and hired Britney Merrick to operate it. Miss Merrick, who studied restaurant and hotel management at Sullivan College in Louisville, likes the place and the town. If things go right, the Brownes plan a 50-seat restaurant nearby which Britney also will manage.

Chester Browne grew up downriver at Charlestown, and is in the insurance business in Indianapolis. His wife is a professional interior decorator. She plans to open an antique shop in Bethlehem.

CHESTER BROWN & BRITNEY MERRICK          -*Joe Young*

* * *

Outside Bethlehem, we turn north on Paynesville Road, leave Clark County, enter Jefferson County, and arrive in Paynesville. It's a town with a Christian Church, a tax service and about fifteen houses.

# Chelsea and Saluda
## "NOT MUCH TO EITHER"

Back on Ind. 62, we drive north, attempting to find the communities of Chelsea and Saluda. There are no markers to either. We turn onto a rural road, see a few houses, but no town-limits sign, no indication of a town. "Where's Chelsea?" we ask two men who are talking at one of the houses.

"This is it," one of the men replies. "Not much to it, is there?"

If this is Chelsea, Saluda must be east across Ind. 62. "Ain't much there, either," the man says. He neglects to tell us about the Chelsea Jubilee, Indiana's oldest community reunion. Come the first weekend in September and the Saluda Park will be alive with bluegrass and country music, games, rides, bingo and flea-market booths.

We drive toward where the man says Saluda is located and find Saluda Township Park, but no indication of a town. The man over in Chelsea is correct. There isn't much to Saluda, either.

What once was Saluda High School, home of the Saluda Lions basketball team, is now a Shrine Club. What students there are in Saluda are in class up at Southwestern High School in Hanover. Only a few houses, no businesses, remain at County Roads 600 South and 600 West.

# China
## LILY OF VALLEY

We have left Madison and are heading for China—that is China, as in Jefferson County, not Asia. Ind. 62, the signs say, is the Chief White Eye Trail. We don't know about White Eye, but a Clear Eye is needed to drive this road.

The road drops down an incline, the speed limit 20 mph, the curves sharp, the hills rugged on each side, the traffic heavy. Suddenly we are in China, where the hills form their own version of the great wall, framing the countryside in its natural splendor.

A half-dozen houses and St. Anthony's Catholic Church are in China, on the banks of the Indian-Kentuck Creek, spanned by a bridge near where the road makes a 90-degree turn. It is an idyllic setting, this valley where water rushes down the creek and cows graze on the slopes at the edge of the settlement.

Just north of China, Ind. 250 joins Ind. 62 into Canaan.

# Canaan

## SMALL-TOWN AMERICA

The hills end, the terrain flattens and we have no trouble entering the land of Canaan. It is another of southeastern Indiana's old towns, having been founded in 1812 by John Cain, who is buried in the town cemetery.

Settlers called the town Cain, but, when they learned another Indiana village had that name, switched to Canaan.

Time has not skipped Canaan, leaving it in the past as a paradise lost. A grade school is still here; so are a store, a gift shop, an antique shop, and, as a sign advertises, a "Watkins Black Diamond Liniment" agent. A marker in front of the grade school notes the site of the old Shelby Township High School erected in 1872, long before many Indiana towns had high schools.

Gale Ferris is president of the Canaan Restoration Council, has been ever since it was formed by about twenty-five residents three decades ago. "We saw tourism as a way to offset the decline in farming," Ferris explains.

The council sponsors the Canaan Fall Festival on the second Friday, Saturday and Sunday in September. It's an affair that attracts an estimated 30,000 visitors to events that include craft displays, demonstrations by working craftsmen, a flea market, an old-fashioned parade, games, turtle races, frog-jumping contests, rides for children and other attractions.

A highlight of the festival is the Pony Express ride. Riders from the Clifty Creek Saddle Club carry official mail —with approval from the U.S. Postal Service—on horseback 12 miles to Madison. Authentic saddle bags are used to hold the mail, which has a special postmark for the occasion.

Ferris, a retired South Dearborn High School teacher, compiled a cook book filled with recipes used in the community for generations. Proceeds from the festival and projects like the cookbook, Ferris says, have allowed the town to restore part of its history, preserve its past, maintain a town museum, operate a gift shop and buy some buildings that are part of the town's heritage.

Semarial Partin operates the Indian Trails Restaurant and Grocery, which is in a building owned by the Canaan Restoration Council. "I thought Canaan needed a community center again," she says. The building, an old frame structure, painted barn-red, has been a store off and on for almost eighty years.

Mrs. Partin, who lives at Manville, down the road a few miles, says, "I enjoy the people." That's obvious! It is April 1, and a sign on a post offers,

"Free Food Today." A disclaimer below it says, "April Fool." Another sign reads, "No Singing! No Dancing! No Swearing! This is a respectable house."

Canaan is small-town America. Folks here like humor, like to banter.

Mrs. Partin points to a board that has risen from the floor. A carpenter who has come in to sip a soft drink and nibble on potato chips looks. "Cheap construction," he laughs about the floor that has been in place almost eighty years.

If Semarial wanted the place to be a community center, she has succeeded. A number of men are in the restaurant at mid-afternoon. Gale (not Gale Ferris), who is there with his son, Bruce, shuffles a deck of cards on one of the tables. Bruce drinks from a soft-drink can.

Someone reaffirms the building went up in 1914. "Were you here, Gale?" Gale smiles. "No, I was out of town."

The men wear caps with John Deere, Agri-Gold emblems. They know each other, ask about each other's families.

A customer asks for an ice cream cone. Gale decides he'll have one, too. A farmer orders a slice of peach pie, then comments on how good it is.

"We bake them here," Semarial explains, pleased that another customer is pleased.

\* \* \*

We return via Ind. 62/Ind. 250, over rugged, scenic terrain to Ind. 7, then take a county road north to an old Jefferson County town called Foltz. There are eight houses, one abandoned, between "Foltz" signs a half-mile apart on an east-west road.

Life was far different in Foltz back when four trains a day stopped and residents gathered at the Foltz post office to get their mail.

\* \* \*

We return to Ind. 7, then take Ind. 250 west to Lancaster.

# Lancaster
### EARLY EDUCATION

What looks like an old three-story church made of native stone is off Ind. 250 at the edge of Lancaster, another Jefferson County town.

It is not a church, however, but the old Eleutherian College, a southeastern Indiana landmark. It was the second school west of the Allegheny Mountains to provide interracial education, being open to freed and fugitive slaves. (Oberlin College of Ohio was the first.)

According to the book *Indiana: A New Historical Guide,* Eleutherian was founded in 1848 with support from the Neal Creek Abolition Baptist Church and the local anti-slavery group. The college closed in 1874, became a private high school in 1878 and was a public school from 1888 to 1938.

The building is now owned by Historic Madison, Inc.

* * *

Ind. 250 makes a 90-degree turn as it exits Lancaster, then follows the Neal's Creek bottoms where Angus cattle graze on new spring grass. The road winds and the speed limit drops to 20 mph at times. Plymouth Rock hens peck at gravel along the road. A big red combine rusts beside an old school with the bell tower still in place. "Leaving Jefferson, entering Jennings County," the road sign says.

# Paris
## GRAND HISTORY

We have entered Paris, as in Jennings County, not France. This Paris has about twenty houses, with no businesses. A few large, well-kept homes are reminders of the days when Paris was a busier place than it now is.

It has a grand history, once considered as a site for the capital of the new state of Indiana. Those were the days when Paris was a major stop on the wagon route between Brownstown and Madison.

For years in the 1800s, Paris was the leading industrial center of Jennings County. The town had a hattery, a cobbler shop, a number of tailors, a grist mill, a woolen mill, a wagon shop, a cabinet shop, a slaughterhouse, a harness and saddle shop, a lumber mill and three or four general stores.

Its destiny changed when a railroad was built to the west, bypassing Paris. It never recovered.

# Paris Crossing
## DOUBLE DIP—40 CENTS

When Paris withered, Paris Crossing, to the west on Ind. 250, prospered. It was founded in the 1870s when the Ohio and Mississippi Railroad sliced through the area, skipping "old" Paris. And like Paris, it too waned when the mode of transportation changed, this time railroads yielding their role to huge 18-wheel trucks.

An old country store, the Paris Crossing Market, remains open, however, a busy spot in late afternoon. It's a place to get a double dip of regular ice cream—none of the soft-serve stuff—for 40 cents. The store offers almost everything except restrooms. A sign that says "No Public Restrooms" keeps customers and travelers from asking.

Bill Willhite stops his school bus, lets off a passenger or two in front of the store, their school day over.

The post office is open, and so is Webster's garage. The old high school, where the Paris Crossing Lions, sometimes called the Pirates, played basketball, is now the Coffee Creek Community Center. Township students now attend Jennings County High at North Vernon.

It has been a long day. That double-dip ice cream cone is mighty tasty as we drive out of town.

## *Trip 20*
# QUAKER COUNTRY

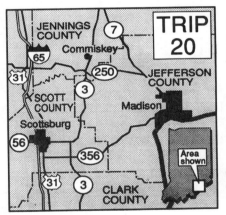

It is a new day, and we are back in Jennings County, where residents take their heritage seriously and make history their continuing education.

We stop on Ind. 3, north of Paris Crossing, at the Commiskey Corner Store, where two men, appearing to be near retirement age, are drinking coffee and talking about Social Security. Commiskey, they relate, is on the country road, a half-mile or so off Ind. 3.

## Commiskey
### MOVIES AND BEDSHEETS

Commiskey's location wasn't planned. It just happened. Historians say the Ohio and Mississippi Railroad wanted the town to be a mile north. When the brakes on a train failed to hold on a slope, the small pre-fabricated depot was dumped off down the tracks on a farm owned by Patrick Commiskey.

The town then developed around the depot. Few residents know Commiskey better than Elisha Layman, who grew up nearby and has been postmaster for the last 32 years. Layman went to high school at Paris

Crossing, where both Marion Township and Lovett students were sent when those schools closed and graduated with a class of 14 seniors.

Layman knows residents by name, asks about their families, keeps them up-to-date on what's going on around town. And he lets visitors know about the annual Fall Festival the third Saturday in September. He keeps a candy tray on the counter, free to customers who don't hesitate to pick up a mint or two as they talk.

It is from the perspective of his interest in the town's history that he can talk about Commiskey. It was a town that flourished when eight passenger trains passed through daily on the B&O, which took over the Ohio and Mississippi. When trains no longer stopped, mail bags were dropped off on a hook.

Layman recalls Saturday nights back in the 1940s when residents came into Commiskey from miles around to watch movies shown on a bed sheet mounted on the main street.

It was the Lurton family, he says, that built a two-story building, turned it into the biggest shopping center of its time, and drew customers from thirty to forty miles away.

"The town has gotten smaller, almost disappeared," Layman explains. "You can stand here and see it all," he says as he looks out the front window of the post office. Down the street are two restaurants, a barber shop, a branch bank, a few other businesses.

At Lurton's Country Cafe, Eva Short, a woman with a Spanish accent, mixes batter as she prepares for luncheon customers in the historic old building that has been a Commiskey landmark since 1884. She indicates business is brisk, that the town has been good to her since she arrived five years ago. Pies, still warm, the toppings high, are indications why the place will be crowded with customers both at noon and in the evening.

It is a Thursday, and she suggests we return that night for ham and beans, "all you can eat for one dollar." Or, she adds, Tuesday is a big night, too. That's when an auction is held in the auction barn that is part of the building the Lurtons made famous. The auctions bring people to town, to bid on furniture and whatever else is on sale . . . and to feast on Eva Short's cooking.

A couple of doors away at the Commiskey Cafe, a woman customer orders a bacon-and-egg sandwich and, as she waits, looks through a waitress's wedding pictures. A male customer comments, "I ain't goin' to look at any wedding pictures. I ain't gettin' married again, I'll tell you that."

Another customer orders coffee. "Twenty-five cents," the waitress says. The coffee is half as cheap, twice as good as a 50-cent cup at a fast-food restaurant.

Another man comes in, sits down and motions his right hand across a chair, a signal for us to join him. "My name's Homer Combs," he says.

"Better get another notebook," he says. "I can tell you enough about myself to fill up two of them."

Combs isn't bragging. He talks freely about himself. "Born in Combs, Kentucky. That's near Hazard," he says, punctuating his sentences.

"Served in the South Pacific, was on Guadalcanal, in World War II. Discharged in 1945 as a staff sergeant. Worked in Green Bay, Wisconsin, after the war, as a chef at the Sportsman Lodge where I got to know all the Green Bay Packers of that era."

He first came to Commiskey in 1957, returned in 1975 to a 40-acre farm where he raises cattle. In the meantime, he was a chef at the Harrison Lake Country Club near Columbus, managed the Jeffersonville Elks Club, owned a restaurant and motel in Houston.

Now, Combs says, he doesn't do much except raise cattle and fish. He seems like a nice fellow, so we agree not to mention where he fishes. "People who live around the lake don't know how to fish," he says. "They come out and if they don't catch something in fifteen minutes, they go back in. You have to know where the fish are.

"We catch most of our fish before June. After that there are so many water skiers and recreational boating, we don't bother."

The notebook is getting full. It is time to move on.

\* \* \*

Commiskey may be on the decline, but the area around it, we note, has shown an increase in population and brought more business to the post office. A rural water system has allowed homes to be built out in the country where wells sometimes failed.

# Lovett
### PIRATES OF THE PAST

We return to Ind. 3, drive north three miles and turn west on a county road at a sign that points to "Lovett." Lovett has 12 houses, no business, no town-limit signs. What looks like an old store is closed; so is what once was a garage.

A stone marker in the bricks of a building, now part of a farm operation, says, "Lovett High School 1901—J.A. Ross trustee." A frame building a few feet away appears to have also been used as a school.

The high school closed in 1940, and the Lovett Pirates basketball team faded into the record book.

# Vernon

### EVENTFUL DAY

Vernon is a quaint community, content to remain that way, leaving commerce and business to North Vernon, its younger but bigger neighbor. Vernon is on Ind. 7, just north of the Ind. 3 junction, and is a reminder of the past even though it is not on the backroads of time.

Vernon is the Jennings County seat, but it is far different from most governmental centers. Few people enter or leave the 135-year-old courthouse on this Thursday morning in April. There are plenty of parking spaces, little traffic, no hustle, no bustle.

It is a town worth a visit for its history. Founded in 1815 on the bend of the Muscatatuck River by John Vawter, it is one of Indiana's oldest towns. Vawter's brick home was Gen. Lew Wallace's headquarters during a brief assignment to defend Vernon from Morgan's raiders during the Civil War. The original town well is beneath the home that also has been used for a school and a funeral home.

Old row houses still line Ind. 3 on the south side of the Courthouse. A log cabin is a half-block to the east. Stores including antique shops are on the west side of the square, and a score or more historical attractions are within walking distance.

A historical marker recalls one of Vernon's most eventful days: "Confederate Gen. John Hunt Morgan demanded the surrender of Vernon on July 11, 1863. Upon the defenders reply that Gen. Morgan must take it by hard fighting, he withdrew toward Dupont."

Morgan, who had several thousand men, planned to destroy bridges on the Madison and Indianapolis Railroad. He overestimated the town's defense, which was made up of no more than 1,000 Jennings County volunteers and Union troops.

It should be added that the defense of Jennings County by these volunteers has also found a place in literary history, in Jessamyn West's popular collection of fiction about Indiana Quakers, *The Friendly Persuasion.* Herself a Quaker, the late Miss West was moved to California from her native Jennings County while still a child but never forgot her Hoosier roots, to which she constantly returned in her novels and stories.

\* \* \*

We head southeast of Vernon, wondering, as we drive over rolling hills and past farms with wood fences, how an Indiana town happened to be called San Jacinto.

# San Jacinto
## NO SURRENDER

We drive several miles off Ind. 7 and locate a community we think is San Jacinto, even though there are no signs. An old school is long abandoned, its windows broken, its ball diamond out front grass-covered, the wire on the backstop rusted. A sign on a two-story frame building says "Temple's Store," but, like the school, it too is closed.

We drive through town, turn at the fork in the road, see an approaching pickup truck, and flag it to a stop. "This San Jacinto?" we ask.

"It is," says the amiable driver. "Ronald Wahlman," he adds, introducing himself. "San Jacinto is a typical little old country town . . . a thing of the past," he says. "Stores can't get suppliers to come out and when they can, they can't compete with the larger stores in bigger towns."

He gives us some history of the town and suggests we talk to his wife, Mary Jo, who has studied San Jacinto's history.

Mrs. Wahlman outlines the town's past: The first settlers in the area arrived around 1810 and formed a community a mile and a half to the east. In the 1850s, the residents moved the town to the confluence of Little and Big Graham creeks and petitioned for a post office. Tommy Bland, who ran the town's store, had read about Sam Houston's victory over Santa Anna at San Jacinto, Texas. He was so impressed he asked postal officials to call the town San Jacinto.

Bland's request was approved, despite suggestions from a few other residents that the village be called West Cincinnati. Nearby residents would come to town to have grain ground at the grist mill on Saturdays and wait for the weekly mail call as Bland, the postmaster, read the names on the envelopes.

San Jacinto grew into a town with a blacksmith shop, stores, and a two-story Knights of Pythias building that still is the town landmark. A house in the area was a stop on the Underground Railroad in the days before the Civil War.

Families who hid the slaves were ingenious. "If slaves made it this far, they'll never be caught," they bragged, using guises to trick pursuers. If would-be captors approached, horses hitched to an empty wagon would be sent in one direction, and once it was followed by slavery sympathizers, the slaves would be sent in another direction.

Mrs. Wahlman also knows about that empty school up the road and about the Temple store. "The school was built for all 12 grades in 1916 for $5,555," she says. She attended school there until it closed in the 1960s and students were sent to Butlerville. High school students from the area now attend Jennings County, grade school pupils the new Brush Creek school near Butlerville.

The Temple store was in the Knights of Pythias Building. It has been the Redmen's Hall and has been used for a lot of other purposes as well. It was gym for high school basketball games back when San Jacinto had a team called the Bearcats, who created a sense of community for fans who came to see them play.

And that post office that gave San Jacinto its name? It's gone, its postmark, like the school, a thing of the past. Residents now have rural Butlerville addresses.

San Jacinto, though, lives in the hearts and minds of people like Ronald and Mary Jo Wahlman.

* * *

We take a county road north from San Jacinto, our mental compass pointed toward U.S. 50 and the Town of Butlerville. The terrain flattens, the land becomes more fertile, there is no traffic and we have time to appreciate the big, old country homes, to rant about junk that detracts from an otherwise scenic drive, to gaze at a grove of some of the beech trees which are becoming an endangered species.

We notice a home that has burned, now deserted, and wonder what has happened to the people who had lived there.

Up ahead, we see traffic on U.S. 50. Our compass has worked. We have arrived in Butlerville.

# Butlerville

## FAMOUS NAMES

It was in the early 1850s when Quakers in canvas-covered wagons rumbled into the Butlerville area and bought land for permanent homes. One of the settlers, John Morris, copied the name of the Ohio town from which he came, became postmaster and opened a general store.

Former President Richard Nixon's mother, Hannah Milhous Nixon, was born on a farm southeast of Butlerville, then moved to California in 1897 when she was 12 years old. Author Jessamyn West, a cousin of Nixon's, also was born near Butlerville and moved to California as a child.

Two schools, no longer in use, remain landmarks in Butlerville. One is marked "Butlerville School - 1922," the other "High School—1904—J.E. Murphy, trustee."

A Shetland pony grazes on grass that once was the school yard. Any Butlerville Bulldogs are now family pets, not Butlerville High School players. Grade-school students attend Brush Creek elementary, older students Jennings County High at North Vernon.

What once was a store is now a residence. A speed bump slows what little traffic there is on an April afternoon. A three-point arc is painted on the pavement, a basketball goal at the edge of the street. A three-tiered bell tower rises above the old Butlerville Baptist Church, not far from the Methodist Church.

A building supply firm is open, but old stores next to the railroad tracks are closed. So are a union headquarters and a grain elevator operation.

An "Allen Loves Tina" sign is painted on the side of a barn almost as big as the "Mail Pouch" letters. It is teen-age love that keeps towns young.

# Nebraska
## Feeling at Home

To the visitor's eye, this could be Nebraska, the state, not Nebraska, the wide spot on U.S. 50 east of Butlerville in Jennings County. Like Nebraska towns, this is a rural community, its only business a general store in a building erected in 1908. But Nebraska, Indiana, was platted by Robert Elliott in 1856, 11 years before Nebraska (from an Osage Indian word for "flat water") became a state.

A sign outside the store advertises "Hot Food. Soup. Pizza. Fish $1.50. Jumbo cheezeburger $1.99." Hey, if you can get a jumbo cheezeburger for $1.99, who cares if it's spelled with a "z"?

Inside, one of the two employees is holding a crying baby. It is of no concern. Men who come in for soup or sandwiches have heard crying kids before. They feel at home. Besides, the employees are friendly. One gives directions to the town of Zenas: "Go north to the T. Turn right, stay on the blacktop, don't go off on any of the gravel roads."

\* \* \*

One-lane humped bridges, their concrete abutments marked with fluorescent paint, slow traffic on the road to Zenas. The roads are hilly, windy, the terrain mostly wooded, a good place for the working sawmill where logs are stacked high. A groundhog waddles off the road as a car approaches.

The road opens into farm land where Angus cattle graze on pastures lush with spring grass. It is quiet, the only sound a bawl of a calf.

The directions have been perfect. We arrive in Zenas although there are no signs to indicate it.

# Zenas
## "King" but No Crown

LeRoy Gaither is out in his side yard, using shovel and muscle to spread a mound of dirt left by a contractor who replaced his septic tank but neglected to finish the grading. Gaither is wearing a brown and white cap from an Osgood store and a checked yellow and brown jacket.

It's soon obvious LeRoy never met a stranger. He's easy to talk with. "My English teacher told me LeRoy was a French name that meant king," he says. "Imagine, LeRoy, the king. Well, that was something for a kid, but I lost my crown a long time ago."

He owns three lots on the corner. "If this lake deal goes through," he says, pointing north to a proposed development, "they'll be worth some money."

He has a few peach, apple and cheery trees, which he says "really get loaded. We let people come in and help themselves."

Towns like Zenas are like that.

"My dad grew up down South and he always told me that to have a good garden you had to live in it. He meant it, too. I found out what he meant, when I came down here."

Gaither was born in Indianapolis, was graduated from Washington High School 1937 and later served with the U.S. military forces in World War II before becoming a truck driver.

He laments the fact times have changed: "When I went into service you admired the President, believed in what the nation stood for, took pride in your country. Now people ridicule the president and criticize the country."

Gaither moved to Zenas in 1969 for peace of mind. "We were living in Franklin," he remembers. "My wife's people lived in Franklin. My people lived in Franklin. So we heard all sides of the [family] arguments. They kept asking us, 'What do you think of this?' or, 'What do you think of that?' We didn't want to take sides, so we decided we had to get away from it.

"I don't think I'd ever been in Jennings County before. Anyhow, we found Zenas and bought this place. The store [now closed] was open, the grade school was over there [now gone]. There was a telephone exchange and a post office, which was in the store."

Zenas High School, where the Warriors played basketball, had closed earlier and Gaither's oldest son graduated from North Vernon, the younger son from Jennings County. "We wanted our daughter to go to a smaller school," he says, "so we leased this place and moved to Westport so she could attend Sandcreek school. When she graduated we moved back here."

Gaither may not be a native, but he has learned much of the history of Zenas, knows that it was once a stagecoach stop on the road from Madison to Indianapolis. I hadn't dreamed Zenas has such a history," he ponders. "At one time they had seven doctors and a dentist here. That old house that looks like it is falling apart, for example, was a doctor's office. Another house has iron rings embedded in stone where horses were tied."

A quick count shows a dozen houses, and a Baptist church, remain in Zenas. No one will be lonesome, though, not as long as there are LeRoy Gaithers to talk with.

*   *   *

A blacktop road with broken pavement leads north off Ind. 7 toward Grammer in southeastern Bartholomew County. A mother, her young daughter and two dogs are enjoying the warmth of the sunshine as they walk along the county road, safe from harm.

# Grammer
## SATURDAY NIGHT LIVE

Flags fly at several of the fifty or so houses in Grammer, a prosperous looking rural town in the midst of prime farm land. A farmer at the edge of town readies his corn planter for use in a couple of weeks when the fields dry and the temperatures rise. Farm supplies are available at Grammer Industries. The post office is open, but the town store has closed.

A township school built in 1899 is now The Rock Church. Signs calls attention to: Matthew 16:18 ("And I say also unto thee, that thou art Peter, and upon this rock I will build my church; and the gates of hell shall not prevail against it."), Acts 2:4 ("And they were all filled with the Holy Ghost, and began to speak with other tongues, as the Spirit gave them utterance."), and Acts 2:38 ("Then Peter said unto them, Repent, and be baptized every one of you in the name of Jesus Christ for the remission of sins, and ye shall receive, the gift of the Holy Ghost.").

Grammer is far different today than it was when Max Friedersdorf was growing up. Friedersdorf, a former Congressional liaison for Presidents Nixon and Reagan and now chairman of the advisory board for the Association of Retired Americans, remembers his hometown:

"In those days, 1929 through the early 1930s, Grammer was a bustling little village with three grocery stores, a butcher shop, barber shop, garage, train station and croquet court. The railroad line (I believe the train ran from Madison to Indianapolis) was the main reason for the town's existence, and once the railroad ceased the town shriveled up.

"My paternal ancestors settled in Bartholomew County just two miles outside Grammer and were farmers. My maternal ancestors settled in Grammer where my grandfather owned and operated his own butcher shop.

"In those days of limited travel, most of the surrounding farm families did their trading in Grammer and on Saturday nights the town was bustling with people.

"The main recreation was the lighted croquet court which lay next to the train tracks, and the games went on until what to me seemed late in the evening. Another focal point of community activity was the Presbyterian church where my grandmother was the pianist. In the summer we all went to Bible School.

"Our roof caught on fire one time and I remember the men relayed buckets of water to the roof to extinguish the blaze.

"I also remember a grain elevator that always seemed busy with the trucks lined up."

\* \* \*

We drive through Elizabethtown, too accessible, too near Columbus, to be called a backroad town. It is a community with churches, nice houses, gift shops, craft stores, a giant grain operation, a grocery and a tavern.

Railroad Street runs along the old Penn Central Railroad that ran through town, its rails and cross ties now removed. Residents, showing pride in their surroundings, have kept the railroad right-of-way mowed.

Sheep that soon will be sheared of their winter fleece graze in a lot at the edge of town.

\* \* \*

Azalia is an old town, just west of U.S. 31 in southern Bartholomew County. It is quiet on this April afternoon. A flag flies over an open square, which, even without playground equipment, appears to be a place kids and adults can enjoy. We are told later that the open area was set aside as the site for a county courthouse before it was decided to locate the seat of government in Columbus.

\* \* \*

We check our mental map, decide we can eliminate some mileage by going cross-country north to Columbus. We are stopped on a curve by the driver of another pickup who asks, "Where am I?" We tell him, the best we can, for we aren't exactly sure where we are, either.

A few miles north, farm land has become subdivisions, home now to families who like the rural life, away from city streets.

# OWEN COUNTY GETAWAY

Small towns change, residents move in and move out, stores open and close, but churches remain as spiritual and community centers.

We are in search of Quincy, in northeastern Owen County, this April morning. There are no highway markers on U.S. 231 to point the way, only an arrow to the Quincy Baptist Church.

The signs become our guide past rural houses, woodland, pastures, a couple of big farms. A squirrel nibbles on corn dropped in the road. This isn't squirrel season, and it holds its ground, forcing a motorist to wait until the meal is finished.

What was once Wallace Junction is now only a row of houses on the road, no longer a place where a railroad line from the southwest merged into the Monon (later the L&N, or Louisville & Nashville).

We arrive at the four-way stop where Owen County Road 1150 North crosses Road 325 East. We have arrived in Quincy, thanks to those Baptist church signs.

## Quincy
### DOWN MEMORY LANE

Quincy is another town that grew up with the railroad, withered when trains no longer stopped. The old Monon tracks still slice through town, but the depot is gone and trains that once helped stimulate the economy and give Quincy an identity no longer stop.

No businesses remain in the old center of town, a sharp contrast to the days when there were two general stores called Beaman's and Sutherland's, a hotel, a barber shop and other businesses. An old two-story business is abandoned, some of its second-story windows out. Another empty store is nearby.

The old high school, whose athletic teams were the Aces, is used for other purposes. What students there are in town now attend school at Cloverdale.

Across from the school, the woods are quiet. The excitement of the Old Settlers Days that once were held there now lives only in memories of residents who enjoyed the picnics, the games, the rides and the farm equipment that was on display.

An old church is offered for sale by a Cloverdale realty firm. The Quincy post office is open, a place for residents to gather and exchange information now that the stores are closed.

As in any town, some of the fifty or so homes are well- maintained, some not. Many of the residences are mobile homes, now called manufactured housing. A few outhouses remain, a reminder of times when Quincy was less modern, yet more exciting.

Zach Dunkin, a writer and editor for *The Indianapolis News,* remembers trips to Quincy where his parents, Eben "Bud" and Florence Ruth "Fon" Dunkin, grew up. "I loved going back to Quincy," he recalls. "I spent most of my spring vacations there and at least two to three weeks each summer. I still have dreams about the homes where my grandparents, Eben and Mae Dunkin and Jesse 'Pete' and Omaden Cummings, lived.

"I've taken my son back there to show him 'the crick' [what most natives called Brush Creek] where I caught my first five-inch blue gill."

Towns change, time marches on, memories remain.

*  *  *

We return to U.S. 231, then drive south to the road to Cataract and turn west at a sign for the "Country Bumpkin Craft Shop." A place called Paw Paw Hills is on the road. A rusting, abandoned hearse sits off the wide paved county road. A camper shell for a pickup rests on blocks.

# Cataract
## A Great Getaway

We are alone at Cataract Falls this Tuesday morning in early April. Picnic tables are still stacked under the roof of a shelter house, awaiting warmer days. A 140-foot-long covered bridge, which carried traffic over Mill Creek for more than ninety years, remains at the site.

It is a scenic recreational area with a spectacular view of the upper falls in Mill Creek which cascade 45 feet downward over graduated drops. A road leads to the west for a view of the lower falls, which drop another thirty feet after a gentle flow from the higher falls up the creek.

It was the falls that attracted Isaac Teal to the area, caused him to erect a small mill around 1820 in an area where Indians dwelled and where bears, wolves, panthers and deer were plentiful. And it was the roar of the falls that Theodore Jennings heard, then visited, as he rode horseback from Louisville to Greencastle to visit his brother in 1841. Jennings bought a thousand acres which included the falls and Teal's old mill.

He soon returned to the area, bringing his wife, four children and other friends and relatives who traveled in covered wagons that remained their homes until houses could be built. Jennings erected a sawmill, flour and woolen mills, blacksmith shop and general store. The area was platted in 1851 and the Cataract community became known for its lumber and its flour.

When the sawmills played out and the use of grist mills diminished, Cataract's businesses declined, but the town remained a good place to call home, and now, decades later, newcomers again are moving to the area for peace and quiet in a scenic setting.

The state of Indiana bought the falls in 1967, a decade or so after the federal government acquired part of the lower falls for a flood-control program.

## Cataract the Village

Wayne and Beverly Snyder's place in Cataract sets the standards owners of most other general stores in Indiana try to meet. "Don't fail to stop at the 'Old Country Store' in Cataract," we have been told time after time by merchants in other towns across southern Indiana.

We are not disappointed. A sign out front offers "sundries, groceries, pottery, knives and gifts." It could have added "and other items too numerous to mention."

Wayne Snyder is at work in the store, just as merchants have been for 130 years. "The place," Snyder says, "was built in 1860, as close as we can figure. And it has been a general store ever since." Snyder has owned the store 26 of those years. He worked for General Motors and was a proofreader in Spencer when he bought a store out on U.S. 231. He kept that five years, then bought the place in Cataract.

He's at home in Cataract. "I was born about five miles away and have lived around here all my life," he says. He's a friendly man, open, candid, seldom lets a visitor leave as a stranger.

Antiques in the store are to view, not to sell. "I like all the old stuff," he explains, his eyes scanning a sausage grinder, a sausage stuffer, harness parts, old desks, cash registers. Most of the items are reminders of days past, when horses provided transportation, when farmers and housewives hand-crafted most of what they needed. Except for antiques, and gasoline, the store offers almost an endless variety of items.

His gasoline pumps became another victim of the Environmental Protection Agency. "We haven't sold gas for about four years. The EPA regulations made it impossible for small businessmen to sell gasoline," he says, adding, "I hope it is proud of itself."

Business slows in winter months, but is picking up as warmer weather arrives. Mushroom hunters will start showing up, turkey season will arrive and campers will begin to filter in for supplies. The area is a good place for mushrooms, but if Snyder knows exactly where, he isn't handing out any directions.

Unlike other towns, Snyder says the Cataract area is gaining population. "There are a lot more people around than there were when we first bought the store. Back then, we weren't quite sure we would make it. But I was still working as a proofreader and that job supported the store for a while.

"The store has been good to us. We raised three children on it," he adds. And town folks, no doubt, think the store has been good to them.

A young man walks in, buys a few items, including a pack of cigarettes, and asks to charge it. "No problem," Snyder replies, pulling out a small charge booklet he uses. "We just have a few people we allow credit. Just a very few," he emphasizes.

*  *  *

It's not every day you can go from Cataract to Cuba in minutes. It's easy, though, if it's the Cuba in Owen County. A winding gravel road, fairly smooth despite the freezes and thaws, is the shortest route between the two communities. We are aware we have reached our destination when dogs run to the road to greet us as we locate the Cuba Baptist Church at Roads 600 West and 600 North.

Cuba, Wayne Snyder has said, was once Santa Fe. It was a thriving little community, but went downhill when the railroads were located elsewhere, creating new towns. Cuba no longer has a school or a post office, just the church, twenty or so houses and more dogs, cats and livestock than residents.

*  *  *

We drive east from Cuba over rolling land, past old, well-kept homes, large farms, toward a town called Carp. We reach a little community of seven homes at the west side of U.S. 231. We can't be sure where we are until we pull out onto the highway and spot a sign that says "Carp."

There are only homes, no businesses, no reminders of the store Wayne Snyder's brother ran from 1963 to 1968. If it weren't for the signs, motorists wouldn't know Carp was on the map.

*  *  *

We drive through Spencer, then head northwest on Ind. 46 past Owen Valley High School, which consolidated the Owen County schools of Coal City, Freedom, Gosport, Patricksburg and Spencer.

Nearby is the big Wal-Mart store, a boon to job seekers and shoppers, a bane to mom-and-pop stores which try to compete with the giant chain.

*  *  *

Vandalia is an Owen County community, a wide spot on Ind. 46 with a few houses, a few mobile homes. The Vandalia United Methodist Church is across the street from an abandoned church.

A shelter where students await the school bus advertises C and R Tool Rental, "We specialize in trenching." A sign seeks work for a well-driller, for there are areas still without rural water.

Ind. 46 runs along the top of a ridge as it winds its way from Vandalia toward Bowling Green.

\* \* \*

We leave Ind. 46 and take a county road north toward Jordan. A sharp contrast is noticeable in the care given homes. Some are immaculate, manicured by meticulous owners who take pride in their property. Others are run-down, junky, domiciles of folks who have other priorities than cleanliness or orderliness.

Off to the east is a housing development on a lake accessible only over a private drive. Home buyers who like the peace and quiet of the country have decided to build here, far from the rat race of urban life.

Up the road, a log cabin, preserved by its owner as a reminder of pioneer days, sits near a relatively new limestone house, uniting the past and the present.

It is a rolling area, and the hills and ravines provide excellent sites for small dams and private lakes. A man eager for the growing season uses a Roto-tiller on a garden plot near one of the ponds.

It is a road of surprises, but we have learned on this odyssey not to guess what is around the next turn. We continue onward toward Jordan.

\* \* \*

We realize we are in Jordan only because of the "Jordan" on the Jordan Presbyterian Church. What appears to have been and old school has been converted to a private home. Only a few houses remain. The only business seems to be B&J—"septic tanks installed, sand and gravel."

It is time to return south to Ind. 46.

# Bowling Green
## HISTORY BY THE BUSHEL

Bowling Green, on Ind. 46 in eastern Clay County, is a historic town that has preserved part of its yesterdays for tomorrows.

Legend has it that David Thomas arrived in the area and bought the land high above the Eel River from Indians for two bushels of corn. Bowling

Green, the first town in Clay County, became a trading post for travelers between Spencer and Terre Haute. Bowling Green remained a busy village until the railroads bypassed the area and the National Road (now U.S. 40) was built to the north, between Terre Haute and Indianapolis.

A community center is in a brick building across from the park, which is in the square that once was the site of the Clay County courthouse. Bowling Green was the county seat from 1827 to 1877, when it was moved to Brazil.

A historic two-story log cabin, built in 1864, sits in the open area that once was the public square. The cabin was on Ind. 59 before it was dismantled and relocated in 1973 by the Bowling Green Historical Society.

A brick county jail near the square, completed in 1865, is now privately owned. The Henry Moss home, erected in 1836, is believed to be the oldest brick house now standing in Clay County. A tin roof covers the house and the front porch.

It is good to see history preserved, the town's heritage maintained, even though buildings like the old Village Mercantile are closed, unable to keep up with competition in bigger towns now that roads are better and cars have replaced horses and buggies.

Still open, however, are the Wagon Wheel Inn, a pizza shop, the Bowling Green Market and houses of worship like the United Methodist Church.

Part of old Bowling Green High School still stands, silent echoes of the days when there was a high school and its athletic teams were called, appropriately, the Pioneers.

It is just before noon, and the Wagon Wheel Restaurant is already busy. Two men discuss business over lunch. A family of five dines at one of the tables, a fitting scene, for this appears to be a town that has kept its family values.

* * *

We drive down a hill from Bowling Green into the Eel River bottoms. Signs warn of high water but there is no flooding, which is good news for owners of cabins on the river banks.

A man filling chuckholes with asphalt nods when asked if we are on the road to Poland. "It'll come out right in town," he says.

# Poland
## "WHERE IT'S AT"

Like Bowling Green, Poland is another Clay County town with a bit of history. The Poland Historic Chapel, built in 1866, and its nearby cemetery are on the National Register of Historic Places. The Gothic Revival-style chapel was organized as a Presbyterian Church in 1866 and dedicated in 1869.

Still a busy community on Ind. 42, Poland has a grocery, hardware store, garage and feed-and-grain business. The hardware is in a big, old two-story frame building with a sign outside for "small engine repair, bait and tackle, marine supplies, plumbing and electrical supplies, lawn and garden." The Poland garage is busy, so is the feed and grain business.

Not as busy, though, as the Hillman Market, where Jerry Hillman is attending to business. Hillman grew up in Indianapolis, later moved to suburban Morgan County, and worked in *The Indianapolis News* and *The Indianapolis Star* advertising department for more than two decades.

He bought a house near Poland, moved there five years ago, then added 40 adjoining acres. "I'm not a farmer, but I enjoy the quiet," he says, explaining he rents the land to a tenant and shares what revenue there is.

He has found his niche in Poland. He uses words like "couldn't be happier" . . . "I love it here" . . . "This is where I want to be" . . . This is where it's at."

He jumped at the chance to buy the grocery when he learned it was for sale. The former owner already had an unsecured offer for it, but no firm deal. Hillman explains, "When he learned how badly I wanted it, he said, 'Give me a dollar as earnest money and I'll tell the other fella who is interested that I already have a buyer.'"

Hillman later built a new building across Ind. 42 and has seen business grow. "I wouldn't leave for any reason," he reiterates. "I like the town, the people, the area and small-town life. It's a sharp change from the pressures of advertising, a slower life style," he says as he greets a customer by his first name.

He plans to add gasoline pumps soon to serve his customers who now have to drive 10-11 miles to the nearest filling station. He does have fuel oil. A customers walks in with a five-gallon can. "Fill it up?" Hillman asks.

"Just two gallons. It's not going to be too cold tonight," says the man who is buying the oil for fuel. Hoosiers don't buy what they don't plan to use.

Hillman walks outside, pumps in two gallons. He runs a convenience store, and he wants it to be as convenient as possible for his customers.

A grandfather comes in with his grandson. He buys a submarine sandwich on display in the meat case, apologizes for taking the last one. The man buys his grandson candy.

It is this kind of life style that has endeared Poland to Hillman. It's a life style where the Volunteer Fire Department can operate on the proceeds of the bingo games it holds on Wednesday nights in the storefront Hillman vacated. And it's the kind of life youngsters, and older residents, too, can enjoy at the recreational grounds in town that are a part of the Clay County park system.

\* \* \*

Ind. 42 is narrow, sometimes winding, as it rolls east from Clay into Owen County.

# Cunot
## SAY WHAT YOU THINK

Any boundaries for Cunot are not defined. No matter! Paul's Garage and Marathon Fuel near Cunot seems like a good place to stop.

We buy a soft drink and sit down at a table with Sue Carroll, who runs the little store inside the garage building. Harry Souders, Paul's brother, is there, too. Paul is gone for the afternoon.

Harry doesn't like all the crime that's rampant in the country, doesn't care about some of the people moving out to the resort area from Indianapolis' Westside. And he doesn't care who knows it. He mentions three "bad" families who have moved into the area and admits he liked things better the way they used to be. He's a man who says what he thinks.

Bill Bellmore walks in. It's obvious he's a regular customer. He and Harry exchange comments, nothing flattering, about each other. They rib each other, call women who talk a lot "typewriter mouths" and dot their conversation with bucolic expressions.

Sue is more interested in genealogy than in character assassination. She leafs through pages of family history. She likes the past, too, but she isn't as vocal about the present as Harry and Bill.

The Cunot area is in transition, and neither man is eager to see change. Indianapolis is only forty miles, less than an hour away, on nearby I-70. Cunot is near the 1,400-acre Cagle Mills/Lieber State Recreation area, near Cataract Falls. Each has attracted permanent residents, each draws visitors seeking relaxation, respites from urban life.

For men like Harry and Bill, life will never be quite the same.

*Trip 22*
# SALT OF THE EARTH

We are back in Clay County, heading south on Ind. 59 from Interstate 70. It is an ideal spring day, a perfect time to visit towns off the main roads.

A sign points the way east to Center Point. Asphalt is peeling off the county road, a reminder of the winter past. Timber has been cut along the bottom land, leaving ruts deep in mud. Wild onions grow in fields along the road.

## Center Point
### BIGGER THAN EXPECTED

We have never been to Center Point, do not expect it to be more than a town with a few houses. We are surprised.

"Welcome to Center Point," a sign says. It is an incorporated town with its own water tower, a community of mostly older homes on streets with names on signs.

The Clay County Genealogical Society library is here, and so are a hardware store, a bank branch, a post office, gift shop and funeral home.

A man is picking up limbs after the previous day's storm.

Center Point turns out to be another town hidden off the beaten path, but one worth revisiting, perhaps when the Old Settlers Reunion is held the fourth weekend each August.

## Ashboro
### NO MORE SHAMROCKS

Eight houses and the United Methodist Church are on Ind. 59 between the town limit signs in Ashboro. It is another town that lost much of its identity when its high school closed. There are no indications now where the Ashboro Shamrocks played basketball before students were sent to Clay City.

Busier than Ashboro is the intersection of Ind. 59 and Ind. 46 just to the south. Motorists can stop there for fuel or food on their way from Bloomington to Terre Haute or from Brazil to points south.

We take Ind. 46 four miles west, then turn south on a county road to Cory, a town in western Clay County.

# Cory
## UNDER THE APPLE TREE

That Cory is an agricultural town is soon evident. A farm at the edge of town has a "John Deere Road" sign—in appropriate green and yellow—at its driveway.

The heart of the town is at Depot and Wright streets. McCullough Feed and Grain, near what once was the railroad right-of-way, is busy this Friday afternoon. The barbershop, however, is closed. So is a building that looks like it was once the town store.

A Perry Township High School sign is at the edge of town, a reminder of the days when Cory had a high school, its athletic teams called the Cory Apple Boys, that being a time before female students demanded their own teams and their own recognition. Cory high school students now attend school at Clay City.

Cory comes alive each year when the town holds its Apple Festival the last full weekend in September. It is an annual reminder of the days when apple orchards planted by E.A. Doud dotted the countryside around Cory.

* * *

East of Cory, a red-and-white sign painted "I.U. Hoosiers Avenue" points down a rural driveway. Back on Ind. 59, south of Ind. 46, a rural road leads west to Saline City. An old drag-line machine is no longer in use, its scoop at rest on the ground, a reminder of the importance of coal to the area. This is strip-mine land now where overburden is removed by drag lines to expose the veins of coal beneath the surface.

# Saline City
## SALT OF THE EARTH

Saline City today is far different than it was when coal mines were underground, labor was cheap and mechanization was yet to come.

The town, it is said, got its name from a salt lick that attracted deer to the edge of town. Founded in 1870, platted as a town in 1872, it grew quickly. By the end of the 1870s, it had two dry-goods stores, a stave factory, two coal shafts and five hundred residents. A hotel, now a private residence, and other businesses, came later.

The old C & EI Railroad depot, red trimmed in white, still stands. A pigeon, free of danger, walks across its rusting galvanized roof. The tracks are gone, the depot now a monument to the days when steam engines chugged through town.

An old two-story store, a porch across the front, is no longer in use. A bread box is out front, next to a door with a Camels cigarette advertisement.

A cat has crawled through a broken window and sleeps inside the store, which is cluttered with reminders of the days when business was brisk. Up the street, a dog house looks almost as big as an apartment. A water pump remains in a yard, a reminder of a time when houses had no running water.

A church remains, but there are no stores, no post office in Saline City. It does have a park, part of Clay County's extensive recreation system. A shelter house, slides, basketball goals and restrooms are available to residents.

Chances are the park is filled each Labor Day when the community holds it annual reunion. It is a time to relive the days when coal was king and more people called "Saline" home.

\* \* \*

Denmark, seven miles east of Ind. 59, has a name as big as a country. But it's a town so small residents have to close the blinds to change their minds.

\* \* \*

Clay City is the business center of southern Clay County, a town that has kept its high school, much of its business and its most famous industry, Clay City Pottery. The pottery business was founded in 1885 by Beryl Griffith, an English-Welsh potter, and remains a family business more than a century later.

The annual Clay City Pottery Festival, sponsored by the town's Lions Club, is the second Saturday in June.

* * *

The hamlet of Martz is just south of Clay City on winding Ind. 59. About eight houses are between town-limit signs and there appear to be no businesses now that Puckey's country store is closed.

* * *

Ind. 59 continues south, twisting, turning, appearing to have been laid out on a trail left by a rabbit trying to elude a dog. Coal trucks rumble along the narrow road, past a giant cedar that has fallen in front of a home. A new bridge spans the Eel River, an indication the state hasn't forgotten this part of the state after all. The river is at its banks after two days of heavy rain, but the bottom lands have not been flooded.

Ind. 59 makes a 90-degree turn near Howesville, heading west, then makes a sweeping turn to the south. The old feed mill is closed, as is an old store. Virgil Marlow, a Pioneer seed dealer, appears to be the sole merchant. The United Presbyterian Church is amid a dozen homes.

# Bogle Corner
### "LAID-BACK, EASY-GOING"

Folks in Bogle Corner don't need an official state highway sign to identify their town.

Ind. 59 makes a 90-degree left turn to the east where motorists must stop for a county road intersection. They are greeted by a homemade sign, "Bogle Corner—USA," under a flagpole flying Old Glory.

Another "Bogle Corner" sign is painted in red on the side of a garage. And a third sign atop a rock pile around a stump says, "Hi! Bogle Corner." People here are proud of Bogle Corner.

T.J.'s paint and body shop is on the corner, Everett Ellis' Agri-Gold business is in town, and so are the Jasonville Water works plant and a shop called Shamrock Acres, "antiques and collectibles bought and sold."

Shamrock Acres is open. We go inside and look around until Ronnie Ireland walks over from his house next-door. Ron and his wife, Mary, own the place, have ever since Ron retired from the General Motors Delco Remy plant at Anderson.

The Irelands live in Bogle Corner by choice. Ron explains: "I got tired of working in the factory after 34 years, so I decided to retire in 1990. We just looked around and looked around and found this place. We liked the location; it was kinda laid-back, easy-going. So we decided to buy and move here."

He no longer has to commute, as he did 24.9 miles each way from his former home in Arcadia to Anderson. It is a welcome relief, he has found. "We love it down here," he says.

He looks out the window behind the shop. "We planted ten of the nicest pine trees you've ever seen out there, built a fence, bought three goats and put them back there to keep the place clean. The first thing the goats went for were those dad-gone pine trees. Boy, were they beautiful pine trees," he says, recalling one of his early experiences in Bogle Corner.

"We built crafts, got tired of doing that, and have dabbled in antiques and collectibles the last three years," he says. It's obvious Ronnie and Mary do more than dabble. The shop which he built himself is nearly full of items. He explains, "We sold about everything we had in here at a sale last June. We've gathered all this in the nine months since then. All of it is ours. There is nothing here on consignment."

He points to an old Buckwell Brewing Company sign he got in a trade. It is wooden, 24 by 32 inches, the first of its kind Ireland has seen. "I'd say it's more than a hundred years old. so I don't even want to sell it. Oh, I told a fellow I might let it go for $10,000. He laughed and said he was going to offer me $5,000 for it."

That's Ronnie Ireland, a man who has found peace and happiness in a place called Bogle Corner.

# Jasonville
## ROCK 'N' ROLL MAYOR

We stop in Jasonville, not because it's a backroads town, but to meet the mayor, Bruce Borders. Borders is not your usual mayor. He's an entertainer as well, an Elvis Presley impersonator, "the mayor of rock-n-roll," his cards say.

Appearing on TV with David Letterman, Oprah Winfrey, Joan Rivers, Entertainment Tonight and CBS Worldwide News, Borders has brought national attention to Jasonville. It's a good way to promote the city of 2,400 residents at the northwest tip of Greene County on Ind. 48 just west of Ind. 59.

We stop at Borders' insurance business, but he is out. A man with three jobs can be hard to find.

Jane Fish works in the mayor's insurance office and also is part of city government. She is president of the five-member Jasonville City Council, a job she has found harder than she thought it would be: "It's a lot more difficult, a lot of decisions to be made. I'm the first and only woman on the council, which sometimes makes it is a little more difficult."

Jasonville, once in the heart of a flourishing coal industry, is now more of a resort community, the gateway to Shakamak State Park. Shakamak High School is at the west edge of town.

* * *

Like many other towns, the biggest competition in Jasonville may be among churches. Case in point: St. Joan of Arc Catholic Church is on one side of McKinley Street, the Church of Christ directly across on the other side.

# Midland

## OUT THE DOOR

Midland, another Greene County town, is off Ind. 59 at County Road 675 North. And it is another community that languished as railroads and coal became less important.

It is an old mining town that has kept its post office and has a volunteer fire department, but not much else. The only advertisement is for scissor sharpening. An American flag flies next to a mobile home. A chicken stands in a street, doesn't move until a horn blows. Mules graze in a pasture at the edge of town.

Three basketballs, perhaps belonging to future Shakamak High School Lakers, rest near a goal, the dirt court covered with water from rains the previous day. Before consolidation, youngsters here would have grown up to play for the Midland High School Middies.

We are reminded of Midland's old quonset-type gymnasium, which was the origin of one of Indiana's humorous basketball stories. It had rained for hours before a Midland game, the roof had leaked and the floor was wet when referee Dee Williams and his partner arrived.

The teams sat on one end of the gym, separated by an aisle to the exit. Williams watched as his partner's feet slipped from under him, sending him sliding through the door into the outdoors. Fans were ecstatic, players stifled laughs. One of the coaches jumped up, closed the door and said, "He should have been out there all night, anyhow."

# Vicksburg
## Mining Their Business

Students are away at school, parents are at work, there are no stores open and it is too early in the season for yard work, so Vicksburg looks like a ghost town on this Friday afternoon in April. Another Greene County hamlet, it is west off Ind. 59 on County Road 450 North.

It is a residential town of a hundred or so houses, some neat, nice and spacious, others small, in need of attention. "We support the UMWA" signs are at many homes, an indication this is coal country and a strong union community. The town has no post office, its residences on a rural route out of nearby Linton.

Vicksburg has open lots and a double-wide prefabricated house is in place on one of them, waiting for its foundation to be shored up. It is just a hundred feet or so from Vicksburg's "Cadillac" of houses.

An old strip mine at the edge of town is now a lake where a sign, "Sorry, Danger, Deep Water," is posted. Across the street, a man checks on his hunting dogs, for a person needs a hobby whatever his profession.

# Dugger
## Alive and Well

It is soon obvious that Dugger and coal are synonymous. A stone in front of the Town Hall-Library marks the town's first 100 years, "1879-1979," with two etchings, one of a mule pulling a coal cart, the other a drag line.

The town on Ind. 54 in eastern Sullivan County was laid out in 1879 at the time the Dugger Coal Mine was opened on the east side of town near the railroad. The Coal Museum is here, has been since 1980 when it opened in what had been a restaurant. Its contents document the history of coal mining for the last 115 years.

Dugger is not a hamlet but a small town of 1,100 where residents can bank, shop for groceries, hardware and furniture, relax at a tavern, dine out, or be treated by a doctor.

And it has kept its high school, Union-Dugger, a 150-student consolidation of Union and Pleasantville.

* * *

Ind. 159 stretches south out of Dugger past the Green-Sullivan State Forest, a number of roads leading east to lakes and camp sites. The forest is on the site of abandoned strip mines, many of which are now lakes where the fishing is good but swimming is prohibited. Old coal mines have been returned to nature.

A road to a home off Ind. 159 is marked "Boilermaker Avenue." Purdue fans are few in this area of Southern Indiana, but those who are here are proud to be.

* * *

Bucktown is not on any map that we have, but it is here on Ind. 159. A store and filling station, its pumps gone, is closed. Only a few houses, back off the road, remain.

# Pleasantville
## GONE FISHING

Ind. 159 ends at Pleasantville, another coal town in southeastern Sullivan County. Off to the west, a giant machine lumbers away from a strip mine. Much of the surrounding land, however, already has been reclaimed, creating small lakes ducks now call home.

This, too, is a union town. "Support the UMWA. Promises are fine. A UMWA contract is better," a sign reads. Others say "We support the UMWA."

George's place is open, offering night crawlers for sale to sportsmen who want to fish in the strip-mine pits. Another store is closed and there appear to be no other businesses. A refrigerator sits in front of a church that no longer is used. Two churches remain. Pleasantville no longer has a post office or a high school as it did when the Blue Streaks basketball team gave residents a sense of community.

A school bus drops off children, who run toward their homes, free for the weekend. Another work day is ending.

*Trip 23*
# LAND BEYOND BATESVILLE

It is time to visit southeastern Indiana, an area that developed early as pioneers filtered into the state from the east and southeast.

We are on Ind. 46 southeast of Greensburg, visiting New Point, a Decatur County farm community where the post office is in an old two-story building with a fading "We sell Bryce's Mother's Bread" sign on the side. A building that says First National Bank with a notation that it was built in 1905 is now a garage.

A driver of a pickup truck waves to us as does a woman hanging clothes on the line on the sunny side of her lawn.

A big farm center is a busy place as the planting season nears. An old store next to railroad tracks is closed and for sale. A liquor store is open. So is an auto body shop.

At the edge of town, the Sharon Brown Trucking Company advertises, "Truck 'em Easy. Truck 'em Safe." Wood-Mizer, a factory that makes portable sawmills, is at the east edge of town.

\* \* \*

We cross into Ripley County, passing through the north edge of Batesville, a prosperous community that is the home of Hillenbrand Industries, and drive on to Morris.

Morris is a little town with several big homes on large lots, giving residents elbow room in a suburban setting. Clothes hang in the sun to dry.

St. Anthony School, built in 1917, and the church are Morris landmarks.

\* \* \*

Back on Ind. 46, new houses blend in with big, old two-story brick homes with ancient wooden window frames. Another farmhouse is a two-story frame with a tin roof that likely makes for peaceful sleeping when it rains.

## Spades
### CLASSROOM LIFE

A dot on the map shows Spades to be south off Ind. 46. We turn on Spades Road, then follow the asphalt trail which separates a cemetery and the rural St. Stephen's Evangelical Lutheran Church.

An old two-story brick, a "1891 Public School District No. 10" marker on the front, is at the north entrance to Spades. It is now an apartment building, with four rural mailboxes out in front.

No signs indicate this is Spades, except for one that appears to have been taken off the old depot that served the railroad. A stone wall lines the bank of the railroad that parallels a road for a short distance.

It is a community of some well-kept homes, but no business, no post office, no school. Outside town, a separator sits on a front porch, a reminder of the days when its crank was turned to spin cream from milk.

\* \* \*

We pass through Penntown, a crossroads community where Ind. 101 crosses Ind. 46, see the Old Brick tavern, which once was noted for its chicken dinners and entertainment, and continue southeast into Dearborn County, the third county formed in Indiana.

# Lawrenceville
## SERVICE WITH SMILE

Ask almost anyone who has been there about Lawrenceville and chances are he or she will mention the Schoettelkotte Brothers store. In a time when stores come and go, Schoettelkotte's has been a general store in the same location for 66 years. "Service with a smile since 1927," it boasts. It has kept residents around northwestern Dearborn County from having to leave town to find what they need to survive another day.

Christine Callahan is at work at the store, just as she has been for the last six years. She tells the Schoettelkotte story: Ray and his brother, John, opened the store in 1927, and had a store at St. Peter's north of here at the same time. "Here they are in this picture," she says, pointing to a photograph on a display case. "Ray retired out of here about nine years ago and his oldest son, whose name is Ray also, bought it."

It is a busy store often visited by motorists from Indianapolis and Cincinnati who like to look over the items in a genuine general store. "We are open every day, seven days a week, so we get a lot of visitors," Christine says.

Customers or sightseers can ease through the cramped aisles, past the groceries, pop and candy and look at the clothing, bug spray, shoes, seed potatoes, wood stoves, stove pipes, garden supplies, horse collars, harness, nails, hardware, shovels, rakes, nuts, bolts, buckets, mail boxes, axes, saws and can hooks.

Christine hands us the store's "Happy Helper Calendar," a tradition started to help farmers record income and expenses so they'll have "a much easier time in preparing federal income tax forms for next year." She also gives us a copy of the *Trailblazers' Almanac and Pioneer Guide Book,* which is filled with helpful information for anyone who farms or cares about the weather or can use household tips.

Lawrenceville is an old town. The white frame two-story store was a funeral home, Christine says, before it was a store.

The Hollywood Tavern, a block away down Tavern Lane, may have been here even longer. It is just after 10 a.m. and a customer steps from his pickup truck for a mid-morning refreshment. Chances are the parking lot will be filled with cars and the tavern crowded with customers for the square dance Saturday night.

A graveyard is across Tavern Lane . . . but any connection with the bar is purely coincidental. We think.

* * *

We head south from Lawrenceville on a county road. It is an old area of Indiana, and aging two-story brick houses are common, a sharp contrast to new homes on scattered lots. Old barns, some with sheep, still stand, having been better maintained than those in other areas.

# Hubbell's Corner
## THE GARDENER

Hubbell's Corner isn't much more than an intersection of Lawrence-ville/Weisburg Road and North Dearborn Road. A few homes are along the east-west North Dearborn pike, but there are no businesses.

We stop to talk with a man who says his name is "Schaffer." Rural folks often don't give their entire name unless pressed. Before we can ask his first name, he wants to know, "You lost?" "Just driving around," we tell him.

He has returned from a walk. "Live right here," he says, pointing to his house. He wears a baseball cap above a three- or four-day growth of beard and talks about his garden. "Planted 'bout everything except Brussels sprouts and rice," he tells us.

People here care about their gardens and their birds. An American flag flies above three martin houses at one home. Other homes also have houses for martins. A cardinal flits across the road, it too, perhaps, looking for a place to call home.

* * *

Lawrenceville Road becomes Weisburg road at North Dearborn Road. We take Weisburg Road, which makes sense, because it leads to the community of Weisburg.

# Weisburg
## DAYS OF YORE

We take a long look at Weisburg and wish we could step in a time machine and go back for a few hours to an earlier time. Time has all but passed Weisburg. It grew quickly after the Lawrenceburg-Indianapolis Railroad started operation in 1853. A general store, blacksmith shop, saloons and a flour mill soon followed.

The old Weis Mill, no longer in operation, still stands, its clapboard siding and gable roof in place. What once was the Weisburg General Store is now filled with antiques and other items. So is the covered porch than runs along the front of the red clapboard two-story structure built about 1885. Its doors are closed on this Friday morning. The town tavern, once the Weisburg Brauhaus, also is abandoned.

All the businesses were down along Tanner's Creek in what area residents call "The Bottoms."

Rudy Oehlman stops his pickup to talk. He grew up on a family farm near here, one of six children. "I'm 71 and most of them [his brothers and sisters] are older than I am," he says, his accent still showing traces of his German ancestry.

Oehlman, who now lives in nearby Sunman, remembers when Weisburg was a thriving town. "It wasn't very big, but the businesses were productive. The store, the tavern and the mill were all busy places."

Now people have to travel elsewhere to shop. Oehlman knows about the Schoettelkotte General Store we have visited in Lawrenceville. "The saying around here is that if you want something, you can find whatever it is at Schoettelkotte's," he confirms.

Oehlman shares our interest in small towns. He has brightened our day.

\* \* \*

We return north on Weisburg Road to North Dearborn Road and drive east to New Alsace.

# New Alsace
## AFFORDABLE LIVING

New Alsace is an old town in the midst of change. Families are moving to this section of Dearborn County where they can buy building sites much cheaper than in Cincinnati, thirty minutes away on Interstate 74. It is a good place to raise children away from the noise and traffic of the city.

New Alsace—pronounced New All-sis by some residents—was platted around St. Paul's Catholic Church, which has stood since 1837, its nearby cemetery almost as old. Klump's Tavern opened soon thereafter and remains across the street from the church, having been in operation long before laws required bars to be at least 200 feet from churches.

The Catholic elementary school is part of the church complex. It is outdoor activities day and the students are romping on the playground, enjoying one of spring's brightest hours.

Jerri Paoletti, one of the area's newcomers, is at work at the New Alsace grocery. She and her husband moved to nearby Yorkville from Cincinnati and took over the store in 1992.

"I love the country," she asserts. "We could afford to buy some land and build out here, which we couldn't afford to do in Cincinnati. Ten acres out here go for $21,500. In the city a quarter-acre lot might be $40,000."

They are not alone, she says, explaining that 37 new homes have been built between New Alsace and Yorkville on parcels sold by farmers. "It's not all blue collar. A lot of white collar workers have moved out here. It's one of the few places people can find to live on the money they make."

She may be new to New Alsace, but she has learned its history. "This store has been here forever, a hundred years at least. It once had a huckster wagon that covered the rural areas. And in the old days, all the meat-cutting was done here at the store," she says.

She has added crafts—those she has acquired and those left by 39 different consigners—to the items available. "The crafts have done amazingly well. We had an open house at Christmas and did $1,400 in one day. There were a lot of open houses in this area the same day and people came out of northern Kentucky and Ohio to shop."

But amidst her delight, there is sadness. "We're going to give up the store," she says, the disappointment in her voice. "You can't make any money in a store in a small town, anymore. We don't own the building, so maybe somebody else will take it over when we close in August."

She explains the problem the store faces: "A lot of people out here now are young with families and they are not going to shop here, not like in the old days when residents shopped here weekly. They are going into the city and buy what they need, like we all do."

A store at Yorkville does better, she says, but it has been established with the same owners for a long time. It also has a gas pump and a bar in an adjoining room which helps attract customers. The New Alsace store also sold gasoline until EPA regulations forced the owners of the building to discontinue sales.

We leave New Alsace with a touch of sadness, with another example of the plight of small businesses in tiny towns.

\* \* \*

On the road to Yorkville we note some of the new houses Jerri Paoletti has mentioned. The air is clear, the only noise the stir of the wind and the chirp of the birds.

The road follows a ridge, offering a view of the horizon in its undisturbed splendor. New homes are mingled among the old, uniting yesterday and tomorrow, bringing together rural and urban cultures.

# Yorkville
## YES AND NO

St. Martin's Catholic Church, built in 1915, is the spiritual center of Yorkville. Widloff's Groceries is the social center. It's a place to gather, exchange information, post signs for lost dogs, tack auction notices, promote fund raising events and announce births.

Customers are buying meat, paying for gasoline from the tanks out front. The clerk isn't all that busy, but she isn't eager to talk, at least on this day, as Jerri Paoletti was. Our attempt at conversation is answered with a few one-syllable replies. We conclude she is preoccupied with other thoughts.

A lone customer is at the bar as noon nears, but he doesn't seem any more eager to talk than the clerk. That doesn't stop us from appreciating the store or the clean little town of thirty houses that is being surrounded by suburban development.

\* \* \*

The county road toward Guilford continues to follow the ridge, winding past new homes, one almost big enough to be a castle.

The ridge ends, and the road drops down a hill through scrub timber, twisting for a mile as it winds its way into Tanner Valley.

# Guilford
### BRIDGING THE YEARS

Its valley setting gives Guilford an appearance of a mountain town locked between hills. Ind. 1 runs north and south along the east edge of Guilford, which was platted in 1850 and developed after the Big Four Railroad (later the New York Central) opened.

A general store, auto-repair shop and a few other businesses remain, as well as the post office, volunteer fire department and the Guilford Covered Bridge Park, named that for the covered bridge, the last in Dearborn County, that sits inside the grounds. The park also has a shelter house, full-size basketball court, swings and slides.

The Tanner Valley United Methodist Church, a Gothic Revival structure built in 1899, remains a town landmark.

High school students, once the Guilford Wildcats, now attend East Central, a consolidation off Ind. 74.

We stop at the general store where "Bud" Scholl is tending to business. "S-c-h-o-l-l," he spells it out without being asked. "I tell everyone my rich uncle was Dr. Scholl. Of course, I stretch the truth a lot when I say that," he laughs.

He's a relaxed, friendly sort, easy to talk to, ready to answer questions. "I don't own the store," he continues. "I just work here. I took early retirement as a truck driver out of Cincinnati when I was 54 last year. I know the people who own it, Jane and Larry Wuestefeld, so I just work part-time to fill in.

"I started working in November. Before that I piddled around at anything. I started out at three hours a night, and wound up working 33 hours a week. I want to go back the other way, though. I didn't retire to work full time, even though I do enjoy it."

Business, he says, isn't too bad for a little store: "People don't come here to buy all their groceries, but they do run in to buy pop, chips, beer, a few dollars' worth of gas—we can't sell enough gas to compete with places that have a lot of traffic. But one pump is leaded gas, which is a convenience for people who have older cars, tractors and lawn mowers."

Jane Wuestefeld's father, John Taylor, owned the store and sold gasoline, tires and oil, and his mother fixed sandwiches. When the tire business went to bigger stores elsewhere, the business became a grocery. "So it has been in the same family for years," Scholl explains.

Bud says he lives "out by Weisburg, a place a lot of people never heard of. I once told someone I was from Weisburg, and this guy wants to know if that's a sandwich."

We tell him we've not only heard of Weisburg, we've been there. Weisburg, he agrees, has gone the way of a lot of small towns. "I like to take the backroads when I travel, and I notice a lot little towns are doing down."

It is a sad fact about modern-day America.

* * *

Ind. 1 north of Guilford is a scenic drive, a winding road that follows the valley, which is now radiantly clothed in its redbud foliage. Old houses built of native stone date back a century or more. A foot bridge, swinging on cables, spans the creek.

# Dover
## WINE AND HISTORY

Like many other pioneer towns, Dover grew up where two roads intersected, the north-south trail between Lawrenceburg and Brookville (now. Ind. 1) and the east-west route between Harrison, Ohio, and Napoleon (now North Dearborn Road).

It was called Crossroads in those days after Jonathan Lewis built the first house. Irish Catholics followed, and St. John's was built in 1824 as the state's second Catholic church (after the one in Vincennes). The present church, a Romanesque Revival brick, was dedicated in 1879.

By 1855, the town had become Dover with thirty to forty houses, more than there are today. An old brick, which was built as a saloon and general store, is still used as a restaurant and tavern on the northeast corner of that old crossroads. Logan's general store is in a new building, reflecting the new among the old, accentuating the ever-changing neighborhoods in which Hoosiers live.

Antique shops are on Ind. 1. So are a monument shop and a funeral home. And the Chateau Pomije winery is here, attracting visitors to its restaurant and offering tours of the winery and displays of crafts and arts.

* * *

We are in search of the town of Bright as we head east from Ind. 1 on North Dearborn Road. The sun is out, the day is clear and the view over hills carpeted with green leafed trees extends as far as the horizon.

Piped rural water now is available in this highland area of Indiana where the view is good and building lots are reasonable. It is a place scores of families have decided to locate and it appears we are in a housing development at the edge of a city instead of a rural town.

Bud Scholl, back in Guilford, talked about Bright. "It has grown from a little country village . . . by leaps and bounds," he told us, adding:

"There are houses everywhere out there. A farmer told me he once farmed two hundred acres up there. Now, he says, the only thing that grows on his land are houses. People like to get out of the city where land is ungodly high. A farmer can't pass up an offer for $1,500 an acre. He can't make that much farming it so he sells it to people who want to build houses. But $1,500 an acre is cheap for someone who wants to move out of the city and have a place where no one can crowd in on them."

There are so many new houses, it is difficult to find the old town. In fact, we don't on our first trip. We continue east on North Dearborn Road, failing to turn onto Stateline Road as we should have, and end up in Ohio.

Such are the tribulations of travelers with often uncharted objectives. We will return on another day, we promise ourselves, to find the old center of Bright.

* * *

We drive south past Lawrenceburg and into Aurora, check to see if "Mose" is on his park bench at the edge of the Ohio River. He is not, but we recall our visit with him a few months earlier.

## On the River
### "CALL ME MOSE"

He sits on a bench overlooking the gentle bend in the Ohio River, silence broken only by the claps of water. He grips his companion, a bottle in a brown paper bag, in his left hand. His cheeks are sunken, his teeth gone. A smile erases the wrinkles as a stranger nears.

"Sit a spell," he says, removing his right arm from the bench's back rest. The stranger does, for this is a beautiful day, a peaceful and serene spot, a respite from the hubbub of the 1990s. The man is no longer alone with his bottle.

He watches a third man walk two white dogs on a leash. "Anyone who takes care of his pets like that is a good person in my book," he offers.

The stranger looks at a grain elevator where barges are loaded with corn. "I'm still mad about that," the other man explains. "Tore down a church and a store where I lived on the second floor to make room for it. It's OK to tear down a store, but not a church."

He glances at his sack. "I'm religious, believe in God. But I do have one fault," He looks at the bottle again. "I do drink," he says, "but not too much anymore."

He had switched to wine after downing too much of a new brand of whiskey. His heart had stopped later out on the street and had to be restarted by a medic. "Almost broke my ribs, he did," the man recalls. "But it saved my life."

"By the way, name's Moses. But everybody calls me Mose." He relives his life, talking about his father and mother moving to southeastern Indiana from Kentucky when he was ten. He remembers life as a sharecropper's son a half-century ago, and talks about his seven brothers and three sisters, about moving from one farm to another.

The stranger nods from time to time, for this is a monologue. "Mose" moves on to his marriage. "She was a pretty thing and I loved her. I tried to do whatever she wanted." He recalls a new Plymouth convertible he bought for her: "It had only 19,000 miles on it when she saw a 1960 Ford hardtop she wanted. "I had money. I worked, she worked, and when you do that you can save some. Anyhow, I saw this Ford hardtop, sand brown, on the carousel in a showroom in Cincinnati, and I bought it for her because that's what she wanted.

It had pleased her for a week or two. "Then she ran off with another man. Took the Ford. Left me with the three kids," he says.

He eyes the sack again, twists off the cap, eases the bottle up to expose the Melody Hill label. He offers the stranger a drink. The stranger shakes his head, hoping not to offend him. Mose slips the bottle back into the sack. He will drink alone later.

They talk for a few more minutes. The stranger says it is time to continue his journey. Mose has turned a nodding acquaintance into a friendship. He thanks the man for the visit, and offers, "If you're down this way again, look me up." "Enjoyed it," replies the stranger, realizing he has said no more than a dozen words the entire time. Lonely men on river banks, awaiting salutes from a barge crew, enjoy company, especially listeners.

"Mose" waves goodbye. He has been a survivor nearly eight decades. The stranger does not worry about him. He senses "Mose" can take care of himself.

*  *  *

We are near the site where the first Indian conflict on Indiana soil occurred—the Lochry Massacre. It was on August 24, 1781, down on Laughery Creek near the site of what is now Riverview Cemetery, that about a hundred Indians under the command of Mohawk Joseph Brant surprised and defeated Col. Archibald Lochry and 107 Pennsylvania volunteers. Lochry and about half of his men were killed, the others taken prisoners.

# Moores Hill
## BEATING THE ODDS

Treasures sometimes are found in unexpected places. Take Moores Hill for example. It's a Decatur County town of six hundred residents 13 miles northwest of Aurora just off Ind. 350. Outside the area, it's seldom in the news; any conflicts aren't broadcast, and its residents go about their lives without much fanfare.

It is a community that saved its old high school and turned it into a cultural center with a library, museum and meeting hall. It conducts weekly bingo games to raise funds to maintain the center and gets help from prisoners who leave the Dearborn County Jail to do community service.

It's a town with a long educational history. The Moores Hill Male and Female Collegiate Institute opened in 1854. The Moores Hill College, supported by the Methodist Church, remained open until 1915 when the institution was relocated to Evansville. A marker on the grounds notes the original college building was erected 1854-56 with funding assistance from the Freemen of Allen Lodge 165, who used the third floor as a meeting hall.

Now Carnegie Hall is the only building that remains of the campus. It was built in 1907 with a gift from Andrew Carnegie. The building later was Moores Hill High School until a consolidation in 1978 sent students and athletes, known as Bobcats, to South Dearborn High at Aurora. Carnegie then was used as a grade school until 1987 when a new elementary was built next door.

Townspeople united then to block the school corporation from razing Carnegie. It is volunteers like Doris Miller and Donna Hopkins, who have turned what would have been an abandoned—even a razed building—into a community center. It is a monument to people who care about their community and spend hours to preserve a heritage that otherwise might be lost.

They organized the Carnegie Historic Landmarks Preservation Society and negotiated a long-term lease from the South Dearborn School Corporation. The result is a building with varied activities, a library, a craft shop, a museum, a site for meals for senior citizens, a place for meetings, dinners and receptions.

Doris Miller works in the gift shop. She graduated from Moores Hill High. So did her children. She escorts visitors through the building, notes the framed pictures of each graduating class, conducts a visit to the museum filled with mementos from the college as well as from the high school. She is proud, as she should be, of what she and others have done.

She directs us to the library, introduces us to Donna Hopkins, the acting librarian, another volunteer position. Most of the books have been donated to the library, which has about a hundred area youngsters involved in its annual summer reading program.

And the volunteers aren't finished. They foresee a time when the building will become a cultural center for visual and performing arts, a center for classes in music and dance as it was when college students walked the wooden floors.

They promise in their pamphlets to "demonstrate the value of preserving that which is significant in our past so that we may integrate past, present and future." Chances are they will succeed.

That's Moores Hill, doing for itself what other towns might ask government to do.

*Trip 24*

# "EAST WILDERNESS"

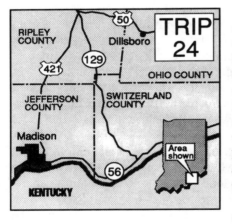

We remain in southeastern Indiana, caught up in the natural magnificence of the area above the Ohio River. Ind. 262 meanders south and east from U.S. 50 at Dillsboro, our destination a spot on the map called Milton, and the towns beyond. It is an adventure in driving. The road is winding and hilly, dropping down a hill that curves, twists and turns back on itself with speed limited at times to 20 mph.

We find Milton across Laughery Creek which divides Dearborn and Ohio County. The highway has been relocated, now skirts the Ohio County town instead of running through it as it once did.

Flags fly from two mobile homes, indications that those of modest means love their country as much as those who live in expensive houses. A 1929 monument honors old settlers, with about forty names engraved on the granite marker. Two men, retirement age, mow grass near the monument.

Not many people remain in the three mobile homes and six houses in town. What looks to have once been a store is closed. A basketball goal is at the side of a street where players can shoot baskets from the pavement without fear of traffic. A bell is still in place at an old school no longer in use.

The Church of Christ at Milton is on a hill above the village. It is in a large quonset hut, large enough to seat the crowds it hopes will attend a revival in a few days.

"Eggs for sale" says a sign on a cut-out model of a chicken. This is rural Indiana.

\* \* \*

Ohio is Indiana's smallest county in size and population, which was 5,315 in the 1990 census. Its rolling hills reach skyward, rock outcroppings adding to the majestic setting.

We continue on Ind. 262 southeast toward Pate. Redbuds and dogwoods decorate the rolling land on this spring afternoon, overshadowing, for a time, trash that has been dumped on the roadside. We stop on a hill to remove a small tree that has fallen across the pavement.

Mail is being delivered on the rural route by a carrier in a black Chevy pickup. Hannah Farms, a polled-Hereford operation, is on the road, the grassy hills lush for grazing.

# Pate

## HOLDING ON

The Old Union Consolidated School built in 1941 is abandoned, the playground stacked with pipes for the Aberdeen-Pate Waterworks extension which is bringing piped water to the area with funds from the Farmers Home Administration.

Pate is more of a stopping-place than a town. We stop at Miller's Country Stop Store, which is also a check station for turkey and deer hunters.

A customer in his twenties is in the store carrying on a verbal dialogue with owner Scott Miller over the amount of the bill he has run up. The customer, good-natured, agrees to pay, says he'll never charge anything again, and leaves. Miller looks at another customer and smiles. "He does that every week," he confides. "But he always come back when he needs something and doesn't have the money."

Miller explains how Pate supposedly got its name: "Two brothers were deeded property, one here, one down on the Ohio. They named the river town Patriot. It grew. This one was named Pate and just kind of fizzled out." He agrees Pate really isn't a town, even though it's marked on the map. "As far as having any boundaries, Pate doesn't have any," Miller says.

The store has been here since before 1876, Miller adds, pointing to a picture taken that year. He took over the business four years ago. "We try to keep a little of everything here," he says. "But it seems like no matter how hard we try, we can't have enough items. We still sell gasoline, but there's not a lot of money in it."

He talks about the competition facing rural stores: "There are four or five empty storefronts within three or four miles of here. Some of the stores closed down thirty to forty years ago. There just wasn't enough business to keep going. This one, though, has managed to hold on."

Miller hasn't faced problems with deliveries like some stores in remote areas. East Enterprise is down the way and trucks do not have to detour to stop at Pate. "If we were three or four miles out of the way, we might have a problem," he says.

Miller also has a construction business, and on weekends exhibits whitetail deer he keeps at his home a mile and a half away. He talks about East Enterprise, a Switzerland County hamlet six miles away where three grocery stores have survived. "That's a thriving little metropolis. If they would put a roof over the town, they'd have a mall," he laughs.

* * *

We drive south out of Pate on an Ohio County Road toward Aberdeen and East Enterprise. An old graveyard with just 14 tombstones is on the winding road near a barn that, like hundreds of others across the state, is collapsing. A yard sale is under way near a dairy farm at the edge of Aberdeen.

Aberdeen is a four-way stop where Ind. 56 makes a 90-degree turn from south to east. Don's Unlimited Store is closed, as is "Marie's Famous Pizza," which is boarded up with a no-parking sign out front. A United Methodist church appears to be the only meeting place in town.

* * *

Ind. 56 continues from Aberdeen toward East Enterprise, crossing the county line where motorists are greeted by a "Welcome to Switzerland County, USA" sign.

# East Enterprise
### CROSSROADS COMMERCE

Scott Miller, up at Pate, has been correct. East Enterprise is a thriving community. All three stores, which are within 100 feet or so of each other have customers. Traffic at this crossroads of Ind. 56 and Ind. 250 isn't heavy, but it is almost constant.

Josie's tavern has some mid-afternoon customers, who are bantering with Joan, the waitress and bartender. They are sipping beer, dining on sandwiches. Josie's is a down-home place, featuring "real home cooking, good food at a fair price," a sign promises.

We ask Joan about the town which she calls "East Wilderness." She is joking. We think. After all, the town does have a bank, a barbershop, other stores and an elementary school. This is a business center for north-central Switzerland County. It is good to see a small town that prospers in a time of discount stores and supermarkets.

*  *  *

We drive out of East Enterprise, where we notice flowers growing in an old steel-wheel barrow.

Up ahead is Quercus Grove (pronounced Quir-cuss), a community, it appears, that once was far busier than today. Neither of what look to have been two stores is in business. This is the day of the auto, and residents can drive to East Enterprise to buy groceries.

Another United Methodist church remains, as does the old Posey Township School, which no longer is a place for students to gather. A golf course near Quercus Grove is open, though, the first tee open for anyone who cares to stop and play.

*  *  *

East on Ind. 250, motorists can almost meet themselves when the road doubles back on hairpin turns as it drops sharply into the Ohio River valley at Patriot, where Ind. 250 meets Ind. 156.

# Patriot
## OLD MAN RIVER

A friendly dog relaxes at the entrance to the Town Hall and the utility office of this old Switzerland County town at river's edge. Some residents, on this April 30, sit in their porch swings and watch the Ohio flow by, much as others have done now for almost two centuries.

The 12-by-12-foot Patriot jail, built 170 years ago, still stands, its thick stone whitewashed, its barred windows slits no bigger than 8-by-12 inches. An old cemetery, as old or older, is nearby.

The Ohio, wide and deep here, brought mills and distilleries that shipped their products on steamboats in the late 1800s. Streets in the town of 275 residents still run along the river's edge. The river now is quiet. So is the town, which has a library, hardware store and post office. It also has a town

park, a liquor store, arcade, gasoline station and convenience store.

It also has a former resident it memorializes. Dr. Elwood Mead, 1858-1936, is called "the engineer who made the desert bloom" by supervising construction of the Hoover Dam. Its Lake Mead is named for him. Mead was appointed director of the U.S. Bureau of Reclamation by President Calvin Coolidge and later served under Presidents Hoover and Roosevelt.

# Rising Sun
### BY NO OTHER NAME

Rising Sun, another old steamboat town, is upriver on Ind. 156 and is the seat of government for Ohio County, the smallest county seat in the state. It was founded in 1814 and, depending on what source you believe, named either for the beauty of a sunrise over the Ohio River, or because a ferry boat by that name was at the site when founder John James arrived from Maryland.

The county seat of Ohio County, its Greek Revival courthouse is the oldest in Indiana, having been in continual use since 1845. The courthouse is away from the business district, not like most others on a square surrounded by law offices, banks and stores.

Row houses are noted for their unusual shape and architecture in the town of 2,300 residents. Visitors can ride a trolley through Rising Sun to see those residences on weekends from Memorial Day through October.

Despite its long, proud history, Rising Sun hasn't always been a popular name. In World War II, some self-styled patriots sought to have the name changed because of Japan's claim to be the "Land of the Rising Sun." Citizens, however, nixed the attempt. Rising Sun was home and its name would not be changed no matter how loud and long the protests.

* * *

We return south on Ind. 156, through Patriot, the road following the river along good farm land some locals call Egypt Bottoms. It is said the land reminded settlers of an area of biblical Egypt which supplied grain for areas that were in famine.

# Florence

IT'S NO LIE

Florence, also on the river, has a general store-bait shop where, chances are, some swear words are heard about the fish that are not caught. This is the town—laid out in 1817 by Benjamin Drake—that once had a 75-member Anti-Swearing Society. Members were fined for uttering profanities, probably even in describing the fish they caught or the game they killed.

The society no longer exists, some of its members buried in the cemetery at the edge of town. But man's inclination to be profane survives.

It is still the river, however, that gives the town a purpose, a reason for the Turtle Creek harbor for small boats.

# Markland

BY A DAM SITE

It was Markland the town first, Markland the locks later. The dam for the locks is 1,416 feet long with 12 42-foot gates, creating a pool upriver for 95 miles. Viewing areas permit visitors to see boats and barges raised and lowered as they go up or down the river.

In Markland, the town, a sign welcomes visitors to the Markland Baptist Church. A newer church is next to an older brick one with a hand pump beside it, a reminder of an earlier time.

A mother in a blue jump suit relaxes with a smoke while her daughter plays in the front yard. A store with rusting gasoline pumps out front no longer is open for the town's hundred or so residents.

Visitors can spend the summer at camp sites between Ind. 156 and the river. Several mobile homes are parked permanently on the river's edge.

# Vevay

A PLACE TO APPRECIATE

Vevay (pronounced vee-vee) is a book within itself, a great little town with an attractive 130-year-old courthouse, the county seat of Switzerland County. It is another community where residents can walk through the downtown area, appreciate the old homes, enjoy the history. There is no reason to rush in Vevay. The streets are wide with little traffic, stoplights few, residents friendly.

The Ogle Haus at the west edge of town off Ind. 56 is an inn on river's edge, far from motels off interstates and hotels in noisy metropolitan areas. Guests can watch life drift by as slowly, as quietly, as barges on the water.

Chances are the Swiss Wine Festival in mid-August is Vevay's best-known annual event, but "Over the River and Through the Woods" the first weekend in December attracts visitors who can sample the tastes, smells, sights and sounds of Christmas.

We have been to Vevay often. And we will return in days to come.

## *Trip 25*
# CLOSE TO KENTUCK

A new day has begun and we begin our drive downriver from Vevay at Brooksburg at the southeastern edge of Jefferson County.

## Brooksburg
### CELEBRATING HISTORY

It is before 8 a.m., and the town north of Ind. 56 is just beginning to stir. A store, an oil tank out front, a "groceries, meat and tobacco" on the side, is abandoned. An icebox is on the porch, a wash tub on a stump nearby.

A park with a shelter house, swing and basketball court is in the center of town. A small building labeled "office" is near the park, probably the headquarters for the "Spring Fling," a festival in June that will mark Brooksburg's sesquicentennial.

It is an event expected to draw folks from both sides of the Ohio River as well as both sides of Indian-Kentuck Creek which cuts through Jefferson County. On the agenda are a parade, a costume-judging, an old-time fiddlers' contest, a band concert, a country dance exhibition, a banana-peeling contest, a pie-eating contest, Driftwood Cloggers and gospel music. Anyone from the Brooksburg area who is over 75 years old is eligible to be one of the parade marshals.

George Miller, a columnist for the *Madison Courier,* recalls that "55 to 60 years ago" Brooksburg was known for the best ham sandwiches available," and the Indian-Kentuck Creek for its good fishing. Chances are those sandwiches, the fishing of days past and Brooksburg of an early time would be discussed throughout the "Spring Fling."

* * *

A map shows a road leading northwest out of Brooksburg to a community called Manville. The road is narrow as it follows the Indian-Kentuck Creek valley. Cows graze on the steep slopes beyond the lowlands where a hot bed, probably for tobacco plants, is still covered.

The sides of the winding road are shored with crushed-stone rip-rap before it crosses the creek, then narrows almost to a single lane as we meander through the hills of southeastern Jefferson County. Houses built on hills have great views and solitude, out here in peaceful serenity.

We do not find Manville. Somewhere we have made a wrong turn and are headed east, we think, toward Moorefield, which is on Ind. 129 out of Vevay. The road rises onto the crest of a hill, then follows a ridge high above most other areas on the horizon. We can see dense woods for miles and look down from the road to the valleys below.

A log cabin is being rebuilt, an old pump kept out front, for effect, for there now is piped water available in the area. A chimney, all that is left of an old homestead, is fenced in, probably a sentimental reminder of an earlier time.

Again, we tell ourselves we are on the way to Moorefield. But we aren't sure. The wooded areas disappear. We are on a plateau dotted with an occasional farm home where bird houses hang from trees. Phlox grows on the sides of banks. Then we spot the Moorefield Macadenia Baptist Church. There is no Moorefield, the town, in sight. A steep hill, its banks laced with wildflowers, winds into another valley to accompany a creek before it crosses through a culvert.

We have been seeking "Backroads Indiana," and we have found it. We have crossed into Switzerland county, but the roads are not marked, and we still are in search of Moorefield. The countryside, though, is showing signs of humanity other than our own. A man uses a gasoline-powered weed-eater to cut grass at 8 a.m. A black cat starts across the road. Our luck holds. He turns back.

We flag down a farmer and his wife who are headed toward us in a red Chevy pickup. We ask them for directions. Thanks to them, we will find Moorefield.

* * *

Pristine Chapman, back in Vevay, has told us Burma Shave Company has granted permission to the Switzerland County Welcome Center to use its old road signs. We spot one on Ind. 129 as we drive toward Moorefield: "A Miss . . . A Car . . . A Curve . . . He Kissed the Miss . . . Missed the Curve . . . Burma Shave."

# Moorefield
## Ice Cream Social

Apple trees are in bloom in Moorefield, a town that, except for a few houses on secondary streets, is built along Ind. 129.

Tractors at the Claas farm equipment dealership are parked facing the highway as if they are about to race at the drop of a green flag. The Moorefield Community Fire Department offers first-aid classes to which the public is invited to participate. Volunteers sponsor an old-fashioned ice cream social each July to raise funds to support the department.

Bennett's garage is closed. So is Miller's general store, even though a sign says "Open 7 a.m." The liars' bench out front is vacant, waiting for tales to be spun. There is no post office in town.

\* \* \*

The community of Pleasant is north on Ind. 129 at the Ind. 250 junction in northern Switzerland County. It has about a dozen houses, a feed mill and a convenience store where a few cars are parked out front.

\* \* \*

We drive east on Ind. 250 past well-maintained farms in this area of Switzerland County that has leveled out beyond the hills to the south. Bennington is a mile or so south of Ind. 250, a country town with a post office where a rural carrier is dropping off mail to be distributed. It is early, and no one from any of the fifteen homes in town has arrived at the post office to pick up his or her bills, catalogues and letters.

Houses are neat, lawns manicured, except for a camper shell left in front of an unpainted garage. The general store is out of business, but the United Methodist Church remains as a place of worship.

As we drive back north out of town we slow to appreciate a picture-book farm with a grain elevator and a number of storage bins. The driver behind, a bit miffed at our speed, zips around us with a burst of speed. He has things to do, places to go on this Saturday morning.

\* \* \*

We drive north on Pleasant Grove Road through the hamlet of Avonburg, notice only a few houses, no one outdoors. The road continues to Ind. 129.

# Cross Plains

## Directions in Detail

Cross Plains is more than a cross roads, it's a busy little country town at the southeast edge of Ripley County. The Cross Plains feed mill is no longer in operation, but Otter's Gas and food mart, "sandwiches, hand-dipped ice cream, deli-made sandwiches," is open for business.

"Cross Plains State Bank since 1906," a sign proclaims. A greeting, "Happy Birthday Steve Chandler," is at Best Buys Grocery. This is a small town. It's hard to keep any secrets, even a person's date of birth.

We spot an historical marker: "Buchanan Station. Fort built in May 1813 by the George Buchanan family as a defense against the Indians. A replica of the original block house was erected on the same site and was dedicated on August 26, 1927."

Two men notice we are reading the marker and offer to help us find Buchanan Station. They are Harold Wilson and his uncle, Elmer Wilson. Harold is wearing a blue shirt with a "Seagram's" label. We learn he works at Seagram's Distillery in Lawrenceburg.

Elmer is retired. He's wearing a pair of Duck Head bib overalls and a Cincinnati Reds cap. They are friendly, helpful, eager to expand our knowledge of Buchanan Station. We listen as they give directions:

**Elmer:** "It's down in a field. Just an old square block building."

We explain that if that's all there is there, we may not bother. After all, it is six miles to the site, the sign indicates.

**Harold:** "It's a little block building. You'd miss it if you weren't looking for it. What road is that on?" he asks his uncle, then adds, "Do you go by the Waddle farm?

Elmer replies, "No, you go to county line."

**Harold:** "That's a gravel road, ain't it?"

**Elmer:** "Well, when you get to the county line you turn to the right and take the gravel road on around."

**Harold:** "I've been down there a thousand times and I forget just how you get there. Or what road that's on."

We say again we probably won't go to Buchanan Station.

**Elmer:** "It's on the county line road."

**Harold,** looking at uncle Elmer: "They'd have to go down there before they get to Jimmy Lanham's . . . ?"

**Elmer:** "You wouldn't go plumb down to Jimmy's."

**Harold:** "You wouldn't go down to Jimmy's?"

**Elmer:** "No."

**Harold:** "Oh, you turn there at Waddle's?"

**Elmer:** "No, go on past Waddle's on down to County Line Road.

**Harold:** "I mean you go on that road past Waddle's. Go on past Waddle's and hit that other blacktop and turn to the left, or rather the gravel to the left."

**Elmer:** "No, you go to county line, go to the right and keep follerin' it around."

We tell him again that if there isn't much there, it may not be worth the time or the effort.

**Elmer:** "There ain't much there."

**Harold:** "It'll be on the left up on the bank near a little old brick building."

**Elmer:** "Of course, there is a graveyard on the right."

**Harold:** "Find the graveyard on the right. A block back from the graveyard on the left is Buchanan Station."

They tell us again there isn't much there. They have us convinced. Besides we don't know where Jimmy Lanham lives or where the Waddle place is.

We talk with the two about mushrooms. "Haven't had time to look," Harold answers, not with helping Uncle Elmer, working at Seagram's, attending an asbestos school in Indianapolis and selling a farm near Cross Plains.

Harold is helping his uncle run water into his house. It is the rainy season and conditions aren't too good. "The trench is full of water and the sides have caved in. If you drive back past here in a few hours, you'll see us covered with mud," Harold explains.

Elmer's house is a small frame bungalow which has depended on a cistern and a pump for water. Now he and Harold are hooking onto the rural water line that runs past the house. "I told him if he put the water in, his worries about a pump and a water supply would be over," Harold says as he looks toward his aging uncle.

Harold lives in Dillsboro, not too far from his job with Seagram's. He commuted from Cross Plains for a time, then lived in Greendale for a while. "That was closer to my work, but I didn't like it there. Had two houses there and sold them. That place is the most overrated spot I was ever in," he says of the community just outside Lawrenceburg.

The sun is drying the moisture from the trench for the water line. It is time to work, nephew for uncle. When you are family in "Backroads Indiana" you help each other. Harold and Elmer are two good men. If we had our work boots and overalls, we would offer to help.

* * *

We drive north on Ind. 129, then take Ind. 62 east to Friendship.

# Friendship

## IN OTHERS' SHOES

At first glance, Friendship appears to be a town out of the past, nestled as it is in the Laughery Creek valley. Ind. 62 winds along the stream before it turns past the Friendship Grocery and General Store, antique and gift shops, Whitey's Auto Shop and Garage, a bank, the post office, tavern and restaurant and a few other businesses. Cars line the street in the shopping area on this Saturday morning.

Friendship is a resort town of sorts. It is the home of the National Muzzle Loading Rifle Association, which sponsors the eight-day National Muzzle Loading Rifle National Shoot in mid-June and a fall shoot in mid- September. Those are times when thousands of visitors crowd into the valley, fill the recreational vehicles park and campgrounds and bring vendors to fill a ten-acre lot with flea-market items.

It is estimated that between ten and twenty thousand people come through the valley for the shoots. The worldwide association has 22,000 members and has attracted visitors from almost every state and many foreign nations.

We enter the Friendship Grocery and meet Raymond West. He's helping his son, Doug, who owns the store. Raymond is congenial, eager to talk between serving customers, for the store is doing a good business at this early hour.

The building has been a store since the 1880s, and West recalls the days when it sent out a huckster wagon to deliver supplies to farms. The upstairs, now an apartment rental, was once a dry goods and apparel shop.

West was "born and raised" on a farm about three miles west of here. "We still have the farm, which my grandfather first acquired," he says. My dad had it, now my sister and I own it, so it has been in the family for three generations. We rent out the land. She lives on the farm and I live here in town.

Raymond left the farm for the same reason a lot of other youths did in the '40s and '50s. It wasn't big enough to support two families, so he became an over-the-road driver for Roadway out of Cincinnati, while continuing to live in Friendship.

"Doug bought the store a little over a year ago," he explains. Unlike most young people, Doug West knew what he wanted to do early in life, rushing home from school one afternoon when he was 15 to say he wanted to go into distributive education. "I want to buy and sell," he told his mother.

He took classes at the career center at nearby Versailles, was given a job with the Jay C Stores while still a student, and stayed with the food chain for 18 years before taking over his own business in Friendship.

Doug is busy with customers, but Raymond takes time to pour his visitors coffee and join them at a round table that is a community gathering center.

"I have a daughter, too," he says. "Her name is Joan. She married a farmer and they live at Elrod, but she is a bookkeeper down at the rifle range here in town."

He pauses to greet a customer: "Hi, Porter." It's a small town, and he knows all the customers, except for strangers, who don't stay that way long.

He talks a while about the primitive campgrounds up the road, then greets another customer, "Hi, Louise." Phil Dyer comes into the store, pours himself a cup of coffee and joins us at the table. Every town needs a place where folks feel at home.

Phil is one of the moccasin-making Dyers. He and his son, Mark, own the "Chief White Eye Moccasin Line." Carl and his wife, Robin, own Carl Dyer's Original Moccasins.

Phil and Carl are brothers. They have separate shops in town; each does a mail-order business that sends shoes around the world. Phil boasts that his moccasins are as "tough as the Indians they are named after." Carl's ads says, "The quality of our moccasins is a direct result of generations of craftsmanship." Neither claim is an exaggeration. Phil and Carl grew up in the shoe business in Yarmouth, Maine, then moved to Lynn, Massachusetts, before coming to Friendship. Their father made the boots Charles Lindbergh wore on his Trans-Atlantic flight in 1927.

Phil talks about himself, about the golf shoes he made for President Dwight Eisenhower and then Vice President Richard Nixon back in the 1950s. They didn't know who made them, but Phil did, and he's proud of that.

He's friendly, expressive, eager to show a visitor his little shop next door to the general store. "Try on a pair of the moccasins there," he says while digging out the right size Chief White Eye T-shirts to give to his guests.

He has adjusted to life in Friendship since his wife died, and he has grown to like the town. "A nice little community," he calls it. "Oh, I go back to Lynn often. I have a son living there." But Friendship is home now. And no one will be an outsider as long as folks like Raymond and Doug West or Phil Dyer are around.

POSTSCRIPT: *Raymond West suggests we return in June for the national shoot. We do, a day after a flood has swept down Laughery Creek, threatening the flea-market stands and doing some damage. The noise of the guns, fired by men and women in clothing of more than a century ago, echo across the hills. It is a chance to see weapons that captured a nation being fired in peace at targets and skeet.*

\* \* \*

Ind. 62 continues to follow Laughery Creek east out of Friendship, past the campgrounds and shooting ranges, around the curves. Ripley County ends and we are back in Dearborn County.

Farmers Retreat is another town that once was but isn't any more. A few houses, some rather new, are along the road. Except for a man mowing grass, another working in his garden, there is little activity.

A nice playground is off the road near St. John's Lutheran Church. A bridge is being rebuilt over a creek at the northeast end of town near a marker that notes "Hayes Brand Mill. Constructed 1835, operated until 1946. Destroyed by fire." The marker was erected by the Farmers Retreat-Quercus Grove Historical Society. Folks in small towns don't forget the people and things that shaped the past and help guide the future.

# Dillsboro
## IT'S IN THE WATER

Ind. 62 ends its long, winding course across the bottom of Indiana at Dillsboro, a town of 1,200 residents just south of U.S. 50. It's not a backroads town, but it has maintained the character of its Italianate, Queen Anne, Free Classic, Carpenter Builder and Gothic Revival style homes. High above the Laughery and South Hogan Creek valleys, Dillsboro was settled in the early 1800s and had a post office by 1828 when the first United Methodist Church was built on the site where a newer version now stands.

The town had a brief fling with fame in the early 1900s when drillers found mineral water, which was said to have medicinal value. The Dillsboro Sanitarium Company erected a "hospital" for up to 75 persons who sought cures through nature's so-called elixir.

# Milan
## AND ITS MIRACLE

We stop off Ind. 101 at Milan, population 1,500, for lunch and meet Mary Tuttle who, with her husband, Charles, owns the *Southeastern Indiana News*. It is a free newspaper distributed over all of Dearborn and Ripley counties and in parts of other Indiana and Ohio counties.

Mary is a teacher at North Dearborn elementary school. Charles is a computer programmer for Hillenbrand Industries in Batesville. Unlike most Milan residents, Mary prefers to talk about Milan native Stephen Harding, rather than about the 1954 Milan state basketball champs. Harding was a Ripley County resident who briefly served as governor of the Territory of Utah during the Civil War.

The 1954 basketball team pulled off the Miracle of Milan, defeating big city Muncie Central, 32-30, on a shot by Bobby Plump as time ran out. The episode was the basis for the 1980s movie classic, "Hoosiers."

\* \* \*

We take Ind. 350 west off Ind. 101 through Pierceville. It was the home town of Bob Plump, who has since become one of Indiana's basketball legends. Plump played for Butler University, then became a success in the insurance business in Indianapolis.

Pierceville is a tiny community. What appears to have been an old general store is closed. The only business is Bergman's Phillips 66 out on the highway.

\* \* \*

Delaware is a Ripley County village, not a state, at Ind. 350 and Ind. 129, but like the state, it's small and compact. A general store is open, the Delaware Township fire department has a good-size headquarters, and residents are up and about on this Saturday morning.

\* \* \*

Lookout is just a wide spot at the crossroads where Ind. 129 and Ind. 48 intersect north of Delaware. It so small it might be called Lookout-For-You-Might-Miss-It. Some maps, including the one listed as "official" by the State Highway Department, do not show it.

What residents there are owe a thanks to Rand McNally for placing it on the Indiana map in its 1992 Atlas.

\* \* \*

We drive west on Ind. 48 from Ind. 129 to Ind. 229 to a place marked Ballstown. We do not learn why it got its name and we aren't sure we want to know. It is another wide spot in the road, with a barn, two houses, two curves and a postal carrier, who stops to slide mail into the rural boxes.

This is good farm land, though. Right outside Ballstown is a big dairy operation, a farm with five tall silos.

We have come from Indiana's hills back into its farms. It is a state of variation, one area unlike another, each with its own personality. Byways that wind and curl have become section lines, one each mile, as true as a surveyor's eye. Fields that were open patches between woodlands now are restrained only by fences and roads.

*Trip 26*
# NO-RUSH TO RUSHVILLE

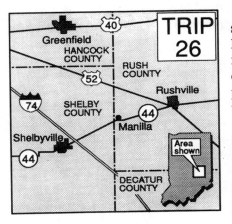

Farming is to Rush County what scenery is to Crawford, Harrison and Dearborn counties. The land is mostly flat, its fields rich, its crops bountiful except in droughts. An estimated 90 percent of the land is used for agriculture.

Unlike counties to the south where farms often are patches in nature's quilt work, fields here extend toward the horizon, contained by property lines, not creeks and hills. Despite the differences, back roads town are similar, each struggling to survive in an era when mobility sometimes overruns stability.

## Manilla
### ON THE ROAD

Manilla is a town on the move, leaving what was once its business center down by the old railroad for the highway traffic of Ind. 44. The Penn Central Railroad that once ran through town is gone, without leaving any tracks.

Buildings are all closed at Main and Cross streets in the old heart of town. Four stores that once occupied one of the bigger buildings are closed. An old grain elevator is no longer in operation, its grain dust replaced by rust.

The only business on the block is the Schutt blacksmith shop. A Farmall tractor with a rake attached is out front. The shop is busy, a godsend for farmers who need parts welded or repaired and other work done on this Friday in the midst of the planting season.

Manilla, as flat as some towns are hilly, appears to have been a bustling town. It no longer is a trading center, but it is home for those who like the quiet pace of small towns. Streets are well-paved, homes clean and neat, yards in bloom with spring flowers. Vegetables grow in weedless gardens.

The post office, the Rushville National Bank branch, most of what business there is, is out near the highway, leaving the old downtown to the ghosts of an earlier time.

# Homer
## MADE TO ORDER

As long as there is "The Sampler," there likely will be a Homer. Just east of Manilla on Ind. 44, Homer is another farm town but better known because of "The Sampler" store, an outlet for cherry furniture, which management says is "not far-out, not fattening, nor free."

The Sampler's address since 1946 has been 1 West Railroad Street. And it boasts, "In an era of assembly-line plastics production, we still build each piece according to individual customers' preferences." Clerks insist that visitors tour the store's sprawling showroom, even offer coffee to browsers.

Homer, a community of fifty to sixty houses, has a post office and a few other businesses, but except for The Sampler, other stores along the abandoned railroad are closed. A grain elevator is quiet, a monument to busier days.

\* \* \*

Cemetery Road, a map shows, leads from Homer to a place called Gowdy. It is a good chance to see the vastness of the farms in western Rush County. Three tractors are at work in one field, preparing the ground, seeding the grain. Some corn, planted before the rains delayed work, is up and growing.

Gowdy turns out to be a crossroads hamlet at Rush County Roads 650 South and 640 West. An outhouse remains on the wooded grounds of an abandoned church. A quick count shows about twenty houses in the rural farm town which has no businesses.

Road 640 West continues south across Ind. 244 at a sign that indicates Moscow is just a mile away.

# Moscow
## NEWCOMER'S VIEW

"Children at Play," a sign warns as the county road rounds a curve into Moscow. Much of Moscow's charm, it is soon apparent, centers around an old covered bridge over Flatrock River. It is narrow, one-lane, 330 feet across, with a three-ton load limit. "Built in 1886 by Emmett L. Kennedy," a notation on the gable says.

We cross the bridge, the planks clattering against the supports as we ease across. The bridge provides a safe crossing and we return through the passage that has tied a community to its neighbors across the river for more than a century now.

We wonder what life was like when the bridge was new and Moscow was a busier place. We are not alone in our curiosity. A Rush County Consolidated School System bus pulls up, and a load of grade school students departs to look over the historic span.

It is the bridge that provides the community its reason for an annual festival each June.

The old three-story brick Moscow school built in 1912 when Charles Owen was trustee is now a residence.

We drive to the southwest edge of town and see the town park, already being prepared for the town's Bridge Festival. A cemetery, neatly mowed, and graves decorated, is across the road near the Moscow Christian Church.

We stop to talk to a man who has just walked out in his yard. "Is this "Mos-co" or "Mos-cow?," we ask.

"I pronounce it Mos-cow," he says. "But people claim that's not correct. But I haven't lived here too long. The people who live here call it Mos-co." The man says his name is "Daum, Herb Daum." He's friendly, soft-spoken, as he talks about the town where he has settled to be nearer his children.

"You make four right turns and you are out of town," he says. "Over there is the carriage business. Bill Schrock is the fellow that runs it and rebuilds carriages. He also has a bakery. He's Amish.

"And straight through there is a fellow, James Wendell, who does mill work, fancy trim. Not just plain boards. "And up on the hill around the bend is another mill operation. That's about all we have."

Daum may not be a native of the state, but he has picked up some Hoosier humor. "A store?" he repeats a question. "Yeah! We got two or three coin-operated soft drink machines out in front of one building down here."

It is true. There are vending machines, but no store, no service station. "People here still talk about the grocery that was here, and about the old mill, even about a toll gate that was on the road," he relates.

Daum has spent the last 30 months remodeling a house on a corner lot. He's not sure, though, how much he likes the town. "I don't know," he says. "We have to drive 12 to 14 miles to a store each way. I came from Iowa. We have children scattered all over and this saves us about a day's trip each way when we visit them."

He isn't accustomed to small lots. "This is the smallest place we've ever had to live. We had 15 acres before to roam around on. The nearest neighbor was about a mile and a half away."

He does say Moscow is a quiet town where he feels safe leaving his tools in an unlocked area of the house, explaining, "I don't have to worry about them. Of course if anyone sees someone messing around, there generally is a gun that comes out to stop that. If there would be any theft or anything like that it would be from somebody not familiar with the area. You'd have to be stupid to be a thief to start with and you wouldn't steal locally if you were. That's a darn good way of getting caught."

"Mos-co" or "Moscow," Herb Daum seems to have a philosophy that fits in well in town.

# Milroy
## ON STAGE

A woman pulls her granddaughter in a red wagon along Ind. 244 in the center of Milroy, a community of nine hundred residents in south central Rush County. Homes and churches are well-maintained. It is obvious people here are family oriented and take pride in their community.

A church, no longer in use, is now the Pleasant Street Playhouse, "home of the Rush County Players." The Anderson Township community building is in town. Milroy is a rural town with a branch bank, a post office, frozen food lockers and other businesses.

The Old Milroy High School where the basketball team was called the Cardinals is now a grade school. High school students now attend Rushville Consolidated High.

\* \* \*

Ind. 244 continues straight as a surveyor's sight across southern Rush County into Richland, a rural hamlet of fifteen houses on the highway.

A woman mows the thick grass of May with a new mower. Down the road, an antique manure-spreader sits beside a nice home. To the east, a board fence painted white lines the road, a big house back off the road, a horse barn in the distance. It is hay harvest, and a farm truck with bales of the first cutting of alfalfa slows traffic.

Farms are large. Silos and storage bins dot the horizons. A farm owner—his fields too wet to work—uses a John Deere tractor to mow the highway right-of-way along the road. Hoosiers sometimes do not expect government to do what they themselves can do.

\* \* \*

Rush County ends, Franklin, the seventh county established in the old Indiana Territory, begins.

# Andersonville
## THE POINT IS . . .

A restaurant and service station at the triangle where Ind. 244 meets U.S. 52 seems to be the center of activity in Andersonville. A station attendant takes a breather between serving customers at the gas pumps to hold his granddaughter, who has just "graduated" earlier in the morning from kindergarten at Laurel. Grandfather is proud of her and she of him.

Customers in the restaurant know each other, exchange comments and taunts. A pickup out front is loaded with flea-market goods, available to anyone who stops and finds something he or she wants.

The restaurant, "The Point," was an even busier place when U.S. 52 was the main route between Indianapolis and Cincinnati. But much of the traffic has moved south to I-74.

* * *

We have moved to an area where the great glaciers of the Ice Age stopped, thawed, leaving the debris ahead to become hills and valleys. The road declines into the Whitewater River valley, which leads north on Ind. 121 to Laurel.

# Laurel
## . . . OF THE VALLEY

A new elementary school is along Ind. 121 at the south edge of Laurel. It will be, we will soon learn, about the only thing new in the historic town. It is a town off the beaten path, remote enough to keep its charm. "Welcome to Laurel, Population 549, Have a Nice Visit," a sign says.

Chances are anyone who doesn't have a nice visit doesn't care for history. It's a town that takes pride in itself and its importance to the birth of the state. It is where the Whetzel Trace began on its way to Waverly in Morgan County, a 60-mile path blazed by Jacob Whetzel and his son Syrus, 18. It was the route most settlers took in the early 1800s on their way from southeast Indiana into central Indiana.

A historical marker notes that Edward Toner operated Toner's Tavern, from which pioneers, perhaps bolstered by booze, started west on the Whetzel Trace to the new purchase in central Indiana between 1816 and 1823.

The Laurel Feeder Dam, which diverted water into the old Whitewater Canal from the river, can still be seen a mile south of town. The village prospered after the canal opened in 1843, becoming a shipping point and a stone-quarrying center. The prosperity was short-lived. Canals succumbed to railroads, and although a rail line went through town, growth and business declined.

It isn't size or business, though, that makes Laurel attractive. It is its old homes . . . and the spirit of its residents. For example, the three-story brick Laurel Collegiate High School, completed in 1852 and used as a school until 1915, still stands. The Masons, who helped finance its completion, still meet there.

The best view of the community is from the old Laurel cemetery high on a hill at the north edge, offering a wide view of the Whitewater River valley to the east, the rugged hills in other directions. Flags fly on graves of veterans as Memorial Day nears. A water tower across the road reaches skyward from a position that assures gravity flow to the town below.

A bandstand sits atop a mound built by Indians as an observation point before the arrival of white men.

There are historic residences to observe, like the circa-1840 Federal-style homes on Conwell Street and the northwest corner of Baltimore and Washington, and what was the White Hall Tavern at the northeast corner of Baltimore and Franklin.

The old, white Italianate Laurel Hotel, Restaurant and Bar, circa 1850, is worth a stop, too. It is said to be the only building in town that faces directly east. It's a good place for lunch or dinner, and it is where passengers sometimes come from Connersville aboard the Whitewater Valley Rail Road to dine.

Guests can order pan-fried chicken, steaks, or seafood from three family dining areas or the bar. Rooms may no longer be rented at the hotel, but there is at least one bed-and-breakfast in town for those who want to stay overnight.

Along the railroad, a sign—"Laurel Welcome You—Have a Nice Day."—greets visitors who come by rail. "The train to dinner" runs from Connersville the first and third Fridays of each month from April through November.

Laurel is a mixture of the new and the old. At least one double-wide manufactured home offers a sharp contrast to the landmarks, blending the past with the present.

Clothes hang from lines at one home. Those who prefer can do their clothes at the Washing Well, a coin-operated laundry.

The old Laurel High School, once the home of the Laurel Panthers, is reopening as the Town Hall, police headquarters, senior citizens center and community center. Norman L. Dant, Sr., president of the five-member Town Council, is busy preparing for an afternoon open house where residents see the changes that have been made in the building.

He leads the way through the police station, a town council meeting room, his office as the Town Council president, the clerk-treasurer's office, two big rooms for Head Start classes, a meeting room where noon meals are served for senior citizens, the gymnasium which can be rented, and the cafeteria which is available for parties, weddings and receptions.

Dant explains the town took over the building in February, 1993, under a five-year agreement with the Franklin County School Corporation. If all goes well, the building will be deeded to the town after that five-year period.

An annual Pioneer Days celebration will start in September 1994 in an attempt to market the town as a tourism attraction. Pride helped build Laurel. Pride among its people may help to sustain it.

Scott Jackson exemplifies that pride. He has just finished lunch at the senior citizens cafeteria. He knows as much about Laurel as anyone, runs the town's waste water treatment plant and the water system in town.

He grew up in Switzerland County, moved to Detroit, then came to Laurel at the start of World War II and worked as an aviation inspector for the Army and Navy in a plant at nearby Connersville that made wings and component parts. Now 77, he is working for the town, as usual, even though the funeral for the oldest of his six daughters was yesterday. "We lost her to cancer," he says softly.

"At one time we had seven taverns, six hotels, doctors' offices," he relates. "That was back in the heyday when the stone business was big. It is a variety of dolomite stone only located in two parts of the U.S. One is in Laurel, Maryland, one in Laurel, Indiana. "That's where the town got its name, from Laurel, Maryland." (Other versions say Laurel was named by the town founder, James Conwell, who came from Laurel, Delaware.)

Jackson talks about the Indian mound up on the hill and shows his concern for how the town looks. "We have to remove those satellite dishes for cable television from in front of the mounds. They [the dishes] are unsightly and the historical society wants to get them off the hill."

Scott Jackson doesn't like other things he sees. "The town has deteriorated. The population has dropped fifty percent, maybe sixty percent, since I came here. We have the same trouble all of Indiana has . . . migrations to other locations where opportunities are better. Indiana is not a progressive state any way you look at it," he insists. "We have spent fifty winters in Florida, so we know we can gauge what other states are doing. Truthfully, this is an economic backwash."

Another Hoosier hates to hear that kind of talk, but agrees it may be true. Jackson continues: "We have real economic troubles in a town like this. All our federal funds have dried up. Revenue-sharing, which was the most necessary thing we ever had, is gone. It left us without any income [except property taxes] and we run deficits now." It is not an unusual complaint.

"When the federal CETA [Comprehensive Employment and Training Act] program was in here—back in the '70s and '80s—I was supervisor for that," he continues. "We worked 22 people here in Laurel under that program and we had the town in really nice shape.

"All we have now is the Green Thumb, sponsored by the U.S. Department of Interior. There are five of us who work in that program under supervision of the town board. We do whatever we can to help, like converting the school to the town center."

Someone mentions that the town has character. Jackson smiles, looks at us and says, "If you had more time, I'd show you the characters this town has."

He claims Laurel once had a reputation as the worst town in Indiana, crimewise. "This was the meanest town there was. If we didn't have two murders a week, we were having a poor week. That was about forty years ago. This was a mean town," he repeats.

So what happened to change it? "Bad characters moved. People don't have enough get-up-and-go now to be mean," he says, jokingly, we think, then adds. "We have a package liquor store, a tavern and the hotel where drinks are sold. That's plenty for a town of 540."

That's Scott Jackson, plain speaker. And that's Laurel, still a hidden jewel even with the flaws he has exposed.

* * *

We drive back south to U.S. 52, east to Ind. 229 and continue south toward Peppertown. Few roads have been more winding than Ind. 229. Warning signs are common, limiting speeds to 15, 20, 25 mph, S and 90-degree turns are frequent, as we move through this area of Franklin County. Reach an open space and the speed sometimes soars up to 40 mph.

A great place for a road race, we think, if any drivers had the nerve to negotiate these roads.

# Peppertown
## German Influence

A two-store building, walled with native stone from area quarries, is being restored in Peppertown, a hamlet of a few homes on Ind. 229. It is just one of the stone structures that reflect the stone masonry craftsmanship of an earlier time.

Peppertown, platted in 1859, was named for August Pepper, a German immigrant and shopkeeper. The German influence remains, for there is a Lutheran Church, but no Methodist or Baptist churches as in most other rural Indiana villages. An old store has been converted to a residence, as has a brick school. An old cemetery on both sides of a county road just outside town depends on contributions for maintenance. A note reads, "Peppertown

Cemetery Association welcomes all visitors and would appreciate any contributions. If you would like to make a donation for the care of the cemetery send it to . . ."

* * *

Ind. 229 becomes less winding toward Oldenburg and a 50 mph speed limit is permitted before a 30 mph warning.

# Oldenburg
## SPIRES AND STRASSES

Three spires rise majestically over the hills on which Oldenburg is built. "The City of Spires" it calls itself. It actually isn't a city, but a village of 770 residents that has retained its European character.

The Oldenburg Freudenfest in mid-July promotes an annual "Volksmarch." On the menu are "Brats, metts, Reuben sandwiches, Sauerkraut Balls." And entertainment like "Die Dopple Adler Musikanten German Band." Plus the 16th "prestigious running" of the 6K called the "Oldenburg Lauf." Advertisements promise that all proceeds will be used for "the beautification and enrichment of Oldenburg."

Named after a province in Germany, Oldenburg has a combination of shops, masonry homes of stone and brick and framed homes with clapboard siding.

Streets carry bilingual names, such as the German Wasserstrasse, with the English name Water under it; Weinstrasse (Washington Street), Hauptstrasse (Main Street).

The town's spiritual center is the Holy Family Church at Haupt and Perlenstrasse (Pearl Street) built in 1862 when Austrian-born Rev. Franz Josef Rudolph was pastor of Oldenburg. Its spire rises 187 feet above the street. Father Rudolph, who came to Oldenburg in 1844, died in 1866 and is buried beneath the Holy Family Sanctuary.

The Holy Family Parish Cemetery and the Immaculate Conception Convent Cemetery are at the north end of Pearl Street. Across the street from Holy Family is the Immaculate Conception Convent, the motherhouse of the Sisters of the Third Order of St. Francis, founded by Vienna-born Mother Theresa Hackelmeier in 1851. The Franciscan Sisters serve schools, hospitals, parishes and missions. The academy for girls in Oldenburg was founded in 1885 and has managed to remain open despite falling enrollment and financial hardships.

A number of other places are worth noting. Hackman's general store, erected in 1861, features ornate tin work, fashioned by the Prussian-born master tinsmith, Casper Gaupel. The Sisters' Cow Barn, a big structure at the south entrance to Oldenburg, once was operated by members of the convent.

It is a busy town, with a lumber company, garage, stores, bank and, of course, as with all German villages, taverns. Koch's Brau Haus offers German dinners the first Tuesday of each month.

Anyone who is not German, or doesn't care for German food, can always stop at Wagner's Village Inn which specializes in fried chicken.

# Enochsburg
## AND ROSSBURG

To reach Enochsburg, it is first necessary to locate Rossburg. And to locate Rossburg, a motorist must first look for the New Point exit off I-74. Rossburg is to the west off the county road that leads north off the exit. Enochsburg is about five miles to the east on Base Road across Decatur County to the Franklin County line.

Enochsburg, too, has a spire to lead wayward travelers to what is another German settlement where the hills level out into a plateau overlooking Franklin and Decatur counties. Again it is a church, this one St. John's Evangelist Catholic Church, around which the community revolves. It has two cemeteries, one behind the church with older tombstones, a newer one across the street.

The few houses that are in Enochsburg, are clean and neat. There is no junk in sight.

The Fireside Inn, a popular dining spot in the area, bills itself as the "Home of the Crisp Chic." It is not open yet on this Friday afternoon.

\* \* \*

Only a few houses are in Rossburg. "Welcome to Rossburg, home of North Branch Golf Course and Gauck Concrete Company," a sign says.

# St. Maurice
## IT'S UP AHEAD

A Decatur County road winds north from Rossburg toward St. Maurice. It is a longer drive than expected and we are beginning to think we are again in nowhere land. But another church spire rises in the distance and we know we are approaching St. Maurice.

A playground is in the center of the tiny farm community where the side of one of the few streets is dominated by the St. Maurice Catholic Church and its school. A Model-T Ford is being restored at one of the few houses in the neat, orderly community. The Kramer Feed Mill at the edge of town is in operation, and two or three area farmers have stopped to talk.

\* \* \*

It has been a good day. We have seen the influences of centuries past on the towns of today, old-world traditions preserved, evidence that disciplines of life did not die with the pioneers who carved out the future in backroads Indiana.

## *Trip 27*
# "TEN O'CLOCK" TRIP

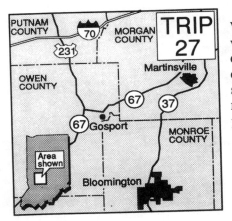

Early morning fog hangs over the West Fork of the White River as it weaves through Morgan County south of Martinsville. A school year is ending, and fresh-scrubbed youngsters, eager to get on with the business of life, wait along Ind. 67 for the yellow school bus.

## Gosport
### Ten O'Clock Shadow

Motorists anxious to reach their destination, focused on the road ahead, miss the pleasures of visiting towns off highways, talking with folks less rushed on the trip through life. On Ind. 67, few drivers heed the "Welcome to Historic Gosport—Established in 1829" sign; most don't bother to drive into the old town and to learn its history.

They may never know Gosport sits on the 10 O'Clock Treaty Line, so called because it parallels the shadow cast by a spear stuck in the ground at 10 a.m. on September 20, 1809. Under the treaty between William Henry

Harrison and Chief Little Turtle, the U.S. acquired almost two million acres of land at a cost of three cents an acre.

Gosport thrived in the days when flatboats plied White River and, later, trains ran often on the Monon Railroad (now the CSX). But the population dwindled over the decades, falling to 729 in 1980. There has been some growth since, reaching 820 in 1990.

Much of the decline came in the mid-1900s after a covered bridge burned, cutting off a route into town from Monroe County, creating hardships for merchants. Another fire destroyed a popular hardware store, and the high school closed when Owen Valley Consolidated opened.

Gosport's two main employers now are Gosport Manufacturing, "the king of tarpaulins" firm that employees 30 to 35 workers, and the Gosport Nursing Home where 65 employees provide health care. A water tower atop a hill dominates the incorporated town with a three-member town council. A farm service, bank, post office, insurance service, food center, tavern and VFW Hall are in the renovated business district.

Homes and lawns are well-kept, other buildings in good shape. This is a another town where residents take pride in the place they call home.

We go south on 5th Street in Gosport to a sign that points the way to "Stinesville-Ellettsville, State Road 46." We follow the road south, crossing a one-lane, wooden-floor bridge over the railroad. On down the road, a modern span crosses the river. It is a scenic drive, up and down hills, over twisting roads.

# Stinesville
## FRIENDS AND LIARS

Size doesn't bother Stinesville's 250 residents. "Stinesville City Limits," a marker at the edge of the community boasts. Stinesville isn't a city, but a town run by a town council, but if people want to call it a city, let them. No matter. It is yet a place where everyone knows everyone else, where no one remains a stranger long.

Stinesville owes its place on the map to limestone. It is said the first quarry in Indiana was opened nearby in 1827. Stone for the Soldiers and Sailors Monument in Indianapolis came from quarries here. It was the mills that allowed Stinesville to prosper until a fire in 1916 destroyed one of the Hoadley Company stone mills.

A grade school is atop the hill where old Stinesville High overlooked the town until it merged with Ellettsville to form Edgewood in 1965. Names of war veterans are memorialized on a five-sided stone marker in McGlocklin Park on Main Street.

An 1894 limestone building that once housed several businesses is vacant. A two-story section, once was used as "Oolitic Lodge—Instituted in 1891."

It now is the Quarry Lad Store, named after the basketball teams at the old high school. A sign outside asks residents to supply pictures of the town and its residents for display at Pioneer Days in June.

Pamela Bayne is at work in the store she and her husband, James, bought in October, 1992, when Robert Summitt, the owner and town postmaster, took early retirement. The post office, on one side, came with the store, and Pamela became postmaster when ownership changed. She operates both businesses while James works at the Indiana University power plant in nearby Bloomington.

"Bob Summitt left on Friday and I took over on Saturday," she explains. "No training, no anything. They just said, 'here it is.' I'm slowly learning, but there is a lot to it . . . It's interesting," she says of this business of being a merchant and a public servant.

"We've had to do a lot of repairs to the store, but one day, we hope, it will be a nice general store," she says. "We've had to make a lot of changes to please the health officials. They wanted us to tile or linoleum the floor [which is the original tongue-and-groove boards] and we absolutely refused. We did agree to put a little linoleum in the deli area. They [the health officials] saw they weren't going to win, so they let us keep it the way it is for now. But we do plan to sand the floor down."

The century-old building has an upstairs, which may be converted to an antique mall. "A lot of people here are into crafts and it would be nice for them," she explains.

It is a building with a checkered past. The upstairs has been an Oddfellows Hall, an apartment, a Pentecostal church, and was used for classes when the school burned. Mrs. Bayne, called "Pam" by customers, says she has been told the building was once used as a gym. "It has been a dance hall, a theater, probably several other things no one has mentioned. A mortician even used the basement as a place where bodies could be prepared for viewing at homes.

"One former owner," she laughs, "kept live chickens down there. If anyone wanted a chicken, he'd go down, wring its neck, and bring it up."

Pam and James own the building across the street that serves as the town marshal's office. "He wanted a place to store items and supplies and the town didn't have the budget to acquire the space," she explains.

The Bayneses' love for the town came with their own romance. Pam grew up on a farm in Owen County. James was from Ellettsville and became enamored with Stinesville on trips through town en route to Gosport when he was in the insurance business. He brought Pam to Stinesville when they were dating and told her, "If you marry me this is where you are going to live." They moved to town 17 years ago.

A few customers pass through the store, some stopping to pour themselves coffee from the pot. It is before 9 a.m. and Pam says the "liars' club" will start gathering soon. "This entire area will be filled with guys who grew up around here," she explains. "They have breakfast and talk about the silly things they used to do to aggravate the town marshals. They talk about the old limestone mills, who ran them, who worked in them, who got killed in them. You learn a lot even though it is hard to soak it all in."

A man walks in and offers a friendly, "Hi, Pam." She returns the greeting and says, "Here's one of the liars now."

The man smiles, says, "Yeah, this is one of them. Carl Kale," the man says, extending his hand. He's open, likable, easy to talk with, a man who adds "friendly" to small towns.

"I graduated from Stinesville High School and lived in Beanblossom Township [where Stinesville is] all my life," he says, "until about 1964 when I moved across the line over into Richland Township and worked at RCA in Bloomington for 34 years.

"I told a buddy of mine when I retired that I was going to start hanging out in Stinesville again. So that's what I do. I come here about every morning and usually stay until about 11:30."

The place wouldn't be the same without him. And he wouldn't be the same if he couldn't stop in at the Quarry Lad each morning.

He continues, "We were sitting on that wall across the street the other day and two people came up. I said to Al Taylor, 'Al, that looks like Jim Halstead.'"

Carl stops to greet another "liar." "Hi, Norman," he says, before continuing his story.

"Al says, 'You may be right.' So I said, 'Hey, what's your name?' He said, 'Jim Halstead.' I said, 'I'll be a son-of-a-gun.' He [Jim Halstead] graduated from Ellettsville in 1950 and I graduated from Stinesville in 1952. Anyway, I asked Jim whatever happened to his sister, Nancy. He said, 'This is her standing right here.' I used to date Nancy and I hadn't seen her in forty years. She lives in Tampa and Jim lives up near Indianapolis."

Another "liar" sits down at the table. He declines to give his full name. He's not interested in seeing his name in a newspaper or a book. But he, too, is amiable, asks about Kale's son, Tony, who is an announcer at a Spencer radio station. Tony is "the best in the business," Mr. Anonymous says.

The conversation turns to a story in the *Bloomington Herald-Times* the past weekend recalling a trip the 1960 Stinesville graduating class made to New York City. That trip led to a feature, "The Yellow Bus," in *The New Yorker* magazine, which portrayed the class as a group of country kids happy with who they were and unimpressed with the megalopolis. Kale says most of the students still live around Stinesville.

The magazine piece quoted graduate Larry Williams, who wasn't overly impressed with New York City: "Back home, you can do anything you please in your own back yard any time you feel like it, like hootin' and hollerin' or anything. You don't ever get to feel all cooped up." He added, "This place couldn't hold me. I like the privacy of the farm."

The topics change. The conversations at the Quarry Lad continue, endlessly. We talk for a while longer. Pam, Carl and Mr. Nameless bid us farewell, but not before inviting us back for the town's Frontier Days the last weekend in June.

We make a note to return. Stinesville is, we decide, a gem among Indiana's towns. And nobody will complain if, as Larry Williams said back in 1960, you drive out of town and do a bit of hootin' and hollerin'.

* * *

We take a Monroe County road south to Ind. 46, drive east to Ind. 43 and head south across southeastern Owen and eastern Green counties toward Freeman, Whitehall, Hendricksville and Solsberry.

The terrain is a mixture of woodlands and farms, the road straight before becoming winding and hilly north of Freeman, speed limits dropping as low as 30 mph. Owners of a home have posted an appropriate sign—"Uppin Downs"—to describe their place.

A few houses are along the road between the Freeman town-limit signs. Then Ind. 43 continues its snake-like maneuvers south; a 15 mph sign alerts drivers to a turn ahead. It is wise to obey it. Curves, some as sharp as 90 degrees, are common.

A number of houses are along the road in Whitehall. What was once a store is now closed and the lot grown up with brush. A newer store, concrete blocks painted green, gasoline pumps out front, is outside Whitehall.

A new diner at the north edge of Hendricksville is not yet open. Twelve houses and an abandoned store are between the town-limits signs, but a lot more residents are to the south. Chances are that more folks than those in the dozen houses call Hendricksville home.

Mowing crews are on a hill to the south, and what few cars there are ease around the tractors, which isn't as difficult as negotiating double 90-degree turns later.

# Solsberry
## A BOY NAMED TANNER

Ind. 43 passes through a graffiti-littered viaduct under the old Illinois Central—now the Indiana Railroad. It was the Illinois Central railroad that helped shape Solsberry's history, put its name on road maps and train schedules. Trains still roar through town, hauling coal from the mine fields of southwestern Indiana. The depot, though, is gone and trains no longer stop.

The high school, where basketball players were known as the Hornets, exists only in memories. Students now wear the red, black and white of the consolidated Eastern High Thunderbirds.

We enter Yoho's General Store, a weather-worn frame landmark with clapboard siding in need of paint, at the corner where Ind. 43 turns from the east to the south. This is a store with character, a place away from the sterile, squeaky-clean, sanitized supermarkets in bigger towns.

Dwight Yoho and his wife, Pearl, have run the place since back in 1941 when each was 31. They've been partners in marriage, and in business, for more than a half-century. This is no part-time, 40-hour-a-week job. This is a seven-day-a-week, round-the-calendar occupation.

The store is a Greene County landmark, an institution, a community gathering spot. Other businesses have come to Solsberry and closed. The town survived those losses and the demise of the high school. It wouldn't be the same, however, without a place like Yoho's Store to give it an identity.

The store hasn't changed much since the Yohos bought it 52 years ago. Coal buckets are still sold here, and chances are some items have been on the shelf since the couple took over the operation. A customer who looks closely can find anything from a can of soup to a football helmet. A stove still heats the place in winter with wood fires.

The town, though, has changed. "Like everything else," Mr. Yoho says. A working man in a blue-collar town, he's wearing a denim shirt over blue jeans. A "Yoho & Sons" cap sits on his head. It's not unusual for customers to buy a hat or a "Yoho Store" T-shirt, reminders of this store that is a step back in time.

We ask about a cup of coffee. Yoho points to an urn. "Help yourself." We pour into a Styrofoam cup and ask the price. "A quarter," he says looking at the cup, "but fill it up. Sugar and cream back there if you need them."

"Much here in town, now?" Yoho is asked. "Septic tank outfit down here, that's it," he replies. "Except for the Greene County ambulance service and the post office."

Yoho's has stayed in business as other stores have closed. Burch's store across the street, for example, is abandoned, a reminder of the days when Solsberry was a busier place.

An excursion train out of Indianapolis stopped here occasionally just a few years ago, letting its passengers spend some time in the store, but that's changed too. The train has moved to Florida where it can run year-'round.

"We're busy, off and on. We try to keep a little bit of everything," Mr. Yoho says, walking down the counter and returning with a small, old-fashioned Coke bottle. It had been filled in Spain, a notation on the bottle says. The world has found its way to Solsberry.

A man enters the store and proudly announces he's a grandfather again. "Two o'clock this morning. Yeah, she [his daughter] had it before we got up there to the hospital. Another boy, Tanner," he announces. "Oh, my," Mrs. Yoho says.

It is a place where people care about each other. And Yoho's is a good place to spread good news.

# The Viaduct
## MONUMENT TO ENGINEERING

We drive west out of Solsberry over a plank bridge above the railroad, past a saw mill, over a road as rough as a washboard. Our destination: the state's highest trestle, a viaduct just south of a road identified on a Greene County map as Plankeshaw Trail.

We slow down, letting three buzzards pick away at their road kill, the pavement their table. They scatter, but only to a perch on a rolled hay bale barely off the right-of-way. They are in their own way a scavenger service in this area which belongs as much to the animals as to the people.

The trestle near Roads 390 North and 400 East is worth the effort it takes to reach it, still standing almost ninety years after it was built, a monument to the ingenuity of American engineering and labor. Its enormity escapes the eye of a visitor until he walks under it and looks at the huge steel columns which rise to the crossing 157 feet above. The trestle extends 2,295 feet across the Richland Creek valley, its 18 steel columns supported by reinforced concrete pedestals, like icebergs, mostly below the surface, as secure now as when the $1.5 million marvel of its time was built.

The steel work is a popular place for graffiti, for this an isolated spot, far from the constant roar of traffic, away from watchful eyes. Hearts in spray paint link initials of couples, here to remain after many of the romances have faded.

Despite fears of deaths during construction in 1905 and 1906, no lives were lost. Now, in the 1990s, it is still in use, allowing trains with as many as a hundred cars safe passage.

# Tulip
## CARDINAL COUNTRY

We continue west on the Greene County road toward a community called Tulip. The road slices through another viaduct under the railroad, two lanes separated by a divider. Again the sides are marked with graffiti, art work, vulgarities, religious messages, all frozen in time, thoughts for the future.

Along the road, a second story is being added to a basement home. Pre-cut rafters rest in a pile, for times have changed and carpenters no longer need to measure, saw and nail them on site.

A cardinal cutout is on a garage near a nice home. "Tulip Tinker Shop," it says. This is Bloomfield Cardinal Country. The home is a sharp contrast to an abandoned house nearby, its roof collapsed. Another abandoned house is on down the road.

Tulip is more of a community than a town. Only the Tulip Church of God identifies the area. It is of no matter. "Tulip" is a place for its resident to call home.

Another viaduct, this one with creosoted posts, rather than concrete, is just southwest of Tulip. Ind. 157 is ahead, past Morning Glory Farm.

* * *

Ind. 157, linking Bloomfield and Worthington, is not a heavily traveled road, but it is becoming a choice building site for homeowners. It is a road that offers a nice view, a panoramic look to other ridges in the distance. New homes are scattered along the road. A housing development, near the Eastern Heights water tower, is another example of what the availability of water has meant to rural development.

We stop in Bloomfield, population 2,600, buy a county map at the auditor's office in the Greene County Courthouse, and head for a place marked Mineral City. It's easier to find on paper than it is in the pickup.

We take narrow gravel roads east off U.S. 231 until we see a sign that indicates Mineral City and Koleen are ahead. The road, also marked Plankeshaw Trail, is paved and smooth.

# Mineral City
## KOLEEN AND PARK

Mineral City is down in the lowlands where Letzinger Branch meets Plummer Creek. We count nine houses, five of which arrived on wheels. A United Methodist church is in town, but there are no businesses.

Koleen is on down the pike, which follows Plummer Creek. It is slightly bigger than Mineral City, has a post office, perhaps ten houses. A place called Park is to the north and we head cross-country in an attempt to find it. We stop for a pony that has escaped from its corral and is walking from side to side, gnawing at the grass in the side ditches. The roads are not marked and driving is more by guess than by design.

Surprise! We arrive in Park, a community of maybe a dozen houses with no businesses. Walnut Creek Church is just to the south. We drive on toward the spot on the map marked "Tanner," passing an old rural school, a junkyard and auto-parts business. We wonder if there is any connection between Tanner the place, and Tanner, the newborn we heard about back in Solsberry.

# Tanner
## AMERICAN BOTTOMS

We cannot find Tanner at the spot on the county map we bought at the courthouse in Bloomfield. The closest thing we can find to a community is the Sylvania Methodist Church. Except for the view, we begin to think this trek to Tanner might be a wasted trip. The map, however, is wrong, we learn. Tanner isn't, or in its case wasn't, at the T-intersection where Road 800 East dead-ends at Sylvania Road.

A man we will learn is Glenn Crowe parks his car at a farm house up 800 East and we stop to talk to him. He looks at the map. Tanner, he says, is east of Road 800. "Turn left down at the T, go past the Sylvania Church, past the gravel road to the right, to the stone road on the right. Turn left. Tanner was on the corner."

He emphasizes "was." Only an old house with an overgrown yard remains in Tanner. Crowe explains it once had a general store that was important to the early history of this area in eastern Greene County.

Crowe was born on the farm where he has stopped, a place he now owns, and he knows the area. He is a retired principal of schools in Monroe County. "I own the 80 acres here, 200 acres over on Clifty Creek and 60 acres where my house is, so I've got plenty to keep me busy," he says. The work is an enjoyable respite from education, but he confesses he misses the daily contact with students.

We look over the map with Crowe and notice an area marked "American Bottoms." We ask about those bottoms and learn about a geological phenomenon. Let's let Crowe tell the story: "This bottom has a creek which is the waterway for what is known as a bowl, so to speak. It starts about a mile to the east, then travels down through the bottom which is totally surrounded by hills. The waterway goes underground about the center of the bowl and continues underground about four miles to the west before coming out near Park.

"During heavy rains, almost the entire bottom is covered because the underground passage is not large enough to carry all the water." He emphasizes again, circling his right arm, "This is a total bowl. And it is known as the American Bottoms." He agrees that it is similar to Lost River in Orange County. "We call it the sink," he says. "There is a big chamber there at the mouth, but I don't think anyone has ever been far into it."

We spend a few more minutes with Crowe, talking about small Greene County towns, then drive past where the creek, marked Bridge Creek on the map, enters the cave. It has been an informative visit, thanks to Crowe, the educator, who has come out of retirement to conduct a class in geography.

* * *

Among the towns Crowe has mentioned is Shawnee. It's not on the map. But we drive by a restaurant on Ind. 54 called Shawnee Trail. It's in another community without town limits or road signs.

It must be a good place to eat, for a Cadillac as well as pickups are among the vehicles parked there. We are not disappointed.

We return to Bloomfield, then drive north on Ind. 157 to a road that leads to Calvertville. We pull to the side of the road to let a six-row corn planter pass. In Indiana, farming in May has preference over sightseers.

# Calvertville

## STILL ON THE MAP

It is the unexpected that adds to the mystery of travels on the back roads of Indiana.

We stop at Hutchens' Sales and Service. "Lawn mowers, chain saws, weed trimmers," a sign says. The owner hangs up the phone. "That man wanted a left-hand mower blade. Didn't know they make them," she says. "I have four of the right-hand blades, but no left-hand," she laughs, then adds, "That's something new to me. But I always say you never get too young to learn."

Meet Luvina Hutchens! Her life alone would make a book. "I've been here 37 years," she says. "The town has changed a lot since we moved here. I'm the oldest person left. This used to be a blacksmith shop.

"We even had a post office, a library, two grocery stores and a feed mill, which burned. The post office wasn't here when I came but the grocery stores and feed mills were. "It was a thriving little community. It's still a friendly place and I love it here."

"Here" is where, she says, "you might find 20 people . . . on a good day. I tell people I'm staying here to keep Calvertville on the map."

Mrs. Hutchens adopted Calvertville, or perhaps Calvertville adopted her. Her late husband, Medus, was a descendant of the Calverts for whom the town is named. "Medus died five years ago and this is what he left me," she says, her bright eyes scanning the business. "So I'm still going at it. I have to keep the engines going for my customers. My son works at Crane [Naval Surface Warfare Center . . . he's an engineer . . . he helps me on Saturdays. My grandson, who attends Indiana State, also helps me when he is not in school.

"So I tell customers during weekdays, 'I'm all you got.' When people thought I might close, they really got upset. They wondered what they would do without me."

In addition to fixing engines, she sharpens chains and blades and keeps belts and parts. Living next-door, she's available 24 hours a day, if a customer needs help. We tell her about an Echo chainsaw we have that won't start. She knows what's wrong immediately, recommending a specific type of sparkplug.

She explains that she had never been to Calvertville until Medus suggested that they stop on a drive back through the country from southern Indiana. She recalls, "We saw this little old place, all growed up, the weeds way higher than our heads, a white picket fence around it. I said, 'Medus, I'd like to have this place.' He said, 'You what?' I said, 'I'd like to have it. The kids and I would be a lot better off here than in Indianapolis with you gone so much.' He was on the road a lot as a salesman for Goodyear."

She convinced Medus by telling him she and the kids could clean up the place and he could come when he was off work on weekends. "We bought it before we went home," she laughs. "It was up for sale and we stopped, saw the realtor, and bought it. It didn't have electricity, running water, nothing modern back then. We put the house in Indianapolis up for sale and I've been here ever since."

She found Calvertville far different than the city: "We lived on Shimer right across from International Harvester, and you can imagine what we put up with. There were 14 kids the same age on that block. I couldn't let my kids out to play, but what a whole gang would join them.

"I think we were all a little miserable in the city because we had been in the country before. We had lived on a farm up near Pottersville [in Owen County] until farming got so bad you couldn't make any money.

"The kids, a boy and a girl, loved it here. They still say they thought they had died and gone to heaven when we moved down here. We had a two-room school out here then [now a residence] and they went out there until they went on to Bloomfield."

Mrs. Hutchens is an interviewer's delight. She continues: "After Medus passed away, my son and his wife—Leland and Sandy—came out one day. They wanted to know if I'd sell that piece of ground across the road. I said, 'I won't sell it to you, but I'll give it to you. What do you want with it?'" Her son told her he wanted to come home.

"I looked at Sandy and asked, 'Do you think you'd be that happy living next-door to your mother-in-law?' She said, 'I think I'd enjoy it.' They got busy and put in a double-wide and they've added on to it. They moved in one Tuesday and had a little boy the next Tuesday. He's a four-year-old now and he loves the yard."

Mrs. Hutchens looks around her shop again and says, "This was his [Medus'] dream. All we had to begin the business was this little room here. Before he passed away, he got to see the entire building go up. But he never got to work here," she says sadly. "He had leukemia for 13 years. He fought a long battle."

In town, if Calvertville can be called a town, a store, its concrete blocks painted green, is closed, the Phillips 66 pumps unused. The Calvertville cemetery is well-maintained, as is the community's church. A mill shapes stone hauled from quarries of Lawrence and Monroe counties.

It is for Luvina Hutchens, however, that a visitor will remember Calvertville.

* * *

County Road 675 North heads east from Calvertville through lowlands past scrub timber where dogwood trees bloom. At Road 650 East, an incline leads into the community of Newark.

# Newark
## STORE KEEPERS

April McAtee is at work at the Newark General Store she runs with her brother, John Edward McAtee. Tell us about Newark, we ask.

"Well, it has been here, I think, since about 1870," she replies, "and at one time it was a big community, unlike it is now. I've been told there were three stores, a blacksmith, a doctor, a lawyer, all those kinds of things."

Like a lot of other towns, it lost out to the railroads. When the tracks went through Solsberry, five miles to the south, businesses followed and Newark went downhill. "There are about, oh, 75 people in this immediate area, two churches and one store," April says. "It's about as podunk as you can get," she laughs.

That doesn't mean she doesn't like the town. She has lived around Newark since she was 12. "My dad bought the store then," she remembers. "I'm 27 now, so it has been in the family 15 years. My brother and I lease it from my dad, John Harris McAtee."

The store still sells gasoline, but April isn't sure how long it can continue to do so, explaining, "The EPA will demand tanks be changed and we just don't sell enough gasoline to pay the $20,000 or so they will cost."

Newark is in remote northeastern Greene County and not all delivery trucks come through the area. The store has to pick up its bread in Solsberry and had to truck its gas to the pumps until a distributor agreed to make the drive.

Some residents in town got their water from a spring at the base of the hill until the Eastern Water Company installed mains through the rural area in January 1992.

This, indeed, is "Backroads Indiana."

* * *

The drive north out of Newark into Owen County is scenic, the roads unpaved and narrow. Many of the residences are mobile homes or prefabricated housing. Three disabled cars are parked in one lawn, perhaps a sign of [[a kind of down-at-the-heels]] affluence.

On some roads south of Spencer, we decide the term "Sweet Owen" wasn't a term give the county by a motorist who had to drive over the gravel or pock-marked asphalt roads. We seem to be driving in circles, but somehow we arrive at New Hope, right where April McAtee said it would be. She has one of the three homes in New Hope, which has a church but no businesses.

* * *

We intend to cross the West Fork of White River at Freedom, but miss the turn and drive over Pottersville Road toward Spencer. A motorist in a van has stopped on the White River bridge into Spencer to talk to a pedestrian. We wait, reading the information on the steel structure: "20 mph speed limit. Chicago Bridge Company, 1897. Trucks, buses cross one at a time."

We take no chances on the narrow structure. We wait for the van to cross. This is a bridge that once carried traffic on old Ind. 43, before it was relocated to the north.

* * *

Communities are known for different things. Whitaker on Ind. 67 at the southwest corner of Morgan County, made news because of its burning sawdust pile that smoldered next to the sawmill that operated there for years.

* * *

Motorists on highways that skirt towns often miss the real heart of these communities. An example is Paragon on Ind. 67. Just a block north of Ind. 67 is a brick building erected in 1898. It was home to the IOOF lodge founded in 1872 and to the Paragon Knights of Pythias Lodge begun in 1895, according to markers on the building. The Lions Club has its own hall, with a notation that it meets the second and fourth Wednesdays of the month.

Many of the buildings that were once stores are closed, a reminder of a time when the town was a trading center. The trade has now moved to convenience stores out on the highway.

\* \* \*

North of Paragon, traffic slows to 20, then 12 to 15 mph, behind a John Deere tractor towing a six-row corn-planter. There is no horn honking, no irate motorists, even though no one can pass because of oncoming traffic. This is May in Indiana, the planting season. Delays are expected. It is a beautiful spring day, a day God made to enjoy, not to whine at a minor inconvenience. The road widens to four-lane south of the Ind. 39 bridge. The cars and trucks move around the farm rig. The delay has been only a minor nuisance.

\* \* \*

It has been a good day, despite some irritations. Some roads have been dreadful, a few of them teeth-chattering, bone-crunching, spine-testing, bottom-busting, good only for shock-absorber businesses.

We have seen the hills, hollows and woodlands of Eastern Greene County, the farms of the central section, both different than the coal mines to the west.

And we have seen scenic sections of Owen County we have never before traveled.

## *Trip 28*
# BROWN COUNTY

Ask any Hoosier to name an Indiana county at random and chances are he may pick Brown. It may be the state's most popular county, not because of its industry, its farms, its schools or its athletes, but because of its natural attractions. Up to four million visitors a year come to Nashville, the Gatlinburg of the north, and other areas of the county to view its wondrous beauty and the display of colors nature paints on the wooded hills each autumn.

Less than a third of the land in the county is farmed, the rest is woods and hills, choice sites, scenic and remote, for those who seek to escape cities and subdivisions.

Residents are far different than they were when Ernie Pyle described them back in 1940, a few years before he lost his life while a war correspondent. Pyle wrote: "The typical Brown County man plays a guitar in the woods, and raises a little tobacco; and goes to church, and drinks whiskey, and is a dead shot with a squirrel gun, and there are even those who can kill a squirrel with a rock as easily as with a gun."

Brown County residents today are more cosmopolitan— businessmen, career women, retired professionals, shopkeepers, lawyers and salesmen, who may drive daily to offices in Bloomington, Columbus, even Indianapolis.

On this summer Saturday, we have chosen to visit, not Nashville, but the back roads of Brown County.

# Peoga
## IT LOVES A PARADE

Peoga isn't very big, but it's large enough to straddle the Johnson-Brown County line.

It is just after 8 a.m. and Jimmy Brock is alone in the Brock and Brock Grocery, a concrete-block building painted tan. Jimmy, who looks to be in his twenties, is eating Frosted Flakes from a bowl while watching Saturday morning cartoons. He's not much for talking, more interested in the cartoons than in a stranger's questions.

He does tell us his name, that he frames houses, that he has lived in the area all his life, and that people in these parts call Peoga, "Pe-o-gie." Anything else, he says, can come from his mother, who runs the store. "She'll be down in about an hour," he says.

We return. Jimmy is still there, a soft drink in hand. His mother, Mary Rhude Brock, is at the cash register. She is friendly, easy to talk with and helpful. Jimmy, we learn, is one of seven children.

Rhude was the name of her ancestors, who helped settle Brown County and who gave Rhude Hollow, over the hill from Peoga, its name. Her father, who was born in 1887, lived his entire life in the area. Mary has so far, and expects to continue to do so. Her mother, she says, was "a Trisler" and she grew up here, too."

Mrs. Brock is involved in efforts to maintain the town's heritage and is secretary of the Peoga Centennial Committee. It was that committee that arranged the Peoga Festival in June, 1993, an event that will be held each year to raise funds for the town's centennial celebration in 1998.

Peoga is older than 100 years; the Mt. Olive United Methodist Church has been here 125 years, for example. But the centennial will mark the hundredth year since a post office put the town on the map.

The post office is gone, but the town's spirit remains. It's a spirit that has been shown at Peoga's Fourth of July parade for the last 26 years. It may be one of the shortest parades in America, just over two blocks long, starting at the Mt. Olive Church in Brown County, proceeding past Brock's Store, turning at the parking lot at Wyatt's Grocery, then returning to the church in 20 to 25 minutes.

The 1993 parade had a prince, Jason Little, a princess, Leighanna Smith-Brock, and a marshal, State Rep. Ralph Foley of Martinsville, and paid a special tribute to World War II veterans. It was a day when the crowd exceeded the population in Peoga.

* * *

We mention to Mrs. Brock that we are headed for Spearsville, about four or five miles to the west. She smiles as she explains how the two communities differ: "Peoga has two stores and one church. Spearsville has one store and two churches."

# Spearsville
## A THREE-WAY STOP

Ask Kenny Burker how many folks live in Spearsville and he'll likely tell you, "It depends on what time of day." Burker has spent most of his life in the tiny Brown County community a few strides south of the Johnson County line. He has seen residents come and go, some finding that ever-elusive contentment, others disenchanted in the solitude of the quiet hills.

More and more people have bought building lots in areas around Spearsville, but the rural water system has reached its capacity and has discontinued hook-ups, he explains.

"Stand at the corner up at the three-way stop," Kenny says, "and you can see all of Spearsville." Besides the store and the two churches—the Wesleyan and Church of Christ—there are a half-dozen houses, including the one Burker owns. Not counted is an old abandoned log cabin at the intersection.

Kenny, to be more formal, is Kenneth W. Burker, owner of Burker's General Store. His dad was Wayne Burker, who was raised by Luna "Tony" Walker, the son of John Walker. It was John Walker who opened the store back in 1885, later turning it over to Luna, who turned it over to Wayne, who turned it over to Kenny. So it has been in the same family for almost 110 years, open continuously except when Wayne Burker was in military service in World War II.

Kenny Burker served his country, too, during the Vietnam War, and returned to Spearsville in 1970 with his Japanese bride, Hiromi. It is here they have raised three children—Doug, a 1993 graduate of Franklin College who now is a Brown County probation officer; Misa, who will be graduated from nursing school in 1994, and Andy, a senior at Brown County High School.

Hiromi enjoys the area, Burker says, explaining they have been back to Japan a few times so she can visit her family. As a high school graduation present, Mrs. Burker took daughter Misa to Hawaii in 1989 where they vacationed with Hiromi's parents.

"It is a good place to be . . . quiet and peaceful," Kenny Burker says of Spearsville. Like life, Spearsville, he adds, "changes every day."

Not as many residents gather at the store as they once did. "A lot of the older ones have died. Younger ones are more on the go. Both husbands and wives work and they don't have much time," he says. "Newer residents wanted to get out of the cities, so they prefer to be alone to enjoy peace and quiet."

Burker's place is an old-fashioned general store, the kind that keeps almost anything a customer might want. There are fan belts and washboard and chimney covers. But not even an operator of a 110-year-old general store can anticipate every request.

A woman rushes into the store, "You have any pantyhose in here, Kenny?" she asks. He walks with her to an aisle. They find no pantyhose. She thanks him and leaves.

We note a three-foot by four-foot framed painting of the store. It is a work of art, the kind for which Brown County is famous, done from a 1916 picture of the store. "My kids saw that at a gallery and bought it for me as a present," Burker explains.

We step outside where Kenny's dog, Cuma (a "Heinz 57 variety with checkered ancestry"), is still on duty as a silent sentry. It would be good to sit on the porch and enjoy the tranquility, but the road calls us to continue our journey.

\* \* \*

We return to Peoga and head south toward Gatesville, skirting Sweetwater and Cordry lakes, driving past houses accessible by fords across Sweetwater Creek, down through Wolfpen Hollow. Off to the right is the Hamblen-Taylor cemetery where a flag flies over a huge gravestone for Job Hamblen, "born July 14, 1762—died Sept. 1, 1833." Hamblen, the marker indicates, built one of the first homes in the area in 1825. A Revolutionary War veteran, he participated in the siege of Yorktown where the British forces surrendered. Hamblen Township, Brown County, was named for him.

# Gatesville
## CREEKS OF GOLD

The road continues along the valley to where Sweetwater meets the North Fork of Salt Creek. A sign at the bridge says, "Entering, Leaving Gatesville—Elevation 661." It is obvious Gatesville isn't very big: a general store, a three-bay fire station, a mobile home, the Gatesville Park (a shelter-house, some benches on a small plot).

Carolyn Wilkerson Hancock is at work at the store, owned by Harlan and Rita King, who are gone for the day. Jamie Cline, a 12-year-old with time on his hands, is there, too.

They talk about gold that sometimes is found in the branch of Salt Creek, point to the gold pans, for sale at $4.99, for rent for $1 a day. Some prospectors, they say, have found gold flakes, enough to show off at the store.

Jamie says, "People come from Ohio, all over the place, to pan for gold. A guy was down here two or three days ago and came out with a fourth of a quart of flakes. One man came down with some kind of a sweeper. He did all right, too."

Mrs. Hancock says it isn't unusual to receive phone calls from out-of-state from people who ask about the gold pans and seek directions on how to get to Gatesville.

The Kings bought the General Store—a Gatesville landmark since 1915—more than five years ago from Susan Stout. It was Susan Stout who developed the park across the road which has become a popular spot for picnics, birthday parties and church gatherings. And it's a good place to enjoy a pizza, which is available at the store on Fridays and Saturdays.

\* \* \*

We reach Harlan King later. The store and the King home behind it, he says, are for sale for $110,000. A general store, he explains, takes a lot of time "and we are tired. We want to get back to family life."

\* \* \*

Gatesville is too small to be on most highway maps, but Taggart is found on a few. Taggart, a half-mile or so to the east of Gatesville, has a few houses scattered along a county road. The two-room school Carolyn Hancock attended back in the 1950s is gone except in the memories of students who attended grades one through four in one room, fifth through eighth in the other.

\* \* \*

A county road to the southwest out of Gatesville rises three hundred feet up from the valley to Panther Lick Ridge, an elevation of 950 feet, in less than a mile. We follow Clay Lick Creek on a road that is partly pavement, partly crushed stone, past small lakes formed by dams in the recesses of the hills.

It is remote, wooded. Scattered homes, an old log cabin or two, have become respites from life's daily grind for their owners. Horses and Shetland ponies graze in small pastures between hills and creeks. Campgrounds for church groups and other organizations offer summer getaways for city youngsters.

# Stone Head
## ROUTES TO THE PAST

We leave the county road, drive east on Ind. 46, then turn south on Ind. 135 en route to Stone Head. Ind. 135 makes a 90-degree turn to the west at Stone Head, a place, not a town. It's a five-foot-high likeness of a man's head carved into a slab of sandstone placed atop a concrete directional marker.

The book *Indiana: A New Historical Guide* credits a farmer, Henry Cross, with the sculpture work done in 1851 "in lieu of the state tax requirement that all males spend six days a year working on public roads or waterways." It is said the likeness on the stone is that of George Summa, a township road supervisor. The towns on the marker, Sparkesferie in Jackson County, and Fairfax in Monroe County, no longer exist.

# Pike's Peak
## "OR BUST"

Pike's Peak, a town rich in folklore, is a mile east of Stone Head out on New Bellsville Pike. It was named, indirectly, for Pike's Peak in Colorado, which is a story itself:

In the 1800s, James Ward prepared to take his family to Colorado, decorating a prairie schooner with a "To Pike's Peak or Bust" banner. The family, he said, would take the trail from Brown County to Madison, where it would travel on the Ohio and Mississippi rivers to Missouri. Already homesick by the time they reached Madison, the Wards returned to Brown County and opened a store in a log building. After that, local residents in need of supplies at Ward's store, would joke that they were going to Pike's Peak to shop.

A store operated on the site for 70 years, proving to be a more lasting venture than Ward's decision to move to Colorado.

Business in Pike's Peak today is conducted at the Crouch Market, owned and operated by Harry and Norma Crouch. It's a store that evolved, expanding periodically to meet the needs of a growing community. It started as a fruit stand, mainly because Harry Crouch was known for his excellent gardens, and grew into a general store, restaurant, "museum," picture gallery and recreation center.

"We started out small 22 years ago. We didn't intend to get this big, but as the community's needs grew we kept adding to the store," Norma Crouch says. "I've told people we have anything from A to Z, apples to zucchini. And if we have several requests for items we don't have, we try to add those, too."

And the growth hasn't stopped. A new addition is planned for plumbing and hardware supplies.

It is a general store to match those of the past. "We've had customers who say they haven't seen anything like this since they left the hills of Tennessee," Norma adds.

She grew up near Tampico in Jackson County. Harry's family has been a fixture in the area for decades. His dad was a blacksmith in Pike's Peak and some of his tools are on display in the store.

The Crouches and Moores are prominent names in the area. Aquilla Moore, 86, is an institution in these parts, but he hasn't been feeling well, we are told. "He's proud of his new grandbaby," Mrs.Crouch says. "He's getting hard of hearing, but he's a great guy who knows everything about the area."

Mrs. Crouch admits, "I'm partial to this area. There are a lot of friendly people. It's just a nice neighborhood."

We browse through the store, filled with groceries, a sandwich bar where workers are sacking huge bags of popped corn, assorted merchandise, all those "a to z" items. Tables for diners are in a back room, one wall partially covered with hundreds of snapshots, mostly fathers and sons, with their catches of fish, and their deer, wild turkey and grouse.

Memorabilia are on the opposite wall—pictures and other items that give visitors a view of the past. Indian artifacts Harry has found in his gardens are in a display case.

"Our family always has been interested in history. People are so busy going in all different directions, they sometimes forget their past," Mrs. Crouch says. "They need to learn to keep their family heritages and histories alive."

For young people and adults who aren't interested in history, there is a pool table and a video game. And an old-fashioned penny scale so a person can check his weight.

Outside, five men have their lunch at a picnic table under the trees in front of the store. There's a place for everyone—either inside or outside—at Crouch's Market at Pike's Peak.

* * *

We return to Stone Head. A few miles south over a meandering Ind. 135 is the town of Story. Well, actually, its not much of a town, if houses and people are a necessity. We recall back 25 years ago when the entire town was for sale for $40,000. Only money and a lack of foresight kept us from buying the place.

Today the town of Story is the Story Inn, a restaurant that has become known for great food, and a bed and breakfast that's usually booked months ahead by visitors who want to be here for the peak of the fall foliage season.

The Story Inn is said to have the best breakfast around, but that may be open to debate because folks who grew up in the hills and woods of Southern Indiana know how to fix a morning meal that will keep a traveler going to well past noon.

* * *

Further south on Ind. 135 at Becks Grove Road is a store operated by Wendell Crouch, the son of Norma and Harry Crouch of Pike's Peak. If he's as ambitious and hard-working as his parents, and chances are he is, the place will soon be a community center for residents of Southern Brown and Northern Jackson Counties.

* * *

We return to Nashville, the Brown County seat and the center of what is called the "Little Smokies." Sidewalks are filled with shoppers and tourists on a Saturday afternoon, people who are spending money to put some "green" into Brown.

Few of them are likely to visit the T.C. Steele State Historic Site out to the west, a mile and a half south off Ind. 46 at a wide spot in the road called Belmont. It will be their loss.

It was T. (for Theodore) C. (for Clement) Steele, who unlike visiting artists who painted and left, bought the 211 acres in 1907, built the "House of the Singing Winds," and made it his permanent studio. He was one of the founders of the Brown County art colony. Steele, who died in 1926 at age 79, has been called Indiana's most famous representational artist, and his works can be seen in the 11-room house named for the winds that blow through the trees.

His widow gave the estate to the citizens of Indiana in 1945, but too few of them take time to visit the picturesque setting and see the works Steele left as his legacy. The estate is part of the Indiana State Museum system and no fee is charged.

Guided tours of Steele's home and studio, hiking trails and gardens are available from 1 to 5 p.m. on Sundays and from 9 a.m. to 5 p.m. Tuesdays through Saturdays. The site is closed in January and February.

* * *

There are other places—on the back roads—to visit in Brown County, places like Helmsburg and its general store, its sawmill and its Cullum Broom & Mop Co. And other places back off the beaten paths, yet unspoiled by commercialization, places best left for tourists who seek their own adventures.

As Ernie Pyle wrote more than a half-century ago, "Brown County is not the same as it was when the artists discovered it. They say it is spoiled. They would go away, except they say it's still better than anywhere else."

## Trip 29
# GERMAN COUNTRY

It is the unknown, the unexpected, that adds to the mystery hidden on the backroads of southern Indiana. Amazement, astonishment, may be around the next hidden corner, for no turn is a duplicate of another, no two places identical.

We are headed west on Ind. 64 from English in Crawford County en route to towns and hamlets in Dubois, Pike and Warrick counties.

## Miffin
### DOWN IN THE VALLEY

A sign at the east side of Taswell points south from Ind. 64 to "Miffin—3 miles." Chances are that not more than one in a thousand cars turn off the road and makes the trip. It is their loss, even though it is a sojourn over a rough road where blacktop turns to crushed stone, where there are no houses. Trees are so thick, foliage so dense, the road seldom sees daylight in spring and summer. Motorists are alerted that they are passing through a "Nature Preserve—Do Not Litter. Everything is Protected."

There must be life in Miffin, we decide, as a car approaches from that direction. We arrive in Miffin, a scenic, remote spot, quiet, peaceful where, the silence is broken only by water that tumbles over the five-feet drop at the falls in Otter Creek.

It is worth the trip. The Miffin Store, an old water pump out front, is open early this Thursday morning, as it is every day of the week. It is not an imposing structure. Its sides are covered with corrugated roofing and there are no fancy signs, no frills. A porch is roofed in tin which covers an ice machine and a gasoline pump that no longer works.

We enter, greeted by owner David Parr, who asks if we want a cup of coffee. "It's free," he says. Parr tells us he reopened the store in 1992 after it had been closed "12 to 14 years." "I always wanted an old country store, so when this place became available, we decided to give it a shot. I like running the place so far, but it's more work than I thought it would be."

He was born in Washington, Indiana, moved to Florida, then returned to Indiana to live at Grantsburg, a community south of English.

Business is getting better, he says, "People are getting used to it now. It's handy." The nearest big grocery is the Jay C over at English. It hasn't been easy starting a store in an empty building, Parr tells us: "There wasn't any equipment or anything in here when we reopened it. At first, nobody would deliver, so we had to go get our own supplies. Now we have an outfit out of Terre Haute and a guy out of Paoli who drop off supplies and produce."

The store is open from 8 a.m. to 10:30 p.m., longer on weekends sometimes. If you are going to be in business, Parr has decided, you need to be open for the convenience of customers. It would cost too much to install gasoline tanks to meet EPA regulations, about $40,000, he estimates. The mark-up on gasoline wouldn't permit him to recoup the cost.

"We did get a pay phone put in, which helps when someone needs to make a call," he says.

The store has become a community gathering spot, he reports. "Men, most of them retired, start coming in about 9 a.m. It gives them a place to talk, and if they want to order food later, we can warm sandwiches and pizza in the microwave.

Parr was a trucker before he opened the store, still drives some, "mostly for myself." He has five children, "one in Colorado, one in Washington, three around here," he says. Son John, a trucker, too, is in the store.

A regular customer walks in. Parr greets him with a "Howdy, Mr. Lloyd." Parr enjoys greeting customers, appreciates the serenity of the valley. "It's pretty around here," he says simply. He points back to the waterfall, tells where there are steps that remain from the days when only a foot log crossed the creek to the church.

Off to the side of the store is a section where craft items are for sale. "My wife and daughter-in-law make some of them. Other people also bring in things they make and offer them for sale," Parr says.

He counts 10 or 11 houses scattered near town, although there are only three or four, plus the church, near the corner where the store is located.

We talk with "Mr. Lloyd," who we learn is Lloyd Newton. He is a big man with bib overalls over a white T-shirt and a handkerchief in his hand to wipe the sweat from his brow.

It is just after 9 a.m. and already it is humid on a day when the temperature will reach 90 degrees. Newton, whose parents once operated a store in the building, sips on a soft drink. He's retired from military service, splits his time between places he owns near Miffin and in Mississippi.

He says Miffin was started when a man whose last name was Sain brought in a wagon load of groceries and started an old store down the creek. The town grew from there, he adds. "I don't know how it became known as Miffin. That was the old fellers. They figured that one out," Newton laughs.

A feed store across the road has been closed for years, Newton says. "The last feller who had it was my brother-in-law. Can't think of his name, right now," he says, somewhat perturbed at himself. "Anyhow, he was grinding feed there one day and someone ran a horseshoe through it. That ruined the grinder and stopped the feed mill. Charles Harlan, that's his name," he suddenly recalls. Newton's brother-in-law, wherever he may be, will be pleased he has been remembered.

Newton and Parr recall the earlier store where chicken, cream and eggs were traded, when customers sold yellow ginseng and mayapple roots at the store. They also remember when there was a school in Miffin (the building still stands up the road from the store), when drinking water was carried to it from the well that remains out in front of the store.

Parr and Newton bid us farewell and continue to talk. We walk out behind the store, look at the waterfall, note the old step where the foot log once was, walk the plank bridge that leads to Miffin Community Church and the cemetery behind it.

This is a place far from torment and terror, a place to forget the whine of the disenchanted, the smog of factories, the trucks and traffic of the highways. We promise ourselves to return in the fall when the leaves turn.

* * *

We return to Taswell on another Crawford County road, crossing over a humpback one-lane wooden bridge over the railroad which has two sets of tracks in the area. Except for the 64 Market, a school at the edge of town and a church, there are only houses, and not many of those, in Taswell.

It is difficult to keep up-to-date on names for railroads. Consider the route that runs through Taswell, Eckerty and Birdseye (on the road ahead). It started as the New Albany and St. Louis. It became the Louisville, New Albany and St. Louis in 1870 and the Louisville, Evansville and St. Louis Consolidated in 1887. In 1900 it was acquired by the Southern Railway and after a consolidation in 1982 it became the Norfolk and Southern.

# Eckerty
## "A GATHERING PLACE"

A sign on Ind. 64 at the road to Eckerty proclaims, "U.S. Post Office—1 mile." It's the only such sign we have seen across southern Indiana and we will soon learn of the post office's importance to the town.

The road leads over a bridge high above the railroad. Eckerty is a town that owes its existence to transportation, from the stagecoach to the railroad to the automobile. And to the post office.

The community was known as Down Hill when postmaster James Speedy operated the stagecoach station on the old Leavenworth-Jasper road. Down Hill became Boston Station in the 1880s when the railroad was built through town and passengers and mail came by train rather than stagecoach. Boston Station was renamed Eckerty in 1888, in honor of Christopher Eckerty, who designed and helped build much of the town along the railroad.

With the trains came development: two hotels, three stores, a flour mill, two restaurants, a drug store, a hardware store, barber shop, churches, schools, a saloon, livery stable, stockyards for livestock and sawmills to cut the lumber needed for all the construction. The town prospered for years, then slowly declined with the advent of the automobile, the Depression of the 1930s and the closing of the train depot in 1952.

About 320 people remain in town, socializing at the post office, a beauty shop, a church and an antique store. The last grocery closed in 1985. Patoka Lake, however, developed in the last decade, has brought growth to the area near Eckerty. A convenience store and a restaurant-tavern are out on Ind. 64 not far from town.

We stop at the Eckerty post office and talk with Cindy Howard, the postmaster, and Linda Kaiser, a rural carrier who has 235 stops on her route. Sixty-five other families pick up their mail at post-office boxes.

Cindy Howard hands us a copy of the post office's history she has compiled. "The post office," she writes, "was the beginning of this community and remains a gathering place for neighbor to learn about neighbor, to keep abreast of local events and world news.

"It somehow renews one's faith in one's self in one's ability to carry on such a rich tradition when we delve into the past, compare it to the present and peek into the future.

"As postmaster," she concludes, "you don't just do a job, but perform a service to all those in your community."

It is obvious Cindy Howard, who has been postmaster seven years, cares about the town. It was she who saw to it the sign out on Ind. 64 was installed calling attention to Eckerty post office. "I told the Postal Service that a lot of people didn't know we were here," she explains. "Families who live around the lake didn't know there was a post office here until we put up the sign."

The lake has added stops to Linda Kaiser's rural route. "People come down for the summer, like the area, and decide to make it their permanent home," she says. Her home, though, has been in Eckerty for twenty years "in what was one of the two hotels back when the trains stopped and scores of wagons waited to load farm produce onto rail cars."

It is time now for the mail to be delivered. Time for us to move on. The town will continue to change, but as long as there are Cindy Howards and Linda Kaisers, there will be an Eckerty.

* * *

Outside Eckerty on Ind. 64, we slow to a creep behind a log truck. It is an area where timber still is an important part of the community's economic health.

# Birdseye
## "A HEALTHY PLACE"

Homesteaders moved to the area in the early 1800s, but the town wasn't known as Birdseye until 1846, when a post office opened. The town off Ind. 64 in southern Dubois County now has a population of about five hundred.

Here, according to legend, is how the town was named: Postmaster George King and his wife, Martha, asked the Rev. Benjamin "Bird" Goodman (who was postmaster at nearby Schnellville) how he liked the site that had been chosen for the post office. "Bird" replied, "It suits 'Bird's' eye to a tee." And so the town became "Birds Eye" and later "Birdseye."

A story attributed to famous Hoosier poet James Whitcomb Riley likely isn't true. Riley is said to have deboarded a train, asked the name of the town and remarked, "It looks like they named it after the wrong end of the bird."

Riley, however, did write, "The town [Birdseye] has such a tranquil atmosphere, a writer could call it heaven." He is believed to have composed at least part of "The Raggedy Man" while on one of his visits to Birdseye.

We stop in an older area of the town at an old brick building called the Sportsman Shopping Center. Only a general store remains in what appears to have been a four-business complex. The general store hasn't opened for the day.

We ask about the owner we met, and liked, on a visit to town ten years or so earlier. She is Mildred "Crickett" Pruitt, we are told. She still operates the store, which hasn't changed much over the years. And she still won't sell the antiques that are there, despite offers from customers.

We regret we won't see her on this trip. We do find a booklet "18-83—Birdseye Centennial—1983," and learn that Miss Pruitt was among the 18 seniors who were graduated from the high school in 1932 and, like most, remained in Birdseye.

The school closed after the 1971 graduation of 22 seniors. The town's athletes, once known as Birdseye Yellow Jackets, now play for the Forest Park Rangers at Ferdinand.

Frances Steffen's antique shop is open up the street and the items there are for sale. She tells us about Birdseye and some of its people, talks about the development around the lake, says she was born in Wickliffe, a few miles away over in Crawford County.

A customer enters the store. It's a hot day, the temperature on its way to 90. He is greeted with, "It's hot out there, isn't it?" "No! Just right," he replies.

We are looking over the Birdseye centennial history we have just bought. The man says, "Everybody's in there but me."

"Why aren't you in it?" we ask.

"Didn't want to be," the man says, introducing himself. "Lonie Cummings."

He flips through the book, stopping at Page 78. "He was my father-in-law, a good man," Lonie says, pointing to a picture of James Kellum, the centennial senior king. The text with the picture quotes Kellum, "It [Birdseye] is a pretty good place to live and a healthy place." It must have been. Kellum, Lonie tells us, died in 1991 at age 101.

Today, Birdseye blends the old of Kellum's day—and of Crickett Pruitt's day—with the new. Big old homes remain at the south edge of town near the town park. Out on the highway, a convenience store and other new businesses have developed to serve visitors to Patoka Lake. Change—like the trains that now run through town—is unstoppable.

* * *

We backtrack on Ind. 64 to Ind. 145, go north a short distance, then turn back west on Ind. 164 and head for Wickliffe. We are near Patoka Lake and there are signs for chalets, resorts, vacation cabins and campgrounds.

# Wickliffe
### A Slab of Bologna

John Stemply isn't awed by all the activity around Patoka Lake. He operates his business on Ind. 164 in Wickliffe, just as he has for years. Except for his store, a United Methodist Church and six houses, there isn't much between the Wickliffe signs on the road. The store is old, imitation brick on the side, weather-worn, paint-chipped clapboard on the front. An old "Drink Double Cola" sign is on the front.

John Lester Stemply sees us as we walk up the steep steps at the front of the store. He stops mowing the grass around the store, turns off his old Ford tractor, the engine sputtering a few times before stopping. Stemply greets us with a friendly welcome and a two-, maybe, three-day growth of whiskers.

"Guess I've had the store for about 22 years," he says, the sweat making his green shirt even darker. "My father [J.P. Stemply] started in here in 1899," he adds, without much emotion even though it's a ninety-plus-year-old family business.

"He started in a building up there," he says, pointing south. "When the road was changed past this place, dad moved down here on the main drag. "There was just this one room until my dad bought the German Lutheran Church and used the lumber to add to the store."

Stemply took over when his dad died. "I worked for Double Cola and Seven Up for 38 years and I was six years from retirement at the time. So I hired a couple of ladies to run the store until I had my time in," he says.

He was a distributor, covering six counties out of Vincennes, so he knows southwestern Indiana. He lives on the west side of Jasper, a 22-mile drive each direction. He sometimes decides to stay overnight at the store rather than make the trip. "I'm spending more and more nights here all the time," he says. "I used to like the drives but when you get to be 81 years old you don't enjoy it quite as much." He keeps the store open seven days a week. It's no wonder he tires of the drive.

He talks about his wife. "Lenora is 73, but she doesn't feel too well. I tell her she lays in bed too much. You can't do that," he says. Business, he relates, was good through last year. "I haven't done so good this year," he says, not sure why sales are down. "I don't think as well as I once did. Don't figure as good or nothing else," he laments.

We look at an old scale in the store, which is heated with wood in the winter. "That [the scale] was bought in September 1920 for $100," he says immediately, indicating his memory is sharper than he may think.

A few horse collars are on the walls. "My wife went to a farm sale and bought five collars for $100. My dad used to sell new ones for $5.65," he says, not as a complaint but as a matter of fact.

We see a soft-drink cooler, the kind that was used a half-century ago. "That was bought in 1934," he says. It is empty, or we would lift the door, flip off the water, pop off the cap and sip a Coke while we are talking.

We use a term that's out of character for us, which sounds silly even as we say it. We call the place "a neat old store." Stemply immediately needles us about the word "neat." He says, "Well, I don't know the meaning of the word 'neat.' It has more than one definition," he says with a laugh. "I see neat in a way, and in another way not so neat."

A customer walks into the store. Without a word being exchanged, Stemply gets up, walks to a refrigerator in the back room, returning with a round of bologna six inches across. The customer meantime has taken two slices of bread from a loaf, spreading mustard over one piece. Stemply slices off a three-eighths-inch wide slab of bologna. The man sticks it between the bread, and starts his lunch between sips of a soft drink.

No words are spoken. Among friends, silence is its own conversation. It isn't until we leave the store that we hear Stemply and his customer begin to talk.

* * *

The Patoka Lake Newton-Stewart Recreation Area is just to the north of Wickliffe. It has brought some development to the area, but Wickliffe remains, for the most part, unaffected by the development around it.

# Dubois
## SPORTS MINDED

Dubois is a busy town of seven hundred residents on the Patoka River in northern Dubois County. In the center of poultry farms, it has a branch bank, supermarket, restaurants, bars, assorted stores, a town park and two factories.

Six men sit together at a round table in a restaurant-lounge at noon. They eat between talk of Little League baseball, coaches and players, for this is a sports-minded community with ball diamonds and playgrounds.

Northeast Dubois High School is outside town, a four-township area once served by Dubois and Cuzco high schools. And it is the school system, the Northeast Dubois School Corporation, organized in 1969, that is the object of hot debate in this searing summer of 1993. Some residents want the School

Board changed, increased from five to seven members, elected rather than appointed.

The current School Board opposes the changes presented by petitioners. It also has rejected a change that would allow the election of members whether or not they own real estate within the corporation. Appointed members, they say, have always been real-estate owners.

It is the kind of debate that makes communities like Dubois interesting.

# Cuzco
## TRAIN STOP

Unlike most small towns, Cuzco still depends on the railroad for recognition. It is unincorporated, somewhat isolated, in northeast Dubois County. There are no state highways into town, but many visitors arrive each summer aboard the French Lick Railroad excursions. Passengers buy soft drinks and refreshments at the little general store, enjoy a quite respite, gaze up at the old church atop the hill and at scattered houses on Persimmon Ridge.

But the school and gym where fans cheered for the Cuzco Bear Cubs until 1948 is gone.

For a brief time, before the train makes the ten-mile return to French Lick, there are more visitors than there are residents in Cuzco.

# Celestine
## SOMETHING TO CELEBRATE

Celestine is all decked out for a big party. Its sesquicentennial celebration, marking 150 years from 1843 to 1993, is only a few weeks away. "Come join the celebration," a sign encourages.

Town streets are being repaved. Red-white-and-blue buntings hang from many homes inside and outside town. A bulletin board headed "Sesquicentennial News" keeps residents posted with a countdown to the big event.

Residents support one another, care about each other. A sign at the edge of town offers, "Congratulations to Celestine Jaycees. No. 1 chapter in the state. We are proud of you." The organization maintains Jaycee Park in Celestine, which is spruced up on this day for the coming centennial. "We support our troops," another sign says.

Aristokraft, which makes kitchen and bathroom cabinets, has a plant in Celestine.

Celestine (pronounced *Sell-us-tine*) is a town with pride—neat, orderly, typical of the German influence throughout Dubois County. Streets are marked with names. Restaurants, convenience stores, the post office, the bank, even the elementary school, are well-maintained.

Father John Boeglin has written a sesquicentennial history he calls *Preparing For The Future From Memories of the Past.* In the book, he relates that Celestine was the county's third Catholic community, after Jasper and Ferdinand. The town and church were named for St. Peter Celestine, a European saint.

"Immigrants," he says, "brought their German traditions and strong Catholic commitment." They are traditions and commitments that still remain, not only in Celestine, but throughout Dubois County.

School consolidation did not come easily, not in other areas, certainly not in Celestine, which is in the Northeast Dubois school district.

In his Celestine history, The Rev. Mr. Boeglin describes the impact of the school consolidation in 1969: "People had become accustomed to freely choosing their own high schools. For instance, many of Celestine's young people attended Jasper High School. With the new law, however, students had to attend the high school in their local districts.

"Consolidation would also mean the end of religious education programs in the school. Religious objects and crucifixes, pictures and garments would no longer be allowed. Naturally, those school systems which had enjoyed the Catholic presence in their schools would feel the change most painfully."

\* \* \*

We turn south off Ind. 164 and drive toward another unincorporated Dubois County town called Schnellville. A ridge offers a spectacular view of eastern Dubois county. A combines slices through a wheat field on one of the prosperous-looking farms.

# Schnellville
## FOUR STREETS

We are greeted by a "Welcome to Schnellville. compliments of Schnellville Community Club" sign. Schnellville is a small town, one where the post office is in room at the side of a residence.

The four streets are named Elm, Walnut, Market and County Road 800 East. The Sacred Heart Catholic Church, established in 1876, is on the highest spot in town, overlooking the surrounding area in all directions. The Brown Derby restaurant, owned by Dianne and Kevin Persohn, appears to be the only business.

\* \* \*

We take a county road into Jasper, stop at the Chamber of Commerce office, and learn that the Dubois County unemployment rate is just three percent, only half what it is in most areas of the state.

\* \* \*

The town of Ireland is almost a northwest extension of Jasper out on the Ind. 56 corridor. It is a town that has grown up since the days back in 1963 when the Ireland Spuds basketball team was the toast of the county, winning the sectional and regional before losing to Evansville Bosse in the semistate. It now is a busy self-sufficient suburb, no longer a part of "Backroads Indiana." And it's a place the Irish come to join in the St. Patrick's Day Festival each March 17th.

\* \* \*

We enter Pike County from Dubois County on Ind. 56 and drive to a place on the map called Cato. Cato turns out to be a community of four houses and a former store now used for storage. We wonder how long it will be before it no longer is marked on Indiana highway maps. West of Cato, land use changes from agriculture to strip mines, some already reclaimed, then back to farm land again.

We reach the junction of Ind. 61 at Ind. 56. Pike Central High School, which covers all of Pike County, is at the southeastern corner of the intersection. It is a consolidation of the former Otwell, Petersburg, Spurgeon, Stendal and Winslow schools.

\* \* \*

Campbelltown stretches along Ind. 61, about fifty houses between town limits on the north and south. It is a town without a focal point, more of a community of homes, where lots are big and horses graze on an occasional undeveloped site.

# Winslow

## PUBLIC WORKS

At first glance on this early summer day, Winslow looks a wreck. Streets are dusty and ripped apart. But it's only a temporary condition. A $3.9 million waste-treatment project, financed in part by the state and federal government, is under construction in this Pike County town of eight hundred residents.

We have entered the town from the north on Ind. 61, where we were greeted by a sign: "Winslow—Home of Dick Farley." It has been 43 years since Dick Farley led the Winslow Eskimos to the Final 8 of the state high school basketball tournament and made the all-state and All-Star teams. It has been 40 years since he played a vital role on Indiana University's 1953 NCAA championship team. He died at an early age, but he'll not be forgotten, not as long as there are basketball fans in Winslow or anywhere else in Indiana.

Winslow, which is on the Patoka River, is a commercial center of southern Pike County with a number of businesses. It's a neighborly place where residents tend gardens behind their houses while carrying on conversations. And it is a town of some blue-collar workers, who show their support of the United Mine Workers by posting signs on their lawns. A Coal Miner Respiratory Clinic is on Ind. 61 in town.

We leave Winslow from the south side of town. Work in that area is finished, the streets repaved, indicating better driving for motorists, less dusts for housekeepers.

* * *

Ayrshire is a community built along a Pike County road a mile west of Ind. 61 south of Winslow. UMWA signs are on almost every lawn. Satellite dishes are outside many homes as the road winds along a ridge past a Baptist church and a school now used as a residence.

# Arthur

### PEACEFUL COEXISTENCE

Arthur has no post office, never had a high school, likely is little known outside Pike County. Most motorists drive through town, note the Patoka Township Lions Club trailer parked along the road, comment on the orderly homes, wonder about the old Sunoco station that's no longer open. Those who do not stop miss the optimism of the entrepreneurs who are here, fail to hear the enthusiasm of its residents.

We stop at the Arthur Country Store. "Antiques and dry goods," a sign says. We enter and find owner Teresa Grady, electric tools in hand, doing repair work as classical music plays in the background. She laughs when we tell her she should be using antique tools.

She, her husband, Don, and their three daughters moved from Evansville to a place north of Arthur 13 years ago. "Very nice," she says of the town. "It's a nice slow life style."

She explains that she and her husband operated the store from 1987 through 1990, then reopened it this year. "It's a wonderful old building," she says. "I think it was built in 1922. It has been a grocery store and a meeting-place for the Oddfellows Lodge here. It was an antique shop 25 years ago, but that's when they called it junk."

She tells us about a coincidence: "We bought our house in 1980 from Fred Beakley. When we bought the store, we learned he had once had a grocery store here. I hope that's all he owned because we don't need to buy anything else."

Arthur, she comments, once was a thriving community. She mentions a grade school, two funeral parlors, two groceries, a blacksmith shop, a variety of businesses. A convenience store remains. Business declined when residents bought cars and drove to bigger towns to shop.

We mention the UMWA signs around the area and learn her husband works as a "company" man. "We are sort of between a rock and a hard place," she explains. It is difficult because almost everyone is in the union or related to someone who is or is involved in some way [in the company-union controversy]. It's a small community. It's difficult for everyone.

"Some miners asked if I'd put up union signs in the store. I said, 'Boy, you are really putting me in a pickle.' They said, 'Well, do whatever you want to,'" proving that people can get along in small towns despite differences.

She agrees each side has valid issues, adding, "We just hope that it all ends soon. It would be unfortunate for the entire county if the mines close. They are the livelihood for a lot of people."

The Gradys' oldest daughter lived in Indianapolis for a time before moving to Rockville. That allowed Mrs. Grady to observe city traffic occasionally, which is far heavier than that out on Ind. 61, where coal trucks almost outnumber what few cars there are.

The Gradys also have a daughter who attends Indiana University and one who is a sophomore at Pike Central. Teresa Grady does not appear to be old enough to have adult daughters. Small-town life seems to help keep residents young.

# Coe

## PICKETS AHEAD

We count 10 houses between the "Coe" signs on Ind. 61. Another sign alerts motorists that UMWA pickets are ahead. A mile or so away, a lean-to made of plywood and covered with a tarpaulin shelter is a temporary home for four pickets.

A big semi loaded with coal rumbles north oblivious of the pickets. Some coal is being mined despite the strike.

POSTSCRIPT: *Months later, the UMWA strike continued, with no indication the strike was about to end.*

# Spurgeon
## UNMERGED

More UMWA signs are in Spurgeon, another Pike County town on Ind. 61. Jordan Memorial Park at the north side of the residential town has a playground and tennis courts. We notice the Spurgeon State Bank. It is good to see one bank whose name hasn't been changed due to mergers. A big cemetery is near the United Methodist Church.

The post office is in an old storefront with a soft-drink machine that may be the only retail outlet in town.

* * *

We continue south of Spurgeon on Ind. 61 en route to Lynnville. Farms are interspersed with coal mines in this area. A giant American flag flies from a flag pole at one of the big farm operations.

Pike County ends, Warrick County begins, and we notice a giant drag line in the distance, evidence of the machinery that has replaced much of the manpower in coal mining.

# Lynnville
## BY THE INTERSTATE

Unlike many small towns, Lynnville has thrived in recent years, its business spurred by an I-64 interchange with Ind. 61. Cars and motor homes are lined up at a convenience store near the exit on this Friday afternoon.

The old high school, once the home of the Lynnville Lindys, appears to have been converted to apartments. Students now attend Tecumseh High School outside town on Ind. 68, where athletes are called the Braves. It's a consolidation of Elberfeld, Lynnville and Selvin.

The grade school remains in the town of 650 residents.

# Dickeyville
## WHERE ARE YOU?

Dickeyville, the map says, is east off Ind. 61 south of Lynnville. We see a "Dickeyville Road" sign and assume it will lead to Dickeyville the town. Asphalt turns to crushed stone, the wheels of the car stir up clouds of brown behind as we begin our search. If there is a Dickeyville, we're not finding it. We continue east, leaving a trail of dust through several miles of wasteland.

A person isn't lost until he stops, we figure, so we keep driving until we see cornfields and reach a place called Jockey. Except for the Jockey Tabernacle there isn't much here. The road is paved, however, and we drive north to Ind. 68, then return west on Ind. 68 to Scalesville.

Scalesville, at the north edge of Warrick County, has a few houses along the highway, but little else. We can say we've been Scalesville and Jockey . . . if not Dickeyville.

POSTSCRIPT: *We check later with the Warrick County surveyor's office in Boonville. We are told that we passed through what once was Dickeyville, which plat books show was a crossroads with a school and a few houses at one time. It now exists only as a name on road maps.*

# Holland
## LEGENDS IN THEIR TIME

Hoosiers do not forget their basketball legends. "Welcome to Holland" markers are followed by "Home of NBA stars Gene Tormohlen and Don Buse."

Tormohlen played for the Holland Dutchman, graduating in 1955. He then starred at the University of Tennessee through 1959 and later played for the St. Louis and Atlanta Hawks in the National Basketball Association. He was an assistant coach in the NBA for 12 years. Buse graduated from Holland in 1968, was a 1968 Indiana all-star, then played at Evansville University before joining the Indiana Pacers.

Tormohlen is in the Indiana Basketball Hall of Fame. Buse was a member of the Hall of Fame's Silver Anniversary team in 1993.

The Holland Dutchmen are no more. Athletes from town now play as Southridge Raiders with those from Huntingburg.

Holland, population 700, is the home of the Holland Dairy, which serves much of southern Indiana, its trucks seen frequently on roads. Holland is a small town that has kept many of its businesses. There is a medical clinic, as well as the Holland National Bank, which has branches at Huntingburg, Birdseye and Ferdinand.

# "ALPS OF INDIANA"

Dawn doesn't break, it bursts over southern Indiana in early summer. The sun, red in the east, rises onto the horizon, enlightens the rolling terrain, glistens on the morning dew, turning unharvested fields of wheat to amber.

Birds chirp, flit from tree to tree, making the most of their short lives. Rabbits run along roadsides, nibbling the tender grass. Beef cattle graze on green hillsides. Dairy cows form a column as they head for breakfast in dairy barns.

Residents awaken more slowly, especially on Saturday mornings. Traffic on the backroads is light. Few customers are in restaurants: an occasional traveler, a few local men who haven't—despite retirement—shaken the habit of early rising.

It is a good time of day. Yesterday is history, the excitement of today is ahead, tomorrow is still a dream.

## St. Henry
### AND JOHNSBURG

No one remains lost for long in Dubois County. Like lighthouses, spires rising from churches built on high ground are visible for miles. We spot one such spire atop a church before we see a "St. Henry—3 Miles" sign on U.S. 231 south of Huntingburg.

We are surprised to find another hamlet on County Road 1100 South before we reach St. Henry. It's called Johnsburg and it's on a section of the Southern Railway. Customers are already at Johnsburg Soil Service at 7:30 a.m., for Saturday is not an off-day for farmers. The Weaver Popcorn Company's Huntingburg facility is in Johnsburg, a town with more employees than residents.

The only houses are a big three-story white frame that sits atop a knoll surrounded by a wheat field and another house, abandoned on a hill across the county road. To the east, houses have been built atop hills to capture the spectacular views of this area of southern Dubois County. White fences rise and drop as they follow the waves in the landscape. Martin bird houses stand tall on the hills.

New houses dot a development at the west edge of St. Henry, where visitors are greeted with "Welcome to St. Henry, established in 1862." Nice houses are scattered around town on the three streets—Market, Clay and West—that join Road 1100 South to shape St. Henry. None of the houses are close together, no more than two per block, in this old town where residents have plenty of elbow room and enough land for gardens.

The Bungalow Bar is in a concrete block building. Nearby is Pat and Denny's Red Barn, a flower shop offering roses, balloons, crafts, stuffed animals, garden supplies. It likely does a good business because residents take pride in their lawns.

The two businesses seem to be the only enterprises in a town dominated by St. Henry Catholic Church, headquarters for a parish that began in 1862. A number of cars already are parked outside the church on this Saturday morning.

# Dale

### "FARM AND COMMUNITY"

Churches are important in this area of Indiana. St. Henry has one spire. Dale has three that help lead visitors into the town at Ind. 62 and U.S. 231 in northern Spencer County just south of I-64.

Dale is not a backroads town, not with 1,700 residents, a newspaper, stores, library, manufacturing firms, an American Legion Post and other organizations. It's a progressive town with water improvements, a plan commission, chamber of commerce and a proposed new sewage plant. And a slogan, "Where farm and community work together."

Once called Elizabeth, it was renamed Dale after Robert Dale Owen, who once represented the area in the U.S. Congress. We wonder whether towns today would be named for a Congressman, considering the low esteem voters hold for lawmakers these days.

# Mariah Hill
## Tasty Town

It is still almost two months away, but Mariah Hill already is promoting its annual August picnic "featuring quilts, famous soup and chicken dinners." Mariah Hill is on Ind. 62, about four miles east of Dale in northern Spencer County.

Like other towns in the area, its activity centers around a church. In Mariah Hill that center is Mary Help of Christians Catholic Church, which conducted its first mass in 1857. Tennis courts and softball diamonds, where girls' teams are beginning to practice for a game this Saturday morning, are part of the church complex. An old cemetery is over a hill from the church.

Mariah Hill was founded in 1846, and by 1860 it had a flour mill, sawmill, brickyard, creamery, two blacksmith shops, two wagon manufacturers, two general stores, two hotels, two saloons, a harness shop, shoe shop, four livery stables, a furniture store, drum shop, gun shop, drug store, doctor, coffin factory, broom shop and wooden shoe plant.

The railroad missed Mariah Hill. But the automobile made residents more mobile, and the town's importance as a commercial center waned. Today it has two restaurants for two different tastes, one called the Chateau, the other La Cantina, which has a "help wanted" sign out front. The town also has a service station, a few other small businesses, an empty storefront or two, and a post office which is part of a residence.

Mariah Hill is the hometown of entertainer Florence Henderson, although she went to school at Dale and is usually said to be from there.

\* \* \*

Ind. 62 rises and falls as it stretches to the east, past clothes that whip in the breeze on lines. West of St. Meinrad, a mine in operation off Ind. 62 adjoins a farm, another example of the importance of agriculture and coal to this area of Indiana.

# St. Meinrad
## "Alps Of Indiana"

Ind. 62 drops into St. Meinrad, back into what could almost be another century, another continent. It is a living landscape, a mural that blends into its surroundings, giving meaning to those who call it "The Little Alps of Indiana."

Almost entirely Catholic, the town is the home of the architecturally-attractive St. Meinrad Arch Abbey, whose twin-spired church, seminary, monastery, and numerous other buildings stand over the town on a broad hill. The arch abbey has been a St. Meinrad landmark since 1854, and the town actually was laid out on monastic property in 1861.

About 150 priests and brothers operate two schools for the education of future preists, a college of liberal arts and a graduate school of theology. About 1,800 alumni now serve the Roman Catholic Church throughout the world.

This is a community that takes care of itself. Street lights were financed by contributions collected by the Chamber of Commerce. The Chamber directed construction of the St. Meinrad Community Center and led the development of a recreation field with athletic facilities and a shelter house.

Rather than decline in population, like other small towns, St. Meinrad has flourished. The monastery-operated Abbey Press and Sausage & Gift Shop provide employment for some of the residents in town. The town also has craft shops, stores, food stores, garage, a Chevrolet dealership, branch bank, restaurant, post office, grain elevator and American Legion post.

And it, too, salutes an athlete with signs at the edge of town—Terry Brahm, a Heritage Hills graduate from St. Meinrad who participated as a runner in the 1988 Olympics in Seoul, Korea.

* * *

We continue east-northeast on Ind. 62, leaving Spencer County, entering Perry County, where the highway runs through a valley spotted with oil wells. At the road to Adyeville, a sign invites travelers to visit the "Steam Engine Barn."

# Adyeville
## STEAMING BUT FRIENDLY

We enter what we think is Adyeville, even though there are no signs to indicate its identity. A woman stops her car in front of one of five houses in town. "This Adyeville?" we ask. "It is," she say, volunteering without being asked that "it's a nice, quiet place."

She has come out early this Saturday morning to visit a friend on the main corner in Adyeville. "Just dropped in to say hi," she says. Just because a person lives in a hamlet like Adyeville, where the store and its gasoline pumps have been long gone, doesn't mean he or she is isolated from the rest of the world.

We cross Rockhouse Branch at Adyeville, go south and find the Steam Engine Barn on a farm a mile or so south of Adyeville. It is a good place to relive the past. A series of dinner bells hang in the yard between the house and the barn. Signs say, "Beware of Dog" and "No Trespassing."

We are greeted by peacocks that have strutted across the paved road. They are among twenty on the farm, we will learn.

Besides the peacocks, there is a billy goat, hogs and other livestock. Walter Troesch sees us approach, leaves his tractor and greets us. We are visitors, not trespassers.

Walter farms 560 acres with his brother. Their dad, Lawrence Troesch, bought the place in 1927. It was he who started collecting steam engines back in 1959, still enamored with the machines he used to run sawmills and threshing separators. The Troesches once showed steam engines in parades and shows.

Walter talks for a while, but he has field work to do. He tells his son, James, to take us out to the Steam Engine Barn. We expect to see just a few steam engines. We are surprised at the collection the Troesches have amassed. But there are also more than steam engines here in this two-story assortment of items out of the past. There are antiques and collectibles, hundreds of items, from corn shredders to corn shellers; from a hearse to a one-horse drill; seed cleaners, binders, ice cream-parlor chairs. A horse-drawn fire wagon. Scores of clocks. Kraut-cutters.

All of them are reminders of eras that have faded into history. Some of the items are for sale, at what seem reasonable prices, at least for those who value the past.

James knows a lot about the items in the barn, has attended steam engine shows, learned about antiques by listening to his dad. He hands us a brochure for the 30th annual Antique Steam and Gas Engine Show at Thresherman's Park in Boonville in late July.

"Beware The Dog" has come out to check us out, but he only barks, seeing that James is here with us.

James, a graduate of Perry Central High School, helps his dad and uncle on the farm but works full-time over at Dale. He is a high school and college basketball fan, as interested in talking about Damon Bailey and the Indiana University Hoosiers and Todd Cochenour and the Evansville Aces as about antique farm items.

We give him our four books about Indiana basketball. It's good to meet young Hoosiers interested in both basketball and Indiana farm lore.

The Troesches do not charge for tours, but there is a collection box where donations can be made. A few dollars for a visit to the Steam Engine Barn doesn't seem adequate for the time and effort the Troeschses have invested to keep the past alive.

We leave the farm, past the peacocks that are along the roadside, and head back to the present. We return to Ind. 62 and head east through the lowlands past a big farm operation with giant silos. This is southern Indiana, where no county is without its agriculture. A man paints a mailbox at the "Home of the Fishers."

A sign points to St. Martin of Tours Catholic Church at Siberia, north on a county road. It isn't every day a person is within two miles of Siberia.

A paved county road cuts through wasteland broken by a few farm fields between hills. A barn on a hill is in danger of total collapse. A farmstead not far away is abandoned, for it is now difficult to make a living where land is rolling and fields are small.

# Siberia
## WARM IN HEART

We can't possibly be near Siberia, we jokingly tell ourselves. It is already 85 degrees and the sun isn't yet directly overhead. Nonetheless, we are greeted with "Welcome to Siberia. Cold in Name, Warm in Heart. Founded 1869." The sign is wood, white letters on brown paint, splattered with white snowflakes.

We drive through Siberia, past about ten houses, past the St. Martin of Tours Catholic Church complex which includes a church, rectory, convent and hall. Some parish members already are gathering on this Saturday morning. The church appears to be both the heart and soul of Siberia, for there are no stores, no other public gathering places.

It was the Catholic parish that gave Siberia its start, and, indirectly, its name. Father Isidore Hobi named the parish after Sabaria, the hometown of the parish's patron. When the town was awarded a post office, it is said, postal officials, certain the name had been misspelled, called it Siberia.

No matter! Chances are the town has received more recognition for being Siberia than it would have as Sabaria. And, somehow, a sign "Welcome to Sabaria. Cold in Name. Warm in Heart" wouldn't sound right.

The original post office is gone. Siberia is now served by the Bristow post office.

\* \* \*

We return to Ind. 62, which continue to parallel I-64, to an unpaved rural road that leads to Doolittle Mills. There are few houses along the road that slices through a section of the Hoosier National Forest.

We reach Doolittle Mills, noting the Bethel Christian Church and a few houses. A stone sign with a 1956 date, has pointers to "Eckerty—6 miles north" and St. Croix—2 miles south."

A Mobile gasoline station is out of business. There is little activity in town.

We return to Ind. 62, a five-mile round-trip in which we have seen no cars. It is an area that belongs more to wildlife than to people.

\* \* \*

We backtrack on Ind. 62 to Ind. 145 in search of Sassafras for nothing better illustrates rustic Indiana than towns with names like Punkin Center, Sassafras and Solitude.

We have two maps, an official Indiana highway map and the "Champion Road Map." Both pinpoint Sassafras just off Ind. 145 to the east, a mile or two south of Ind. 62.

We drive south, looking for clues to Sassafras. We find none, seeing only two roads in that direction. We decide to drive south on Ind. 145 to Bristow to ask directions.

# Bristow
## MILLING AROUND

The Bristow Milling Company appears to be a busy place, for Saturday is not a day off for farmers.

What looks to have been a hotel in this town on Anderson Creek is closed. A storefront is vacant, a one-time grocery a thing of the past. The Friendly Inn, "beer, wine and food," is not yet open. Neither is a building called a shopping center offering "auto supplies, clothes, grocery, jewelry, health and beauty aids."

Like hundreds of other small towns, Bristow has lost its high school. Athletes who would have been Bristow Purple Aces are now Perry Central Commodores.

We stop in the post office in Bristow to ask about Sassafras. "Nothing there, except the Mt. Sinai Church," we are told. "It's about halfway up the big hill north on 145."

# Sassafras
## A FAMILY AFFAIR

We look at the map again, just to reassure ourselves the town is to the east of the highway. We turn east on a narrow one-lane gravel road midway up the Ind. 145 hill. Finding nothing, we start back toward the state highway. A pickup truck approaches and we ease toward the side-ditch and signal the driver to stop.

We ask about Sassafras. "It's down at corner," the driver says, nodding his head back toward the highway. "Not much there." He claims that "Sassafras really was supposed to be See-far-us, or something like that, and someone spelled it Sassafras, so it stayed that way."

It seems an unlikely story, not with sassafras being as Hoosier as persimmon pudding, paw paws, apple pie and basketball. But we have passed Sassafras, we decide, and we didn't know it. We return to Ind. 145, cross the road, find Mt. Sinai church, located in the wildwood. It's west, not east, of Ind. 145. The road maps we have are wrong. It has happened before in our travels through backroads Indiana. We should have taken the Hoosier National Forest Map. We check later and it pinpoints Sassafras—or what there is of it—exactly.

Mt. Sinai no longer has a congregation. And Sassafras has only a house or two, four or five house trailers, "manufactured homes" in this era of political correctness, and a junkyard, now referred to as "a salvage yard."

We see a man loading debris and junk onto a trailer behind a Farmall tractor. He is Harold Spurgeon and he's friendly, eager to talk. We are, indeed, in Sassafras, he confirms: "They used to call it Mt. Sinai, because of the church. Then a post office came in, which Oral Beard ran, and they named it Sassafras back in about 1950." The post office remained open about ten or twelve years, then closed. "We get our mail out of Bristow now," Spurgeon says.

He continues, "My grandpa, Willie, lived on top of the hill. My dad, Bill, got this place from my grandpa and that's how it all started out. We cleared this all out. It was nothing but woods before that . . . I was born in this house back in 1942, a year after it was built."

He can name everyone who lives in Sassafras, though he claims, "I don't really know how many people live here. But Marion Lindsey lives over where the post office used to be. He bought the church and keeps the grass mowed there. My brother Lawrence and his wife live back there in that trailer. I live here. My mom lives over in that trailer and also owns the double-wide and that other trailer, which she rents out. Alvin Walker lives there.

"Our family has been around here, Lordy, I don't know how long. Dad was born here and he was 69 when he died 14 years ago. All us kids were born here, all of them up on the hill except me. I don't really know when my grandpa moved here, but he was 77 when he died."

Spurgeon attended Bristow High School. "I went two years and, due to Mom and Dad's health, I had to quit and go to work. I would have loved to have finished high school, but that's the way it goes. You gotta do what you gotta do. I sure hated it when they tore that school down," he says.

Spurgeon is his own man and he loves the independence, explaining, "I do a little farming, have some hogs, work out at different jobs, mainly just tinker-tom around. I'm my own boss and I like it that way. I ain't got nobody pushing me, or telling me what to do. It really works nice." He talks about his garden. "I think it's about the prettiest garden around," he says, without bragging.

We tell him Sassafras needs a road sign along the highway. He agrees. "I may talk to the highway department about that," he says.

After all, there really is a Sassafras, and other Hoosiers ought to know where it is.

*　*　*

We close our notebook, turn off the tape recorder. We have traveled 6,037 miles, visited 290 towns and villages, thirty to forty cities, talked with hundreds of Hoosiers on this odyssey. For the most part, we have found "Backroads Indiana" alive and well.

# A POSTSCRIPT

Indiana isn't found on interstates where motorists stop, check in at motels, eat at fast-food restaurants, stay a few hours and depart, oblivious to where they are. Interstates are for speed, for motorists in a rush, unaware of the people and the places beyond the billboards and the chain-link fences.

Life in the real Indiana is to be found on the backroads, in the small towns, in village stores, barbershops, post offices and cafes. In those places, it doesn't matter much whether a person runs a bank or a bulldozer, lives in a clapboard shack on the creek or a mansion on the hill. Individuals are weighed by their character, not by pretense, not by appearance.

It is there, beyond the barn roofs painted "Mail Pouch Tobacco" and "See Meramec Caverns" that the innately deep qualities of old-fashioned Hoosier honesty, courtesy, friendship are to be found. And they are to be found in old stone houses where rivers almost reach the road, and in bungalows, mobile homes and century-old farmsteads.

Indiana, genuine, with little pretense, is waiting to be discovered along roads that gallivant on undefined courses, roads that attempt to follow the contour of the Ohio as it weaves, curls and twists to shape the state's southern border.

And it is there on roads that wind over brooks and up hills, across plateaus, past small tobacco patches and endless fields, that the heritage of the English, Scots-Irish, Italians, Germans, French and Swiss blend into a people called Hoosiers.

\* \* \*

It has been almost 75 years since a man named Herman Ramsey wrote a poem about a small "Backroads Indiana" town. Here is part of that poem, which is as apropos now as it was then.

## Heltonville

Sort of scattered in the valley
And a-stragglin up the hill,
Is a little Hoosier village
By the name of Heltonville.

With this town of friendly neighbors
It's your character that counts
In establishin' your ratin'
And not your bank accounts.

They don't care about your money,
Nor your job or motor car,
It's the way you love your neighbor
That reveals just what you are.

None of them are very wealthy,
But none of them are poor;
None of them would fail the needy;
Turn the hungry from his door.

They won't hold it much against you,
If you're dress up fit to kill,
But your overalls are good enough
For folks in Heltonville.

When there's sickness every member
Of this faithful little band
Stands beside you like a brother
To put forth a helping hand.

Why, your confidence is bolstered,
And your patriotism thrills
When you think our mighty nation
Is made up of Heltonvilles.

# The Author: WENDELL TROGDON

Wendell Trogdon is a native Hoosier, born in Lawrence County near Heltonville, where he was graduated from high school. He earned his Bachelor of Arts degree from Franklin College.

After serving for three years in the U.S. Army's Counter Intelligence Corps, he returned to Indiana to begin his newspaper career at the Logansport *Pharos-Tribune* in 1954, then worked in the agricultural information department at Purdue University. He joined *The Indianapolis News* in 1957 as a reporter, serving as city editor, then news editor, and retiring as managing editor in September 1992.

He continues to write the "Quips" which are a page-one feature of each day's *News,* as well as his Saturday column "Those Were the Days," based on his growing up in Southern Indiana during the Depression years and World War II.

He has won numerous state awards for journalism, including recognition for "best column" and "best feature."

He is the author of nine other books, four of them about life in Southern Indiana in the 1930s and '40s. The other five deal with basketball, Indiana's favorite sport.

Wendell Trogdon and his wife, Fabian, have three grown daughters and live in Mooresville, Indiana.

# Cover Artist: GARY VARVEL

Born the same year Wendell Trogdon joined the staff of *The News,* Gary Varvel grew up at Danville, Indiana, where he was graduated from high school. While attending the Herron School of Art in Indianapolis he drew cartoons for the Danville *Gazette.* He later was production manager and editorial cartoonist at *The County Courier* in Brownsburg, Indiana.

He joined the staff of *The Indianapolis News* in 1978 and has illustrated Wendell Trogdon's "Quips" columns since then. He now is the newspaper's chief artist and in 1992 was named Indiana's best editorial cartoonist by the Society of Professional Journalism.

As an illustrator he has developed and refined a whimsical, highly identifiable style.

He and his wife, Carol, live in Danville with their three children.